LOOKING
FORWARD

LOOKING FORWARD

AN OPTIMIST'S GUIDE TO RETIREMENT

ELLEN FREUDENHEIM

ILLUSTRATIONS BY STEPHEN QUINLAN

STEWART, TABORI & CHANG
NEW YORK

Text copyright © 2004 Ellen Freudenheim

Illustrations copyright © 2004 Stephen Quinlan Illustration Ltd.

Published in 2004 by
Stewart, Tabori & Chang
115 West 18th Street
New York, NY 10011
www.abramsbooks.com

Canadian Distribution:
Canadian Manda Group
One Atlantic Avenue, Suite 105
Toronto, Ontario M6K 3E7
Canada

Library of Congress Cataloging-in-Publication Data
Freudenheim, Ellen.
   Looking forward : an optimist's guide to retirement / Ellen
Freudenheim ; illustrations by Stephen Quinlan.
       p. cm.
   Includes index.
   ISBN 1-58479-342-2
   1. Retirement—Planning. 2. Retirement—United States. I. Title.
HQ1062.F65 2004
646.7'9—dc22
                                        2004014925

DISCLAIMER: The information in this book does not lessen the need for, nor take the place of, legal, financial, medical, or any other professional advice.

The author and the publisher shall have neither the liability nor responsibility to any person or entity with respect to any loss or damage caused, or alleged to be caused, by the infomation contained in this book.

Designed by Lynne Yeamans/Lync

The text of this book was composed in Garamond and Knockout.

Printed in the United States of America

10 9 8 7 6 5 4 3 2 1
First Printing

Stewart, Tabori & Chang is a subsidiary of

LA MARTINIÈRE
G R O U P E

To my dear brother Richard,
and in memory of our parents.

Contents

Acknowledgments

I would like to tip my hat to the scores of people between the ages of 45 and 90 who were willing to offer me tidbits and tales of their lives before, during the transition to, and in retirement. The first to be acknowledged are the retirees who were interviewed in person, in focus groups, and on the telephone during this project. A tip of the hat also goes to those folks with whom I engaged informally in long, short, and even fleeting conversations about life, work, the aging process, and retirement. To those whose names don't appear in these pages, thank you, too; please know that every single conversation spiced and flavored the stew of ideas that produced this book!

Dozens of experts made themselves available to be queried on innumerable topics from mental health to religion to demographic to Internet use patterns. The first person to kindly open the door was Michael Markowitz, director of the Institute for Retired Professionals at the New School University. A network of public health professionals also proved an invaluable resource. I'd like to raise a toast to the baby boomers, for their unsettling habit of forging original twists on American life as we move through the decades.

It takes a village to raise a child, they say, and it took a team to produce this book. Jennifer Lang, my skilled editor at Stewart, Tabori & Chang, has steadily steered the manuscript toward a very clear vision of the final product. I'm thrilled to be working with her, the STC staff, and Stephen Quinlan, whose artwork greatly enhances the book. Wendy Sherman and Jessica Lichtenstein of Wendy Sherman Associates have been dreamboat agents. To Anne Kostick, whose generosity in sharing her Rolodex proved key in making this book a reality, thanks once again. Three cheers to talented researchers Natalie Bell, Jennifer Benepe, Karen Krone, Jill Max, and ace librarian Laura Pinhey. To Eileen Judge, Laura Lambert, Ilana Polyak, Sarah Richards, Ellen Leach, and Eileen Schnurr, a huge thank-you each for your wonderful contributions. Warm thanks to Anne Savarese, Greg Cohn, and to Cynthia Cohen Congress, my brainstorming partner. Pals Jean Halloran, Gloria Martin, Fran Nankin, Barbara Oliver, Jane Roe, and Carole Schweid pitched in with support and suggestions. Hugs to my mother-in-law, Eva Wiener; to Jeff Oppenheim and Marshall Beil for legal direction; to Maureen Gaffney; and the inimitable Richard J. Freudenheim for support. Finally, I'd like to express sheer wonder for the luck of having a terrific nuclear family: my smart, funny husband, Daniel, and our talented children: David, age 20, and Anna, age 17. Their constant love is my secret weapon.

Introduction

What is it, exactly, that people *do*, when they retire? The question hadn't occurred to me until my active, healthy mother-in-law seemed at a total loss upon her retirement as a trilingual salesperson selling $300 scarves at an upscale French shop on Madison Avenue.

So I set out to answer the dreaded, unspoken question of my own workaholic generation: Is retirement, well, terminal? Could I—should I—retire? Can anybody afford it? My friends shuddered at the R-word, and my (younger) husband started talking about getting old; I had recently done a sprint triathlon upon turning 50.

This book is the result of my personal peek over the generational fence into a future retirement. It's based on interviews with over 200 middle- and upper-middle-class Americans, from age 45 to age 90, in urban, suburban, and rural settings—as well as scores of experts—conducted between 2002 and 2003.

The currently retired paint a surprisingly active picture of their mature years. Octogenarians are studying Ancient Greece, getting college degrees, and going ballroom dancing. Septuagenarians are starting businesses. Early retirees, men and women in their 60s who were hard-driving careerists, are blossoming into the artists, dancers, political activists, and nurturers that they never were before. They're traveling the world, climbing mountains, making new friends—and taking internal journeys, too, to write their memoirs and explore spiritual terrain. And, they're "giving back," starting nonprofit organizations, joining boards of directors, volunteering, and lobbying elected officials.

And salaried work? Jobs, home businesses, and part-time work have become a feature of contemporary retirement. Many glide from semi-retirement to work, and back to a nonworking phase of retirement again.

There's not really a new word for "retirement" as it's being redefined today. (Nor is there a word describing the millions of active people over 65 who steadfastly reject the terms "senior" and "elderly.") Thanks to the improved medical management of chronic diseases and the increased life span of our well-fed, increasingly well-educated older population, some people may stay "in retirement" for as long as 30 years or more.

If there's one moral of this book, it's this: People can reap big dividends by investing in their future social, emotional, and intellectual lives. "Investing for retirement" is more than just a financial strategy—it's a smart life strategy.

I've had to coin some new phrases in order to describe what I discovered in my research. THE RETIREMENT ZONE describes a life phase, regardless of whether a person is employed. "Anchor activities" are the compensatory activities that fill the "work void." "Anchor relationships," of course, refers to those people in our lives to whom we turn for love, support, reassurance, and reality checks. These terms, to my knowledge, haven't been used before in the context of retirement. How any individual fits all these pieces together in their own idiosyncratic way determines the rhythm of their retirement.

It's true that for those who find themselves financially dependent only on Social Security, and who lack money for, or access to, adequate health care, aging in America can be shockingly harsh. But in the years ahead, millions of Americans *will* have some stewardship over their own fate and will face decisions about their own retirement (or *un*retirement, as the case may be). All the more reason for younger people reading this book to begin now to plan ahead for their later years, so as to be able to enjoy an unprecedented gift of time—a longer life span—fully.

As we go to press, my mother-in-law has just turned 76—and has returned to work as a salesperson once again, standing on her feet for long hours during a classic New York City Christmas rush, selling silk scarves to New Yorkers and busloads of tourists. And when the holiday rush is over, she says she's off to tour Japan. *Her* rhythm in retirement seems to be work a little, play a little, cha-cha-cha.

What's *yours?*

WHY AN "OPTIMIST'S GUIDE"?

op-ti-mism I: *a doctrine that this world is the best possible world* **2:** *an inclination to put the most favorable construction upon actions and events or to anticipate the best possible outcome* —*Merriam-Webster's 11th Collegiate Dictionary*

The meaning of "optimism" is so obvious to us moderns, it's a surprise to learn that the term first appeared in 1737, in a French account of a German philosopher named Leibniz. It refers to his doctrine that this is " 'the best of all possible worlds,' being chosen by the Creator as that in which most good could be obtained at the cost of least evil."*

Old Leibniz invented differential and integral calculus (independently of Newton), and worked on calculating machines, clocks, windmills, submarines, and even the binary number system. It's no coincidence that this bright-eyed polymath who peers out from history's portraits found life engaging.

This book is dedicated to the proposition that the ultimate twenty or thirty years of life can be "the best of all possible worlds." Because there are so many myths and wrong-headed notions about the "retirement years," that's almost a radical proposition.

In the pages that follow, you'll meet mature adults who describe what it's like to be going back to school, running marathons, getting political, teaching inner-city children to read, and yes, just smelling the roses. You'll find 90-year-olds who act young, and 50-year-olds who fear aging. Among the rock stars of the book are older people who tell stories of what they've discovered about themselves, and about life, during retirement—whether it's an old passion, a new love, or a sudden urge to give something back to society.

An 80-year-old optimist? Well, why not?

*The Shorter Oxford English Dictionary, 3rd ed., Oxford University Press, 1973

HOW TO USE THIS BOOK

Part I describes the changing face of retirement in the United States. **Part II,** complete with worksheets and suggestions for getting a handle on your future, helps you figure out what to do in the post-work phase of your life. **Part III** gives a detailed, insider's snapshot of many interesting and popular activities such as volunteering, traveling, going back to school or work, and special hobbies. **Part IV** briefly covers three practical matters: financial planning, caregiving, and de-cluttering. Throughout you will find tips, informational tidbits, data, anecdotes, and profiles of some wonderful people doing some wonderful things.

This book is for you if
- you're thinking about retiring, or you're retired
- your spouse just entered semi- or full retirement, or is thinking about it
- your parents are retired (or not) and their life could be more fulfilling

Look for these icons for some particularly helpful bits of information.

 HEALTHVIEWS Suggestions and insight into the health angle of over a dozen topics, from volunteering to going back to school

 INSIDER'S GUIDE The inside scoop about, say, the kinds of educational or travel opportunities that people can choose in retirement

 PRACTICAL TIPS Shortcuts, tips from experts, and helpful suggestions

 WORKSHEETS AND QUIZZES Quick, fun do-it-yourself tools

 YOUR MONEY MATTERS Practical tips on costs, savings, and how to do what you love without losing your shirt

Note to Reader On page 346, you will find a handful of general retirement resources. In addition, Resource Guides at the end of most chapters list selected publications, organizations, and Web sites. (Inclusion here does not imply a recommendation or endorsement of the products, services, or public statements of the organizations or reports listed.)

PART I

Exploring the Retirement Zone

Whether you are currently retired, a never-gonna-quit workaholic, or counting the days until you leave work, the question of how you deploy your assets—financial, emotional, spiritual, physical, and creative—in the last third of your life is worthy of an answer.

From sex among septuagenarians to the advantages of aging, a national dialogue is about to drown the airwaves—about the graying of America. It's likely to start very soon, because the oldest baby boomers reach Social Security eligibility age, 65, in 2011, and some become eligible for benefits as early as 2008. An important part of the dialogue, one that may affect you, has to do with jobs, work, and retirement.

Your "retirement" promises to be as different from your father's era as your laptop is from his Corona typewriter. For boomers and their older sibs, now 60-somethings, the "retirement years"

WON'T BE an uninterrupted period of time in the rocking chair

WILL BE a complex patchwork quilt of different stages and activities, including family time; work; laughter; volunteering; smelling the roses; exploring; travel; love, sex and (maybe) rock-n-roll; creative adventures; spiritual moments.

CHAPTER 1

Welcome to the Retirement Zone

What's THE RETIREMENT ZONE? It's a new term for a new stage of your life. Locate THE RETIREMENT ZONE on your internal map somewhere after major career building and your kid's first year of college. If you're open and plan ahead, it can be a place full of opportunity. You're there if you're old enough to be thinking about what to do with the rest of your life, now that you've grown up.

THE RETIREMENT ZONE IS AN ACTUAL TIME OF LIFE

You've entered THE RETIREMENT ZONE when the idea of dropping off the traditional work-career track becomes a tangible reality. You might be thinking about leaving the workforce. Or anticipating that you'll die with your work boots on. Or you might already have retired, ten years ago.

The vast majority of Americans do not work past age 65. And while recent studies have shown that some percentage of boomers predict that they will "work some" past age 65, so far fewer than one in seven people actually do, according to the Bureau of Labor Statistics.

In the 21st-century RETIREMENT ZONE, you'll find older people doing younger people's things: Going back to school. Dancing the tango. Publishing first novels. Americans, especially those with some financial cushion, education, and reasonably good health, are moving through their mature years open to change and new experiences.

What's a "zone," anyway? We'll use the term here for a life stage or shared generational experience, as in: *The 1950s Conformity/Elvis* Zone. The chilly *Cold War* Zone. The *Counter Culture 1960s* Zone. The *Everybody Just Get Stoned* Zone. The *Tick Tock, Biological Clock* Zone. The *Middle Age* Zone.

THE RETIREMENT ZONE IS A MINDSET

The new mindset is flexible and open-ended. It's defiant in the face of ageism and stereotyping. It's the voice, after a look in the mirror, that says, "What the heck, I'm going to live life as fully as I can."

Just in case you didn't get it, THE RETIREMENT ZONE is not the Sunbelt. It's anywhere in the world that you want it to be, from a bare bones sailboat to a solar-powered home in Maine. You're likely to spend 20 to 30 years in THE RETIREMENT ZONE. "Parenthood" starts the minute your first baby is born—and often lasts, if not forever, until the youngest is in his or her mid-20s. Similarly, THE RETIREMENT ZONE isn't one long dreary experience, an endless landscape of sameness. Things happen within it. There are phases. Hey, it's life.

Dorothy, when will *you* land in THE RETIREMENT ZONE? You've arrived when you get that cheery solicitation letter from AARP around your 50th birthday. You arrive when you look hard at that 401K plan. You arrive, after 20 years of service or age 55, whichever comes later, when you are first eligible for your company's pension benefits. When you find yourself worrying, daydreaming, planning to delay or hasten your retirement—well, like Dorothy in Oz, that's when you, too, have landed in a new world.

YOU CAN REINVENT YOURSELF IN THE RETIREMENT ZONE

Your 21st-century experience promises to be different from your parents' 20th-century retirement. Increasingly, the post-work phase of life will have cycles—some years of work, some years of play, some time for volunteering, some time for self renewal and retraining and retooling.

You might work in The Retirement Zone. Or, apply the skills and know-how you've paid for so dearly with your time in some new way. For instance, if you're a doctor or nurse, you may decide to teach health promotion to teenagers. If you're a corporate manager, you may find a less stressful job with a nonprofit organization.

In The Retirement Zone, you'll enjoy "anchor activities" and "anchor relationships" along with adequate finances and, hopefully, good health. Anchor relationships with people you can turn to, and anchor activities that structure your time and provide a way to contribute to the world and live life meaningfully, define the zone. Your Zone, that is.

In The Retirement Zone, you'll be one of the hottest commodities in the nation. In Dad's days, retirees were decidedly uncool. But with projections of 14 millon households transitioning into retirement by the end of the decade, The Retirement Zone is going to be a huge market.

In The Retirement Zone, there's no reason not to date a younger man or older woman, move to Bali, learn to make movies, get a PhD, or ride a motorcycle—or do whatever it is that you wish to do, in your own pursuit of life, liberty, and happiness.

When you are in The Retirement Zone you are likely to take trips and see more of the people you love the most. You might also liberate yourself from the nuisance of owning too much. You don't have to act old, and you don't have to get a face-lift to look beautiful (though you might). You don't have to accept as status quo corruption in government and corporate scandal. You can return to sender any birthday cards with punch lines about being "over the hill." You are invited to be enraptured, outrageous, whimsical, and nostalgic.

"At YOUR Age??"

Meet feisty 78-year-old Estelle Ravage. When she and her husband retired and sold their wine store in Westport, Connecticut, she anticipated "doing all the things we wanted to do." But after two years, she found herself bored to tears. She opened a part-time craft gallery-gift shop featuring the work of American craftspeople in a mostly residential area of nearby Bridgeport, which is a depressed city. Not the sort of place you'd expect a gallery to succeed, but it has—for 15 years.

"When I first opened, I had a wine and cheese party and invited a lot of friends and family. The main thing I heard from everyone was negative comments: 'At your age, what do you need this for?' I said, 'You know what? I do need it!' I was just sixty-three! Everybody needs a reason to get up in the morning. There are many people who make TV and grocery shopping the highlights of their day. This is not enough for me! That would drive me up a wall. I'm reasonably healthy, mentally and physically. My doctor recently asked me, 'How's the store going?' I said great. He said, 'Stay with it, as long as you can.' Not that he had to tell me, I want to anyway. 'I see people who retire completely, and within two years,' he said, 'they're ill.' There's nothing like success. I think it keeps you young."

Resource Guide

PUBLICATIONS

American Demographics, November 2000: "Active Retirement."

Fountain of Age by Betty Friedan (Simon & Schuster, 1993).

The Third Act: Reinventing Yourself After Retirement by Edgar M. Bronfman with Catherine Whitney (G. P. Putnam, 2002).

FREE GUIDE

Staying Sharp: Quality of Life by AARP Andrus Foundation and the Dana Alliance for Brain Initiatives (2002). Available free as download or booklet: www.aarp.org.

CHAPTER 2

One Little Chapter on Four Big Issues

By 2050, there will be enough people over 100 in the United States to populate the city of San Francisco. So, what do you care?

You may be one of them.

Men and women in nearly 14 million households are predicted to retire by about 2010. If you were born in the 1940s, 1950s, or 1960s, you, too, may help transform the nation's financial, consumer, and cultural landscape in the decades ahead. So, before tackling the important task of deciding how you want to spend your 60s, 70s, and beyond, this chapter gives a quick rundown of four "big picture" factors—things beyond any individual's control—that will impact your time in THE RETIREMENT ZONE.

THE "NEW" ECONOMY

"What's good for General Motors," they used to say, "is good for the country." Of course, that might have been true for much of the 20th century. But factory jobs are becoming a smaller and smaller part of our U.S. economy. With globalization and a shift to an "information" economy, a growing part of the workforce is now made up of "knowledge workers," as well as global workers, contract workers, and at-home workers. The list of mega-transformations of the workforce includes the unprecedented entry of women into and the aging of the workforce, as well as outsourcing, immigration, and globalization.

The job landscape already has changed for both white- and blue-collar workers now in THE RETIREMENT ZONE. Many jobs no longer offer pension benefits, and health care costs are increasingly shifted from the employer to the employee.

Even the future structure of Social Security and solvency of Medicare—two pillars of retirement life for decades—are the subject of intense public debate.

For those who expect to continue working part or full time, continuing education may become a necessity for career survival in this technologically fast-changing world. "Jobs Won't Dry Up, but the Wage Gap May Grow" alerts an April 2, 2004, *Wall Street Journal* article. In order to qualify for higher-paid positions people will need to be adept at using the latest information technology in their respective fields, and must be willing to retrain frequently in order to keep up. The person who lacks computer or technological skills relevant to his or her field will be left on the poorer side of the wage gap, filling traditional service jobs such as restaurant worker or retail clerk. While the aging of the population itself will spark new demand for certain services—such as physically demanding positions like janitor and nursing home aide—the better-paying managerial positions even within these fields will require competence in information technology.

Many baby boomers joke about working until they die. It's a joke riddled with ambivalence; underneath the usually rueful smile is a generational question: Will the 20th-century institution of retirement even be an option for me? It's a question worth asking. If historical trends prevail, most people will continue to retire in their mid-60s when they become eligible for Social Security. Still, before any one individual can make that commitment to full-time freedom, he or she will have to think about sustaining their own personal finances and ongoing employability in our new, not always kind, economy.

BOOMER DEMOGRAPHICS

A tidal wave of Americans are poised to cross that invisible shoal known as Social Security eligibility. Most statistics you'll see compare today with the truly distant shore of 2030. But as in any large storm, the first part of the wave will come sooner. Much sooner.

By the year 2010, the over-65 population will approach 40 million. That will include

- Enough people between the ages of 65 and 70 to populate the entire state of Illinois or Pennsylvania (12 million);
- Enough 70-somethings to equal the population of Florida (16 million);
- Enough 80-somethings to take over New Jersey (8 million);
- Enough people between age 90 and 100 to populate all of Houston (8 million);
- Enough centenarians to fill one-half of Glendale, Arizona (120,000).

Demography is destiny, they say. Every year that passes, we hear of more octogenarian marathon runners, more elderly politicians holding sway in Congress, and seasoned, mature actors, businesspeople, writers, and activists having an impact in their respective fields. The average ages of the dearly departed described in the newspaper obituary section creep higher. As our older citizens seem to be getting, well, *younger* by the year, the meaning and implications of aging, too, are in flux.

Even if on an individual level old ain't so old anymore, the aging of America is prying open a Pandora's box of unknowns. It's enough to worry policy wonks and make millionaires of marketing consultants. How and where will mature, active people choose to live? Work? Will they adopt healthier lifestyles and stay fit until the end? Will they bankrupt Social Security, Medicare, and Medicaid? What new products, geared for the mature market, will go mainstream? How will boomers react to discovering they are not, in Bob Dylan's words, "forever young"? These are the questions that will determine the shape and quality of THE RETIREMENT ZONE in the early 21st century.

Snapshot of an Older America

2010

65 to 69 years	12.1 million
70 to 74 years	9.0 million
75 to 79 years	7.1 million
80 to 84 years	5.6 million
85 to 89 years	3.5 million
90 to 94 years	1.6 million
95 to 99 years	556,000

Source: Population Projections Program, Population Division, U.S. Census Bureau, 2003

BABY BOOMERS Seventy-six million Americans were born between 1946 and 1964. Boomers will turn age 50 at the rate of roughly 10,000 per day for the next decade. This demographic reality will define THE RETIREMENT ZONE.

But wait. Will those unpredictable baby boomers actually retire at all? Yes. No. Maybe. Sometimes. And in their own way.

The characteristic baby-boomer reply might be this: "What, retire? I'm fifty-five and I'm just finally doing the work I want to do! Finally figured out my work wardrobe, work persona. The mom dilemma doesn't bother me for the first time in twenty years—because my kids grew up and went to college. I have big plans ahead and I'm just now, finally, making the big bucks. I love having a career. Maybe I'll take some time off, live in Italy for a year when I'm sixty-five, and then come back and start a little consulting thing, I could do *that*."

Surveys show that a majority of baby boomers say they intend to land a job or start a business after they leave their primary career. Many say they expect to work part time. Of course, that's gazing into a crystal ball. For financial reasons, some will keep right on trucking at established careers. A segment will go back to work in another field that provides challenge, or meaning, or just something new. Some will consult; many will work from home via the Internet. It's a mobile, wired, experience-seeking generation that will redefine retirement.

LIVING LONGER

At age 77, Senator John Glenn came out of astronaut retirement. In 1962, he'd been the first American to orbit earth. Thirty-six years later, in 1998, this septuagenarian became the oldest American to ride the space shuttle.

It's a defining characteristic of THE RETIREMENT ZONE that most of us seem to feel younger than our chronological age. Nearly half of older Americans consider themselves to be middle-aged or young, and only 15 percent of those over 75 consider themselves "very old," according to the study *American Perceptions of Aging in the 21st Century* by the National Council on the Aging (NCOA).

Americans Defy Chronological Definitions of Age

When asked "Do you consider yourself young, middle-aged, old, or very old?" here's how a cross section of over a thousand American men and women age 65 to 74 replied:

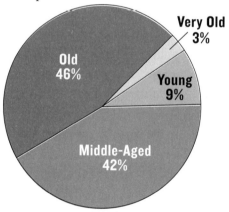

Source: *American Perceptions of Aging in the 21st Century*, National Council on the Aging, 2002

Feeling younger than our actual ages isn't just blind optimism. Americans are actually living longer. Life expectancy has increased two and a half years every decade for the past 100 years. In the United States, the age group that experts call the "old-old," meaning people over 85, is one of the fastest-growing groups, jumping nearly 40 percent in the decade from 1990 to 2000. The boundaries between middle-aged and old are blurring.

The Surprising Lives of Octo- and Nonagenarians

Many people of quite advanced years simply aren't playing their roles. They live longer, consider themselves younger, and act and look that way, too. Retired financier Helmut Friedlaender lives at a pace that some people half his age couldn't match, including flying to Europe for holidays, managing an office, collecting rare books, and attending opera performances. He jokes, "When I tell someone that I am ninety, if they are polite they say I look sixty; if they are realistic they say I look seventy."

Eighty- and ninety-year-old people are blasting through expectation barriers. A quick look at the *Guinness Book of World Records* or even your local newspaper lends new meaning to the term "robust old age." Guinness informs us that at age 107, Scotsman David Henderson had a pacemaker implanted. At age 99, American Hildegarde Ferrera risked a tandem parachute jump over Mokuleia, Hawaii. The oldest recorded living person was Jeanne-Louise Calment, a French woman who lived for 122 years (1875-1997). She took up fencing at age 85, rode a bicycle at 100, and played herself in the film *Vincent and Me* at age 114! These are the champs, the stars of THE RETIREMENT ZONE. They define the realm of what's possible.

"More and more elders . . . demonstrate that they are able to contribute far longer than society had thought. It is not exceptional to have a person highly engaged in civic life in their eighties," says gerontologist Nina M. Silverstein, PhD, an associate professor at the University of Massachusetts. She recalls a student who completed his degree at age 84, relocated from Boston to Seattle, where his daughter lives, and then took an MSW degree—and flying lessons, too. "We talk a lot about functional, not chronological, age," she says.

Will *You* Live to be 100?

A 21st-century phenomenon is the appearance of an entirely new category of person, the 100-year-old man or woman. You may recall that Bob Hope, George Burns, and Strom Thurmond all lived to party on their 100th birthdays. Once a rare blip on the demographic radar screen, the centenarian is a member of one of the fast-growing groups in the nation, numbering 70,000 in 2000, nearly double that of the previous decade. By 2010, the "centenarian club" is projected to grow to 130,000, and further increase to 324,000 by 2030. Imagine a Cincinnati-sized city, every citizen a centenarian!

One has to admit, the prospect of living until 100 or 110 casts retirement at, say, age 60, in a whole different light. Many people haven't given much thought to the implications of living a very long life. As Connie Acton, a 70-something retired school administrator, says, "I didn't even expect to live this long! It surprises me every day. Here I am." Clearly, if you're thinking about leaving work or planning for fun in THE RETIREMENT ZONE, you'll need to know how long you'll be paying bills.

It's a daunting question: How long will *you* live? Of course, nobody can predict on an individual basis. The following table is based on projections for the population as a whole.

Your Average Life Expectancy, According to Your Age Today

If you were ___ years old in 2000, your average life expectancy would be ___ more years.

	WOMEN		MEN	
	White	Black	White	Black
45 years old	34.7	33.1	32.6	28.1
55 years old	27.5	24.9	24	20.7
65 years old	19.2	17.4	16.3	14.5
75 years old	12.1	11.2	10.1	9.4
85 years old	6.6	6.5	5.5	5.7

Source: *National Vital Statistics Reports*, December 19, 2002.

Check out this Web site: www.livingto100.com, just for fun. It promotes a book called *Living to 100*, and for no cost it will make a projection of your potential length of life, based on your inputting basic medical and lifestyle information about yourself.

How Long Can Life Be Extended?

If medical science can eventually lick cancer, heart disease, diabetes, and other major causes of death, will people live to age 150, 200, or forever? Well, no. "There are 131 causes of death that can be listed on death certificates," says Dr. Leonard Hayflick, author of *How and Why We Age* (Ballantine Books, 1994). "And even if you eradicated every single disease tomorrow, you'd still find that people die, if not from disease then from the process of aging itself. Just as your hair goes white, your skin sags a little, similar cellular processes are going on internally," he explains. It's the aging process. Others aren't so sure. Commenting on a study conducted when he was director of Duke University's demographic research program, Dr. James W. Vaupel says, "There may or may not be some limit at some advanced age—it is impossible to tell, given current empirical data and theoretical knowledge." That research, which was reported in the May 10, 2002, issue of *Science* magazine, shows "there is no limit that we are about to bump up against." Vaupel, now of the Max Planck Institute for Demographic Research in Germany, maintains that the average human life span may reach 100 by 2060.

Another open question is whether science can shorten the period of disease and diminution prior to the end of life. Experts call it the "compression of morbidity"—in other words, cramming the unpleasant phase of decline into shorter and shorter periods. In reality, says Dr. James Carey, a demographer at the University of California at Davis, you can't eradicate all disease. After studying six million fruit flies over a 15-year period, he says, "It's a fact of life, whether you are a fruit fly or a human being, that toward the end of life there's a period of sickness and disablement. But you might be able to shorten the amount of time people feel ill before dying."

A variety of factors contribute to long life, including the ability to cope well with stress. Good genes help, of course, but you don't have much control over that; however, good habits *can* make a big difference—eating a good diet, exercising regularly, and staying active and engaged in life.

Is it a good or a bad thing that more people are living longer? Pessimists will point out the stresses an aging society places on health services, housing, and social welfare programs. Books have been written warning of future generation wars over scarce resources. But success has its own terms. Beyond the real, if mundane, issues of resource allocation is the very fact of life itself. That people are able to live longer while enjoying better physical health than at any earlier stage of history has rightly been called one of the great achievements of modern civilization.

What about "Anti-aging" Medications?

Modern medicine is helping people live longer and more productively. But don't hold your breath until they discover the Fountain of Youth; not everything that promises can actually deliver. If you're in THE RETIREMENT ZONE, you're in a target market for a slew of so-called anti-aging treatments—even if the safety and efficacy of some of them haven't been established yet. Buyer beware!

AGEISM AND INVISIBILITY: Fuggedaboutit

Ageism is an "ism" that doesn't have a home in THE RETIREMENT ZONE.

For years, it's been the case that at some age threshold—maybe 50 for women, older for men—people begin to gripe that they feel invisible, like Casper the Ghost, or Cosmo Topper's pals George and Marion Kirby. You'll hear disgruntled middle-aged women say, "You can go anywhere in the world and nobody bothers you." And older gents complain that they're bypassed when standing in line at a store.

Anyone over 60 could be forgiven for wondering if they will see their true reflection in society's mirrors—in films, art, theater, advertising. As of this writing, you can find three or four parenting magazines on the newsstand. In contrast, there's barely a single mainstream magazine dedicated to the heroes, experts, exploits, and life challenges of mature men and women, outside of AARP publications. And anti-age discrimination provisions were written into federal law for darned good reason.

Of course, "isms" feed on misinformation and stereotypes. *The Myths and Realities of Aging*, published by the National Council on the Aging (www.ncoa.org), shows that Americans of all ages—from 16 to 75—associate aging with nursing homes. In reality, only 5 percent of people over 65 reside in them. The same research finds that over half of adults under age 65 consider older people to be

the worst drivers. In reality, U.S. Department of Transportation data show that older drivers are involved in fewer fatal motor vehicle accidents than drivers aged 15 to 35. And the beat goes on.

A particularly fascinating comparison was done to gauge the difference between how older people and younger people assess the problems facing people over 65. The results suggest that people over 65 are in much better psychological shape and are far less worried overall than the public at large assumes (see chart below).

Is This a Serious Problem for People 65 and Over?

DO YOU THINK . . .	Percentage of those 18-64 answering yes	Percentage of 65+ answering yes
Money is a serious problem for people over 65?	88	36
Health is a serious problem for people over 65?	92	42
Loneliness is a serious problem for people over 65?	84	21
Crime is a serious problem for people over 65?	82	36

Source: *American Perceptions of Aging in the 21st Century*, National Council on the Aging, 2002

Given the abundance of myths, will sheer population pressure force a shift in the winds of ageism? Maybe. Here are three reasons:

First of all, consider the dynamism of the generations in and about to enter THE RETIREMENT ZONE. Among existing retirees are the very people who brought us post–World War II successes in science, medicine, art, industry, transportation, technology, and more. And according to the 2000 U.S. Census, huge numbers of highly qualified professionals will be age 65 or over in 2005. Among them count more than 140,000 CEOs, 130,000 teachers at postsecondary schools, 20,000 high school teachers, 70,000 physicians and surgeons, 20,000 dentists, 110,000 registered nurses, 23,000 engineers, 12,000 bakers, 10,000 police officers, 4,000 airline pilots and engineers, 4,700 legislators, and over 500 nuclear engineers. And that's just the tip of the iceberg; baby boomers start hitting age 65 in 2011.

Second, older baby boomers are a growing market, to say the least. Don't be surprised if marketers figure out a way to spin "older" as "cooler." Or if the new joke becomes "Don't trust anyone *under* 60."

Lastly, invisibility is just not a strong suit of baby boomers. This is a cohort that's familiar with yokes of gender and racial discrimination—and used to noisy public policy debates over these "isms." Is it likely that in the face of ageism, the now-60 somethings and their boomer baby siblings are going to "go gentle into that good night," as in the Dylan Thomas poem? Without a party or a fight? Without leaning out the window and collectively screaming, like the character in the 1976 movie *Network*, "I'm mad as hell and I'm not gonna take this anymore"? *Fuggedaboutit.*

After all, it's cool to be older.

Investing in Your Future

Curiously, most books and Web sites about retirement pertain strictly to the realm of financial planning. But your life possibilities add up to more than just the sum of your investments!

In Part II, discover how to invest in *yourself* to stay fit in all ways—your mind and your body, your social relationships, and even your mental attitude—so that you fully enjoy your retirement years. *Life's About More Than Money* is an invitation to identify and marshal your personal, social, and health resources, and to build on them, just as you might build on a successful financial investment. Regardless of what age you are when you start, you'll enjoy life more if you maintain a healthy lifestyle, and pursue the things that enrich you personally as well as contribute to society. In *Forge Your Personal Path* and *Look Inward, Angel,* you'll learn what the transition into retirement entails beyond simply dollars and cents.

LIFE'S ABOUT MORE THAN MONEY

Remember Dr. Spock, the pediatric guru of the 1950s and beyond? His commonsense advice guided generations of parents. He was a plainspoken advocate for a sensible, balanced life, building on simple things, like getting a varied diet, enough sleep and exercise, opportunities to learn, and lots of love. Spock was right—for grown-ups, too.

A 10-year study funded by the MacArthur Foundation found that among a large sample of people aged 70 to 80, those who performed in the top third in terms of mental functioning shared three characteristics—but only in *combination*, not alone. The highest functioning people were all:

1) more mentally active,
2) more physically active,
   and
3) had a sense of their own effectiveness in the world around them. (That is, they felt that they were making a contribution to their family or society.)

Having one characteristic without the others didn't do the trick.

It is with a deep bow toward that notion of balance that much of this book describes specific ways you can stay mentally and physically active, and become emotionally, creatively, and socially engaged in activities that feel useful, life affirming, and fun.

CHAPTER 3

Attitude

ACCENTUATE THE POSITIVE

Attitude counts. How you approach THE RETIREMENT ZONE may influence both how well you live and how long you live.

Like a good raincoat, optimism can help protect you from stormy weather. Optimists seem to cope better when life rains on their parade. So if you aren't feeling great about your age, or about being in non–retirement, semi-, or full retirement, take charge of the situation. Steer your mindset in a different direction: Have more fun, make more of your social opportunities, do whatever it is that rocks your boat, makes you happy, and expands your horizons.

WHAT IS OPTIMISM?

The glass half full.

The brighter side of the moon.

The knowledge that "it's not what happens to you, but what you make of it" that counts.

"Optimism is about the ability to project prior (or previous) successes into the future," notes Canadian psychology professor Gary Reker. In his research, he found, too, that optimists are realistic. "They focused on things that were realistically attainable—not winning the lottery. That differentiates optimism from wishful thinking," he said.

One thing you can do to increase your own level of optimism is to look ahead, create options, and plan for a future you hope to realize. Helmut Friedlaender, an active 90-year-old, says, "One of the key things to a successful retirement is not to waste your time on what is gone and to be interested in what you can do in the present."

A positive outlook is potent medicine. People with positive views of aging live longer—by as much as seven years, according to Yale University researchers working on the Ohio Longitudinal Study on Aging and Retirement. This represents a *huge* gain in longevity, accounting for more years of life than such standards as low blood pressure, low cholesterol or healthy weight, not smoking, or exercising regularly. The two-decade-long study also found that people with an optimistic attitude toward aging enjoy better functional health over the long term. And reams of other research has shown that attitude can influence how people interpret events and experience sensations—even some of the very things, such as physical pain, that make us fearful of aging.

The reverse holds true, too. Negativity can be a self-fulfilling prophecy. People who hold low expectations about what aging may bring in terms of physical and mental capacity, social life, and life satisfaction may also believe it's not important that they seek medical attention, likely leading to poorer health. It's a downward spiral.

Less surprising, perhaps, is that optimism and its twin sister, openness to experience, are important ingredients in keeping the psychological soufflé *up*. Not *everything* is in one's mind, of course. Disease, chronic conditions, and accidents cannot always be prevented. But protected by a generally positive outlook, you're better prepared to ride through life's inevitable storms.

The Best Years of Your Life?

Well, you may sniff, optimism is just fine and dandy. But what's so great about being old enough to have arrived in THE RETIREMENT ZONE in the first place? The answer, in a nutshell, is that every life stage has its wonders and unique benefits. Life continues to offer choices, daily. About half of Americans aged 65 to 69 agreed that "these are the best years of my life," in a study conducted by the National Council on the Aging. That compares to two out of every three Americans of all ages who described the present as their best years. (Two fifths of people in their 70s and one third of people in their 80s agreed.)

The point is, people find and create their own good news.

Take the case of an 80-year-old artist, who is brimming with projects, including worldwide travel plans. She details some of her recent health problems, including a loss of hearing. "A couple of days ago," she says matter-of-factly, "another problem came up, this lichen planus. It's a skin disorder, not contagious. I have it *everywhere*. I itch constantly. It is horrible, as bad as shingles. And they don't know what causes it, maybe a reaction to taking stuff for high blood pressure. It's miserable, all right." Then she laughs and in a long drawl adds, "And it's *uuugly* too. That just gives me more reasons to stay home. The good thing is, I will get to do more in my studio."

"If doors close on certain things, you reestablish that optimism by focusing on alternatives," notes Reker.

You Can Learn to Look on the Bright Side

If "natural optimist" doesn't describe you or your loved one, are there ways to *become* an optimist? Many psychologists who study attitudes say optimism *can* be learned. If you are interested in a structured approach to changing your outlook, there are various resources. Dr. Martin Seligman, a University of Pennsylvania psychology professor and past president of the American Psychology Association offers suggestions in his bestseller *Learned Optimism: How to Change Your Mind and Your Life* (Alfred A. Knopf, 1991). One quick trip to the local bookstore or library will yield a treasure chest of other books, such as *The Science of Optimism and Hope: Research Essays in Honor of Martin E. P. Seligman,* edited by Jane E. Gillham (Templeton Foundation Press, 2000), *Optimal Thinking: How to Be Your Best Self* by Rosalene Glickman (John Wiley & Sons, 2002), and *The Resilience Factor: 7 Essential Skills for Overcoming Life's Inevitable Obstacles* by Karen Reivich, PhD, and Andrew Shatté, PhD (Broadway Books, 2002).

Are *You* an Optimist?

Take the quiz below to determine your own degree of optimism. It's the short version of a tool called the Life Orientation Test (LOT). It was developed by psychologists at the University of Florida to assess individual differences in generalized optimism versus pessimism, and has been used in a good deal of research on the behavioral, affective, and health consequences of optimism.

Please be as honest and accurate as you can throughout. Try not to let your response to one statement influence your responses to other statements. There are no "correct" or "incorrect" answers. Answer according to your own feelings, rather than how you think "most people" would answer, using the following scale:

A) I agree a lot
B) I agree a little
C) I neither agree nor disagree
D) I disagree a little
E) I disagree a lot

1) In uncertain times, I usually expect the best. _____
2) It's easy for me to relax. _____
3) If something can go wrong with me, it will. _____
4) I'm always optimistic about my future. _____
5) I enjoy my friends a lot. _____
6) It's important for me to keep busy. _____
7) I hardly ever expect things to go my way. _____
8) I don't get upset too easily. _____
9) I rarely count on good things happening to me. _____
10) Overall, I expect more good things to happen to me than bad. _____

To score, see key on page 37

Scheier, M.F., Carver, C.S. & Bridges, M.W. (1994). Distinguishing optimism from neuroticism (and trait anxiety, self-mastery, and self-esteem): A re-evaluation of the Life Orientation Test. *Journal of Personality and Social Psychology, 67, 1063-1078.* ©1994 by the American Psychological Association. Reprinted with permission.

Practical Tips: 8 WAYS TO THINK LIKE AN OPTIMIST IN THE RETIREMENT ZONE

1) Focus on what's achievable in the future—things that you look forward to.

2) Review your past successes in life. "Sometimes I ask people to tell me about the things they've done in their life," says Reker. "They are often quite surprised by their achievements. They say, 'Well, I have accomplished quite a bit in hindsight; I've had some successes here and there.' So they realize that they have had their downs and also their ups—and in the end, they feel more positive about the future."

3) Often, the news media presents the statistics of aging in a negative way. So try inverting the numbers, and see how it reads. For instance, "Nearly 80 percent of Americans age 65 and older don't have any chronic disabilities," instead of, "Among people 65 and older, 21 percent have chronic disabilities."

4) Get out and see friends.

5) Volunteer to help someone or some cause.

6) Pursue whatever religious or spiritual path appeals to you.

7) Get regular, vigorous exercise that combines aerobic and strength training.

8) Every day, write down one thing you are grateful for. As the saying goes, count your blessings.

A NOTE ON THE DEEP, DEEP BLUES Sometimes life can get you down. Certainly there's a time for grief and mourning. But if things don't brighten up after an appropriate period of time, you may want to find help. And, if you've got the garden-variety blues, address it. Isolation is associated with depression, so you can fight it: You can pick up the pace of your social life and exercise regimen, or volunteer to help others. Also, cut down on drinking if you turn to alcohol; don't overuse or misuse medications; talk to a member of the clergy or spiritual mentor; and don't forget to eat a balanced diet. And, of course, get counseling.

Remember, the "leg bone's connected to the . . ." and your brain and emotions are connected to your body, too. The blues can affect your health. Even mild depression that lasts longer than 18 months may suppress the immune system, according to research done at the Johns Hopkins School of Medicine. So if instead of singing "Accentuate the Positive," you're more prone to the old spiritual, "Sometimes I Feel Like a Motherless Child," then please, consult your physician. There's no cause for shame (lots of people have similar experiences). And yes, you can get help, and get through it.

Being depressed isn't the end of the world—as long as you know when to blow the whistle. So if your spouse seems like he or she is just a little too blue a little too often, check it out (or do the same for yourself). Have a friend administer this little test for you:

 ## Are *You* Depressed?

Choose the most accurate answer for how you've felt over the past week.

1) Are you basically satisfied with your life? yes/**no**
2) Have you dropped many of your activities and interests? **yes**/no
3) Do you feel that your life is empty? **yes**/no
4) Do you often get bored? **yes**/no
5) Are you in good spirits most of the time? yes/**no**
6) Are you afraid that something bad is going to happen to you? **yes**/no
7) Do you feel happy most of the time? yes/**no**
8) Do you often feel helpless? **yes**/no
9) Do you prefer to stay at home rather than going out and doing new things? **yes**/no
10) Do you feel you have more problems with memory than most? **yes**/no
11) Do you think it is wonderful to be alive now? yes/**no**
12) Do you feel you are pretty worthless the way you are now? **yes**/no
13) Do you feel full of energy? yes/**no**
14) Do you feel that your situation is hopeless? **yes**/no
15) Do you think that most people are better off than you are? **yes**/no

To score, see key on page 37

Source: *Geriatrics at Your Fingertips* 2003, 5th Ed., American Geriactrics Society.
See www.stanford.edu/~yesavage/GDS.html

If you're reading this book for a spouse, friend, or parent, know that attitude can influence your loved one's health. If he or she is upbeat, support that sunny view! Do your best to help him or her reinforce a positive future orientation.

ANSWER KEYS

To score quiz on page 34, "Are You an Optimist?"
Do NOT score items 2, 5, 6, and 8. These are fillers.
Otherwise, give each answer for the remaining six questions a score:
A=5, B=4, C=3, D=2, E=1. The highest possible score is 30.
The closer to 30 your score, the more optimistic you are.

To score quiz on page 36, "Are You Depressed?"
Score one point for each bolded answer. Cutoff for normal is 0 to 5.
If your score is above 5, that suggests depression; it's a good idea to seek professional counseling.

Resource Guide

The Art of Happiness: A Handbook for Living by His Holiness the Dalai Lama and Howard C. Cutler, M.D. (Riverhead Books, 1998).

Learned Optimism: How to Change Your Mind and Your Life by Martin E. P. Seligman, PhD (Alfred A. Knopf, 1991).

Loving What Is: Four Questions That Can Change Your Life by Byron Katie with Stephen Mitchell (Harmony Books, 2002).

Man's Search for Meaning by Viktor E. Frankl (Washington Square Press, 1997).

Toward Positive Aging, a newsletter by Ken and Mary Gergen, available online at www.healthandage.com, sponsored by the Web-based Health Education Foundation (WHEF), an independent nonprofit organization.

CHAPTER 4

Heart

ANCHORING YOUR SOCIAL LIFE

You're a wealthy person indeed if your life is full of loving, positive relationships. Staying connected is one of the markers of people who enjoy their time in THE RETIREMENT ZONE. Social support networks can make an enormous difference when confronting life's inevitable challenges. Whether you're an extroverted "people person," and count your bosom buddies by the baker's dozens, or you're an introvert, with just two one or two close friends, your relationships color the quality of your life—and your health, too.

ANCHOR RELATIONSHIPS

As you're sailing through the journey of life, having "anchor relationships"—people you can count on, and who can count on you—makes all the difference. It's true—maybe even more so—in the post-work period.

Consider THE RETIREMENT ZONE a frontier of opportunities, including social opportunities. Nothing can replace an intimate circle of close friends and relatives. But throughout life, men and women can, and do, find new relationships. They fall in love again, and sometimes marry. They know how to fan the little sparks from a casual encounter into a friendship. And many forge mini-mutual-aid societies of all kinds with one another, from carpooling to being travel buddies.

At age 75, Barry Benepe juggles two homes and a dizzying array of civic roles. Benepe is the retired founder of two highly regarded New York organizations. He says, "I have a handful of really close relationships. And I have a large family, including five children and grandchildren." If anything, Barry's biggest social challenge is not who to see and what to do, but how to schedule his time so he can cram everything and everyone in.

"I laugh, because when I worked for IBM, my wife used to complain I don't have friends or a hobby; now she complains I have too many of both," says 64-year-old George Fox. He returned to work after retiring at IBM and has made new friends in his second career as a programmer. "I have good friends whom we meet at church on Sunday," he says. "We have lunch and maybe watch the football game sometimes. But the rest of the week, my close friends are my fellow workers—and the golfers."

It's a myth that retirement automatically spells isolation. Retirement-age people are as capable of "connecting" as anybody else, at any age. A National Council on the Aging study, *American Perceptions of Aging in the 21st Century*, reports that when asked whether loneliness is a very or somewhat serious problem for them, four in five people over 65 said it was not. That's reassuring.

Reality Check: Relationships Take Work

On the other hand, relationships are complicated. Long-standing "issues" with grown children, siblings, and spouses don't automatically get easier to deal with over time. Relating to grandchildren has its challenges. Love relationships, whether new or old, gay or straight, require nurturing. And with a high divorce rate, some people over 55 years of age are simultaneously facing retirement and living alone for the first time in what may seem like eons. Relationships with friends, partners, coworkers, and neighbors may take work.

Alas, that last paycheck doesn't come with a manual on how to strengthen, connect, rebuild, or form meaningful relationships. However, life in THE RETIREMENT ZONE may provide you with a precious asset for improving relationships: time.

BE PROACTIVE: Think about your social capital as well as your financial capital

You've heard of financial planning for retirement, and financial capital, of course. Let's assume that your relationships are valuable, just as stocks, bonds, and 401K plans are. So when planning ahead for retirement, consider this brilliant idea proposed by Dr. Gene Cohen, director of the Center on Aging, Health and Humanities at George Washington University.

Think of your social relationships as assets. Analyze your social strengths and weaknesses objectively, thinking ahead to possible future situations. Think of your social needs, he suggests, in the same rational way you'd assess your financial needs—and plan ahead. Going perhaps a step further than the average person, Cohen suggests thinking specifically about identifying friends and family with whom you could do enjoyable activities even if your mobility were severely curtailed, or if you had little energy. In other words, he suggests, plan your social life for a rainy day. And if relationships are as important (or more so) than money in THE RETIREMENT ZONE, he's got a point.

In an article called "Social Portfolio, The Role of Activity in Mental Wellness as People Age,"[1] Cohen writes, "the idea of an individual developing a social portfolio has not been deemed nearly as important as building a financial portfolio. A social portfolio contains diversified activities and interpersonal relationships that become sound assets to carry through later life." He continues, "The financial portfolio has three major concepts that influence its growth and development:

1) Assets from which to draw, with emphasis on diversification;

2) Insurance back-up should disability or related loss occur;

3) The idea that you start early and build up over time—though it is never too late."

The *social* portfolio, Cohen says, is analogous.

1) A person's assets are diversified interests and relationships from which he or she can develop and draw.

2) The insurance back-up is addressed by focusing on two areas: high energy/high mobility versus low energy/low mobility activities and group activities versus individual activities. The concept here is that should a loss occur in the form of a decline in physical health, not all of the interests a person has developed would require high energy or high mobility. Similarly, if the loss of a friend or a spouse occurs, in the transition of dealing with such a loss, a person has interests that he or she can draw upon that do not require the involvement of another.

3) The idea that a person starts early and builds relationships and activities, even though it is never too late to build. Thus, if a person has an interest in writing, he or she can start by taking a course on creative writing, and in retirement, write the Great American Novel."

Remember the 1950s hit TV show, *This is Your Life,* hosted by Ralph Edwards? (Yes, fans, he also hosted *Truth or Consequences.*) If you were producing a *This is Your Life* episode about yourself, who would be on the master-list of people in your life? Think of acquaintances; friends; family; current and past bosses, employees, and work colleagues; classmates from college or even elementary or high school; members of your faith community; neighbors; people in the town where you live; your doctor, dentist, insurance agent, banker, barber or hairstylist, car mechanic—and so on.

YOU MIGHT FIND IT HELPFUL TO THINK OF THEM IN GROUPS SUCH AS

The intimate circle: Parents, adult children, grandchildren, spouses, siblings, lovers—these are the characters who occupy center stage in our minds and hearts. The intimate circle often includes partners and close friends. For many people, the intimate circle is life itself—the only set of relationships that really count.

Through volunteer work or other activities, sometimes people stumble on significant relationships. Retired early from public middle-school teaching because of his epilepsy, John Vanier found himself dedicating a significant amount of time, energy, and even money to a church outreach program to help detained immigrants who, while seeking asylum in the United States, were being held in isolation in local detention centers. "I never thought I would be this involved," he says. Through his work in the program, John, a modest, soft-spoken man, has developed meaningful and lasting relationships with detainees who have become more like family than friends.

Friends, buddies, pals: Perhaps not quite "intimate circle status," but good friends nonetheless, sometimes these people fade in (or out) of your focus. An important subset is the "ex" or "old" category, as in "old friend," "ex-neighbor," and "previous coworker."

Friends-in-a-box: They might be coworkers, classmates, or covolunteers—with very defined boundaries. Usually there's something shared; that's the "co" part. What's interesting about these relationships is their potential to grow—to come alive outside the box.

Concentric rings of community: Often people think of community as geographic, as in your town or subdivision or neighborhood. But we've all got lots of communities: a civic, alumni, or fraternal organization; a church, ethnic association, or church choir; a book club, Weight Watchers meetings, exercise class, or quilting circle. Relationships aren't all talk all the time, either. As Quakers build community in silence, musicians build it playing music together. What are *your* communities?

Managing Your "Social Portfolio" in THE RETIREMENT ZONE

Indulge in a little advanced social engineering. Of your own social life, that is! This may seem a little like planning your next New Year's Eve date on January 2. But who wants to be caught late in life without having made decent investments, whether financial or emotional?

The idea here is that you have social resources for all contingencies: things to do when you are alone and full of energy and good health, and when you are alone and not so well; when you are with other people and full of energy and good health, and things you can enjoy with others when you aren't as mobile or energetic.

So run through the following exercise, and if you come up short in one category or another, think about finding a buddy to do some of your favorite things with.

The chart opposite shows how you can list the things you like to do that require a lot of mobility and things that don't require much mobility, and to identify people you can do each kind of activity with.

LOTS OF ENERGY/ABILITY TO DRIVE, WALK, MOVE AROUND		NOT MUCH ENERGY OR MOBILITY	
Social Activities	People I can do this with	Social Activities	People I can do this with
Skiing	Sara David	Playing chess	Richard David
Hiking	Joanne	Watching movies	Joanne
Traveling	Bill Gabriel	Investing club	Gabriel Jonah
Solo Activities		Solo Activities	
Exercising		Reading	

[2] Adapted with permission from Cohen, G. (See citation at end of chapter.)

With less time committed to the office, store, plant, or job, you've got an opportunity to refresh relationships and make new ones. A popular small-business owner whose shop was always filled with neighborhood people reports upon retiring, " I have fewer superficial contacts, but I have a better time with people now. I have more time to really listen. We can have real conversations."

 HEALTHVIEWS

"In London, when you go to the doctor these days, you'll likely be asked how your relations are with your siblings," says one British psychologist. Only half-jokingly she adds, "And if you've gone for corns, well, they figure your feet will feel better if you're on good terms with your brother or sister."

Intuitively, you know that having a solid, if not large, network of social support is "good" for you. Duh! Of course it is! Having friends, sharing laughter, being able to ask for and give help might be the easiest and cheapest preventive medicine around. Reams of scientific articles document it, too, although you might need a PhD in biology to understand them. Suffice it to say, there's apparently an association between good social relationships and the body's ability to resist, and recover from, disease.

For instance, older men who have few personal relationships may have increased risk of heart disease. "Social isolation may influence inflammatory markers and may be one way social relationships influence our health," said Eric B. Loucks, PhD, at Harvard School of Public Health, whose research has gauged social relationships based on such elements as marital status, number of close friends and family members, and extent of religious and social-club participation. "People who have a low variety of social relationships may not have people to support them in behaviors such as exercise or in stopping smoking." He explained that stress can raise levels of certain elements in the blood, and may be another pathway by which social isolation can influence health.

A different study of hundreds of men and women over age 58 found that friends, family, and positive experiences accumulate over a lifetime to help counteract the normal wear and tear of life. Men and women who had good childhoods and good marriages scored considerably better on a measure of aging that includes a broad range of biological risk factors for disease and death, according to findings published in the May/June 2002 issue of *Psychosomatic Medicine.*

Individual components of the measure, known as allostatic load, include blood pressure, cholesterol levels, blood sugar metabolism, and hormonal levels. Those components often do not significantly affect health outcomes, but assessing them together has been shown to predict risk for disease and death, says lead author Teresa E. Seeman, PhD, of the UCLA School of Medicine.

The researchers found that allostatic load was generally higher in the older group of men and women, consistent with the idea that allostatic load represents the normal wear and tear of aging. Men and women who had a lot of supportive friends were much more likely to score low than those with two or fewer close friends. Women, and to a lesser extent men, also seemed to benefit from good relationships with their parents and spouses.

"Relationships likely affect a range of biological systems as cognitive and emotional qualities of social experiences are translated by the brain to downstream patterns of physiological activity," she says.

> **If you're reading this book for a spouse, friend, or parent . . .** heads-up! You may expect that without a full-time job, they'll spend more time with you or their grandchildren. Don't be so sure! They may have other things and people—even new love interests—claiming their time as well.

Practical Tips: 9 WAYS TO MAKE NEW CONNECTIONS IN THE RETIREMENT ZONE

After years of work experience, raising families, and living life, you probably know how to network effectively. Use those skills to benefit your social life, too. If you would like to make new friends, reach out. Throughout this book you'll find lots of ideas to pursue, both fun and serious. And voila! Here are a few ways to expand your social horizons.

1) Think positively about yourself.

2) Pursue something you love or are interested in, in a place where you will meet like-minded people.

3) Get a dog and walk it where you are likely to meet other dog walkers.

4) Join an activity at your local church, civic organization, or political group.

5) Get in touch with old friends, local or distant.

6) Think about making friends of all ages.

7) Join an organization related to your skills, profession, union, or business.

8) Learn how to use a computer and make cyber friends in chat rooms, or e-mail your relatives and acquaintances.

9) Travel with a group that has a high percentage of mature, single travelers.

(See Chapter 18, Loving Makes the World Go 'Round, on page 246 for Online dating information.)

Resource Guide

Difficult Conversations: How to Discuss What Matters Most by Douglas Stone, Bruce Patton, and Sheila Heen (Viking, 1999).

Rebuilding: When Your Relationship Ends by Bruce Fisher, EdD, and Robert E. Alberti, PhD (Impact Publishers, 1999).

[1, 2] Adapted by permission from Cohen, G. (2003) The social portfolio: The role of activity in mental wellness as people age. J.L. Ronch and J.A. Goldfield (Eds.), Mental wellness in aging: Strengths-based approaches (p. 117). Baltimore: Health Professions Press. (Adapted with permission from Cohen, G.D. (2000). *The Creative Age: Awakening Human Potential in the Second Half of Life.* NY, Avon Books).

CHAPTER 5

Head

TAKE YOUR BRAIN TO THE GYM

You're as sharp now as you were at 20, right? And with a wide range of interesting pursuits awaiting you in THE RETIREMENT ZONE, you might want to take good care of that precious gray matter.

Technically, of course, a mind is not a muscle, like your biceps or quadriceps. Your brain is a mass of nerves that probably outdoes the complexity of, say, the World Wide Web. But the experts say, treat your mind like a muscle. Take care of it. Exercise it. Stretch it. Challenge it. Pamper it. Pay attention to it when it's stressed out, undernourished, or in need of stimulation.

MARVELOUS MATURE BRAINS

It's clear that mature brains are doing quite well, thank you very much. At age 90, Studs Terkel was editing interviews for a new book. At age 102, Ray Christ, dubbed the nation's oldest practicing scientist in 2002 by the *Philadelphia Inquirer*, was researching a way to clean polluted water—despite being almost blind. Senator Bob Byrd, at nearly 90, delivered blistering foreign-policy critiques in 2002 from the Senate floor, invoking Greek and Roman classics to argue against a U.S. war with Iraq. Eva Zeisel, legendary ceramicist, made news at 95 with her designs, now sold at major museum stores. Art Linkletter, Hugh Downs, and sexologist Dr. Ruth Westheimer draw large crowds to speaking engagements.

As poet Marianne Moore wrote, "The mind is an enchanted thing, like the glaze on a katydid-wing."

FACT OR MYTH: Is your brain power sputtering out? Brain researchers are finding that an aging brain is more resilient, vigorous, and fertile than previously believed. A breakthrough discovery in the late 1990s at Princeton University identified a process called *neurogenesis*—literally, the birth of new neurons—in the brains of adult primates. The same process in humans was subsequently documented at the Salk Institute.

An emerging consensus is that the adult brain possesses more plasticity than previously thought, and that it is capable of making *new* connections, regardless of age. As reported in the October, 2002, issue of the *New England Journal of Medicine*, just reading a challenging book, doing mental math problems, or even working out the crossword puzzle on a daily basis may provide protection against diseases of the brain such as Alzheimer's. Dr. Joseph Coyle, a Harvard Medical School psychiatrist, wrote, "The cerebral cortex and hippocampus, which are critical to these activities, are remarkably plastic, and they rewire themselves based upon their use." How does this work? Scientists aren't sure yet of the precise mechanism.

EXERCISE YOUR MIND LIKE A MUSCLE. Is retirement good or bad for mental fitness? This is a good question. It's not unusual to worry, or at least wonder, about whether your memory and other mental faculties will remain as sharp as the years fly by.

The simple answer is that it depends in part on what you do with yourself. (Hint: Vegging out in front of the television set for hours every day isn't highly recommended.) Intellectual stimulation is one key to remaining mentally agile throughout life. Staying mentally active may help keep a person emotionally healthy. And feeling intellectually and mentally strong is good for self-esteem. Lastly, scientists hypothesize that there's a connection between depression and your immune system, which, in turn, influences your ability to ward off physical ailments.

You can tickle your brain in lots of different ways. Experts recommend doing crossword puzzles, using a computer, reading books, listening intently to music, and going to lectures and concerts. Take Patricia S. in Rochester, Minnesota, who does math exercises for ten or fifteen minutes a day, just for fun, over her morning coffee. "I'm the fastest, so I'm always the one to split up the bill when us gals have lunch," she chuckles. Ted Couch, an athletic 70-something who realized he was bored intellectually, combines two things he loves: reading and hiking. He says, "I have a general interest in European and American history. I just happened onto a book on Lewis and Clark a few years ago. It became a tar baby for me! I have done *a lot* of reading on it. I've led a ten-week course on Lewis and Clark at the local college. On my own, I've retraced most of Lewis and Clark's trail. There's a Lewis and Clark Trail Heritage Foundation, a national organization, which I have joined."

Practical Tips:
9 WAYS TO STRETCH YOUR MIND

1) Take a brisk walk for 45 minutes, three times a week.
2) Reconsider your relationship with your television. It's passive. Limit your TV viewing, as you might limit a child's, to a few hours daily.
3) Arrange situations where you read and talk more with other people in an in-depth way about problems, books, politics, or whatever interests you.
4) Learn to play chess, bridge, or even take up fencing (all are strategy games).
5) Listen to music, take up an instrument, and go to concerts.
6) Make up your own challenges. If you read mysteries, diagram the plot and see how you think it will end. Buy and play a Brainteaser game designed for teenagers and adults.
7) Start your memoirs. Go back to Elvis, sock hops, the Beatles, and the Cold War.
8) Take a class or go back to school.
9) Dance! Believe it or not, dancing has brain benefits.

HOW MUCH BRAIN WORK IS ENOUGH? Nobody knows. So far, no expert body has issued specific guidelines on what to do to keep mentally agile. But experts recommend that you challenge it on a regular basis. For a stumper, try the Mensa Brain Teaser (www.mensa.org).

 ## Brain Quiz

While you're reading about stretching your mind, why not do it? It doesn't have to take long, or hurt. As long as you are reading this book, here is a little quiz to get your brain brewing.

TRUE OR FALSE?

1) _____   If my brain's going to go, it's going to go.
There's nothing I can do about it.

2) _____   Brain cells can't regenerate, which some other cells in the body can do.

3) _____   A person's mental performance in older age has nothing to do with his/her social life at that stage of life.

4) _____   What I eat doesn't impact how well my brain works.

5) _____   Aerobic exercise is recommended for a healthy heart, etc., but not for improved memory.

6) _____   It's better to stick with established routines when you're older than to be in an environment where there's a lot going on and a lot of choices to be made.

7) _____   An older person who's experienced some decline in cognitive functions can improve his memory by training and special activities.

To score, see key on page 52.

For information on related topics, see Resource Guide on page 52 and also *Successful Aging* by John Wallis Rowe, M.D., and Robert L. Kahn, PhD (Dell, 1998).

OTHER WAYS TO LOVE YOUR BRAIN: Exercise, Diet, and Sleep

Thinking holistically, everything you do impacts your brain.

Exercise: The Greeks Were Right

Healthy body, healthy mind. The mind-body connection is as strong in THE RETIREMENT ZONE as it was in ancient Greece. If sheer vanity (or the desire to look like a Greek god or goddess) doesn't get you back into the habit of exercising, then these studies should. Three key areas of the brain adversely affected by aging show the greatest benefit when a person stays physically fit, according to a study reported in the February 2003 issue of the *Journal of Gerontology: Medical Sciences*. The findings provide the first empirical confirmation of the relationship between cardiovascular fitness and neural degeneration. "Older adults show a real decline in brain density in white and gray areas, but fitness actually slows that decline," said lead author Arthur F. Kramer, a professor of psychology and member of the Beckman Institute for Advanced Science and Technology, at the University of Illinois. In 1999, in the journal *Nature*, Kramer and colleagues also reported findings that previously sedentary people over age 60 who walked rapidly for 45 minutes three days a week can significantly improve mental-processing abilities that decline with age. And of course, physical activity can be an antidote to mild depression, in varying degrees.

Some experts have found that more than 30 minutes of exercise per session, combining both aerobic exercise and strength training, produces the greatest benefit.

Diet: Blueberries Benefit the Brain

Eating certain foods (and avoiding others) may help protect you from heart disease, some types of cancers, and other illnesses. But can your diet help protect your brain if you should suffer a stroke or accidental head injury, or keep your thinking and memory skills strong as you age? It's hard to sort out marketing hype from scientifically grounded fact.

For instance, a National Institutes of Health study found Ginkgo Biloba confers no benefits to memory or brain function in *normal* older people, although it might help people with moderate Alzheimer's. On the other hand, there is evidence that eating antioxidant-rich foods such as blueberries may help keep cognitive skills strong during old age.

One thing's for sure: you shouldn't believe every claim for herbal and other supplements that you read about. Before you take any over-the-counter supplement, check with a resource such as the American Pharmaceutical Association's *Practical Guide to Natural Medicine*, talk to your physician, or get information from another reputable source.

National Brain Awareness Week

"What's gray, wrinkled, the size of a ham, and only uses a fraction of its power? Stumped? Try the brain!" That tag line was one way to draw attention to the National Brain Awareness Week blitz of lectures, exhibits and teach-ins held annually. If you're interested, check out the programs held at dozens of science museums during the second week of March, or visit www.dana.org/brainweek.

Sleep: Those Zzzz's Are Important, Too!

If your image of retirement is a happy siesta every day, you might be surprised to learn that sleep problems are often associated with aging. It would be a shame to lose time in THE RETIREMENT ZONE just catching up on lost sleep when you could be gardening, changing the world, or seeing friends instead. A few sleep tips for the chronically snooze-deprived, from *Geriatrics at Your Fingertips*, published by the American Geriatrics Society, include the following: Get out of bed at the same time each morning regardless of how much you slept the night before; get adequate exposure to bright light during the day; and limit or eliminate alcohol, caffeine, and nicotine. Surprisingly, one of their recommendations at bedtime is not to read or watch TV in bed, presumably so your body gets the message that bed is for sleeping.

Focus for a minute on a body part that's more essential to you than your troublesome hairline or lovely thighs. Yes, that magnificent brain, the one that got you this far down the path of life, through the third grade, high-school geometry, and a long life—and into THE RETIREMENT ZONE. Whatever you do, don't underestimate the power of your own brain—its power to learn, adapt, grow, imagine, and create. Just like making an investment in even a moderate daily exercise regimen, a little mental gymnastics can go a long way.

In the 20th century, the U.S. public was educated about *physically* healthful habits–diet, exercise, sleep, and avoiding risks like alcohol and tobacco. Perhaps a 21st-century prescription for well-being and longevity will read thus: "Balanced diet, daily exercise, six to eight hours of sleep, meaningful engagement with family or community—and vigorous mental exercise several times a week."

If you're reading this book for a spouse, friend, or parent . . . become their partner in a game of intellectual tennis. Be available to play bridge, work together on a tough crossword puzzle, or take a class together. Adult children can use e-mail and the Internet to challenge their parents' brains, from genealogy programs to online computer programming classes.

ANSWER KEY

To score quiz on page 49, "Brain Quiz"

1. false   2. false   3. false   4. false   5. false   6. false   7. true

Resource Guide

PUBLICATIONS

Keep Your Brain Young: The Complete Guide to Physical and Emotional Health and Longevity by Guy M. McKhann, M.D., and Marilyn Albert, PhD (John Wiley & Sons, 2003).

The Memory Prescription: Dr. Gary Small's 14-Day Plan to Keep Your Brain and Body Young by Gary Small, M.D., with Gigi Vorgan (Hyperion, 2004).

The Relaxation Response by Herbert Benson, M.D., with Miriam Z. Klipper (Avon Books, 2000).

FREE GUIDE

Staying Sharp: Memory Loss and Aging by AARP Andrus Foundation and the Dana Alliance for Brain Initiatives (2001), www.aarp.org.

CHAPTER 6

Body

EXERCISE IS FOR EVERYBODY

The Surgeon General Has Issued This Warning: PHYSICAL *IN*ACTIVITY IS A MAJOR RISK TO YOUR HEALTH.

Travelers' advisory for THE RETIREMENT ZONE: Getting older is nothing to worry about, but becoming sedentary *is*. From the perspective of the National Institute on Aging (and they should know, right?) when people lose the physical ability to do things on their own, it generally doesn't happen just because of chronological age. More likely, it is because they have become *inactive* as they've grown older—barring, of course, a medical crisis.

And, now that you're not putting in 80-hour work weeks and spending time every day commuting, you can probably find the time to schedule in a vigorous walk, bike ride, or even a game of golf or tennis.

Some people may wonder whether it's risky to start exercising at age 50, 60, or even 70. Sure, occasionally you might overdo it in yoga class or pull a muscle dancing the cha-cha. And it's sensible to consult your physician if you've got specific concerns, or before you undertake a strenuous regimen of pumping iron or running long distances. Overall, though, regular exercise helps rather than hurts most people as they move up in years. According to the NIA, people 65 and over become sick or disabled more often from *not* exercising than from exercising.

And of course, exercise makes you feel good. For 72-year-old Jack Hobbs of Morristown, New Jersey, mental and physical fitness go hand in hand. "I see myself like a person in their forties," Hobbs says. "And I behave that way." He works at his consulting business, plays the drums, and just finished writing a trilogy autobiography over the Internet with two other men born the same year, one of whom is Chinese and the other Japanese. "I'm an advocate of regular exercise, so I keep in pretty good shape," Hobbs says. "I see people who are my age that can hardly walk. I attended a fiftieth class reunion and everyone was so old! I don't see myself as that age."

LESSONS OF THE BUSHMEN

Take the long, evolutionary view. After all, human bodies would look different if we were really designed to sit all day. "Hunters and gatherers walk for miles, find food, and carry it back," says Dr. Bernard Roos, director of the Geriatrics Institute at the University of Miami. He should know. An expert in aging and exercise physiology (musculoskeletal function), he spent some time observing Bushmen in Botswana in 1985. "By virtue of their walking 30 miles on an average day, Bushmen maintain ideal musculoskeletal function," he said. "That's a very tough routine, but it's their lifestyle."

Decreasing levels of physical activity to the point of an almost complete lack of exercise is a recent by-product of modern life. "Until about one hundred years ago," Roos continues, "people rode horses, or walked, or biked. People walked up stairs because there were no elevators. They pulled up the potatoes and cut them, and cooked them, instead of driving through at McDonald's, eating in the car, parking in a garage, and then sitting again before going to sleep."

The point is, the body's a machine that can do many things. It's a brilliant high-function design. The human body—*your* body—has potential that's just waiting to be used. And that's true at any age.

Curiously, though, the "exercise establishment" doesn't look at the whole body machine. If you go to the gym, lots of people are focused on only one function. For instance, people take aerobics classes but don't do weight training. Most exercise tapes and machines and techniques are marketed on the basis of a single promise, such as "six-pack abs" or "thin thighs" or a "flat stomach." And many media-saturated Americans are obsessed about only one dimension of their body, anyway: appearance.

It's not just aerobics you need. Or muscle strength. Or flexibility. It's a combination of things that your body needs to do in daily life. You need them all: strength, flexibility, power, and endurance.

The lesson of the Bushmen is this: Think FUNCTION.

Dr. Roos's number-one recommendation for exercise is **dancing**. "The jitterbug, waltz, samba, and fox trot, and do them to different tempos," he advises. "Just stop when it is not fun anymore. Dancing is probably the single best physical maneuver you can do to prevent the loss of function." Other modes of exercise that address the multifaceted needs of everyday life include lifting weights, yoga, or aquatic exercise.

While most people should exercise more, even those who do sometimes get in a rut. We choose to do the things that we're good at, and we're good at the things that we do. Distance runners often hate to stretch, because they are already suffering from a limited range of motion. If you look at the part that you dislike doing the most—aerobics, strength training, stretching, for instance—that's probably the part that needs work, some experts say.

Dr. Roos suggests that you use everyday life to challenge yourself. His take-home message: the joy of movement. "Most people think, 'I'm a walker and I have to walk.' We want people to swim, walk, to bike, to stretch, to dance, to do it all. Get off your fanny and exercise."

GETTING PHYSICAL IN THE RETIREMENT ZONE

You're never too old—or too young—to start. Whatever phase of THE RETIREMENT ZONE you're in—planning for it, just retired, retired and still working, or whatever—it's important to invest some time and energy in physical fitness.

Older persons may benefit even more than those in middle age from physical activity. Even 90-year-olds who've become physically frail from inactivity can double their strength through simple exercises in a fairly short time.

What follows are suggestions based on the booklet *Exercise: A Guide from the National Institute on Aging*, available free of charge to anyone who requests it. Call NIA at 1-800-222-2225 or go to www.niapublications.org. Obviously, if you have any chronic diseases or risk factors, check with your doctor before increasing your level of physical activity.

How Much Exercise is Enough?

Here's what the Centers for Disease Control and Prevention (CDC), along with the American College of Sports Medicine, recommends: that adults ages 18 and older participate in a minimum of 30 minutes of moderate-intensity physical activity on most days of the week.

Does that mean you have to go to the gym endlessly? No. Physical activity is not an all-or-nothing proposition. Even moderate types of exercise provide health benefits, according to the CDC. You can count daily physical activities such as gardening, vacuuming, and brisk walking to do errands, in addition to more traditional forms of exercise.

But, experts say, exercise *as much as you can*. The goal is to improve from wherever you are right now, and gradually build up four aspects of your ability: endurance, strength, balance, and flexibility. Start with one or two types of exercises that you can manage and that fit into your schedule. If you aim to work your way up to a vigorous level, check with your doctor first.

INSIDER'S GUIDE:
The Fundamental Four Exercise Groups

1) ENDURANCE EXERCISES like walking or jogging improve the health of your heart, lungs, and circulatory system. Having more endurance not only helps keep you healthier; it can also improve your stamina for everyday tasks and may delay or prevent many diseases, like diabetes, colon cancer, heart disease, and stroke. The more vigorously you exercise, the more you benefit.

Experts recommend choosing any activity that raises your heart rate and breathing for extended periods of time. Do at least 30 minutes of endurance activities on most or all days of the week. If you prefer, divide your 30 minutes into shorter sessions of no less than 10 minutes each. Activities shouldn't make you breathe so hard you can't talk, or cause dizziness or chest pain. Stretch afterwards.

2) STRENGTH EXERCISES build your muscles and make you stronger. They also increase your metabolism, helping to keep your weight and blood sugar in check. That's important because obesity and diabetes are major health problems as we mature. Strength exercises also may help prevent osteoporosis.

Experts recommend doing strength exercises for all your major muscle groups at least twice a week, but not for the same muscle group on any two days in a row. These exercises may make you sore at first, but they should never cause pain.

3) BALANCE EXERCISES help prevent a common problem in older adults: falls. Falling is a major cause of broken hips and other injuries that often lead to disability. Some balance exercises build up your leg muscles; others require you to do simple activities like briefly standing on one leg.

Experts recommend adding balance exercises to your regular regimen for lower bodywork, such as leg lifts—but go slowly so you don't fall! Or do "anytime, anywhere" balance exercises. One example: Balance on one foot, then the other.

4) FLEXIBILITY EXERCISES help keep your body limber by stretching your muscles and the tissues that hold your body's structures in place.

Experts recommend being aware that stretching exercises alone don't improve endurance or strength. If stretching exercises are the only kind of exercise you do, do them at least three times weekly, up to every day. Stretching may cause mild discomfort but not pain.

How to Stick with It

Just knowing that physical activity can improve your health and abilities can be enough to keep you exercising, but you might need extra motivation sometimes. For those times, try exercising with a friend, listening to music, charting your progress, marking your calendar for exercise sessions, giving yourself exercise "assignments" ahead of time, and rewarding yourself when you achieve your goals. Integrate exercise into your life: Walk instead of drive to the store, post office, or local coffee shop for an afternoon break.

If you stick with your exercises for more than a month, it's a good sign that you are on your way to making it a permanent habit.

EXERCISE IS AN INVESTMENT

People are always talking about investments in THE RETIREMENT ZONE. *Financial* investments, that is. If you start treating your health as an investment, you'll have a "ten-bagger," to borrow a Wall Street term for an investment that increases in value ten times over. By putting in as little as the equivalent of one half-hour TV show's worth of time, you could save countless hours in doctors' offices, and the untold cost of aggravation, fear, and inconvenience of developing a serious chronic condition. CDC Director Dr. Julie L. Gerberding urges: "It is important for all of us to remember that sedentary lifestyles increase our risk of obesity, heart disease, hypertension, diabetes, and other chronic diseases. The burden of these diseases can be reduced with a minimum of thirty minutes of moderate-intensity physical activity five or more days a week."

6 Simple Good Health Habits

You *can* impact your own health. Regardless of whether you are 54 or 99, there are specific low-cost things that you can do to stay physically healthy and even get *healthier*. You've probably heard this before:

1) Stop smoking
2) Exercise regularly
3) Lose weight if you are overweight
4) Eat nutritious meals
5) Prevent falls by adding safety measures to your home
6) Get preventive medical screening tests on a timely basis
   (the basic ones are covered by Medicare)

> The good news . . . is that people can benefit from even moderate
> levels of physical activity.
>
> —Surgeon General of the United States

If you're reading this book for a spouse, friend, or parent . . .
Challenging exercises and physical activities done regularly can help
many adults improve their health, even when done at a moderate level.
Exercise may prevent or delay a variety of diseases and disabilities associated with aging.

Resource Guide

FREE GUIDES

Exercise Guide, booklet by the National Institute on Aging. Call 800-222-2225
or visit www.niapublications.org. Also available as a free download (with video,
$7.00).

Pocket Guide to Staying Healthy at 50+, booklet by the Agency for Healthcare
Research and Quality and AARP (2003). Call 800-358-9295 or visit
www.ahrq.gov/ppip/50plus.

Special Recommendations for Older Adults, Web page by the Division
of Nutrition and Physical Activity, National Center for Chronic
Disease Prevention and Health Promotion, CDC (2004). Visit
www.cdc.gov/nccdphp/dnpa/physical/recommendations/older_adults.htm.

ORGANIZATIONS AND WEB SITES

The following nonprofit organizations offer information about exercise and exercise programs for older adults. Some sponsor physical-fitness events as well. Ask
for free publications about how to exercise safely.

American College of Sports Medicine
P. O. Box 1440
Indianapolis, IN 46206-1440
www.acsm.org

American Heart Association
7272 Greenville Avenue
Dallas, TX 75231-4596
800-242-8721
www.americanheart.org

Centers for Disease Control and Prevention
1600 Clifton Road
Atlanta, GA 30333
800-311-3435
www.cdc.org

National Association for Health and Fitness
201 S. Capitol Avenue, Suite 560
Indianapolis, IN 46225
317-237-5630
www.physicalfitness.org

National Institute on Aging/National Institutes of Health
Building 31, Room 5C27
31 Center Drive, MSC 2292
Bethesda, MD 20892-2292
800-222-2225
800-222-4225 (TTY)
www.nia.nih.gov

The President's Council on Physical Fitness and Sports
200 Independence Avenue, SW
HHH Building, Room 738 H
Washington, DC 20201
202-690-9000
www.fitness.gov

FORGE YOUR
PERSONAL PATH

The chapters that follow touch on two topics that people sometimes worry about but often don't discuss, in regard to moving into the post-work phase of life. One is whether life without work leaves a void of meaning. The second topic concerns transitions in the early phase of retirement.

Transitioning out of work is likely to be a mixed experience. The truth is, work fills many roles for people other than a paycheck. Throughout this book we suggest that you invest yourself in "anchor activities" that can help compensate for whatever it is that work might have given you in your life, other than a paycheck, for instance:

- A sense of identity
- Friendships, both close and casual
- Someplace to go in the morning, wearing real clothes and not your pajamas
- News and information about other people's lives
- A predictable rhythm
- Mental challenge, stimulation, and new learning opportunities
- Social status, a sense of control, accomplishment, and power
- Perks, fun, laughs

TRAVEL ADVISORY FOR COUPLES: Needless to say, one person's anchor is another's albatross (which can pose marital challenges when, for instance, he loves to sail, but she gets seasick).

CHAPTER 7

Zen and the Art of Meaning

Dig back into the floppy disc of your memory and you may recall Robert M. Pirsig's 1974 book, *Zen and the Art of Motorcycle Maintenance*. One of the first popular efforts to try to integrate Eastern sensibilities with modern Western rationalism, the book addressed the meaning of life. It also hinted at a fulsome way to live it. Just *owning* a copy of *Zen and the Art of Motorcycle Maintenance* made some people feel better about life.

But of course that was *then*. The 1970s are as antique as a VW bug jammed with college kids. When you were 16 or 26 and engaged in a search for meaning it may not have occurred to you that the search is a lifelong process.

When Archimedes sat in his tub and (as the story goes) exclaimed, "Eureka!," he was, after all, conducting a scientific experiment. That is, he had formulated a question, observed what happened, and drew his own conclusion. Life isn't always that neat. Neither the questions nor the answers are crystal clear. And constructing "proofs" is damn difficult.

From Plato to Stephen Hawking, the brilliant British theoretical physicist, scholars, philosophers, and writers have puzzled over why the universe and mankind are as they are, and whether there's a larger purpose in it all.

Not everyone has an existential crisis during life's transitions such as retirement. Either you feel a pressing need for a clearer sense of direction and purpose in your life, or you don't. But you just can't duck it if you're feeling this prickly, discomfiting question coming on:

WHAT'S THE MEANING OF LIFE? OF MY LIFE? The search for meaning describes more than just an acceptance of the struggles of life. There's a striving for integration, for wholeness, to "finally max out my potential," as one septuagenarian described it. How do I decide what I really want? Is it possible to pursue perfect love, nirvana, or a connection with some spiritual force? What's wisdom–is there such a thing? Does my day-to-day reality have any meaning, really? What's my place in the world? What inner resources do I have and how might I use them? What will my legacy be?

IF YOU'RE SEARCHING FOR MEANING, THAT DOESN'T MEAN YOU'RE LOST. Carving out a new path, you might find yourself standing right where you were when you began the internal journey of exploration—in the same religion, same marriage, same roster of daily activities—but with greater calm, more appreciation. On the other hand, you might engage in a re-ordering of relationships, activities, and priorities.

If you've been spiritually inclined, you might become more so; if you haven't explored this realm, you may decide to now. If you've spent your life acquiring things, you may start to divest yourself of all that "stuff." If you've been a hard-charging executive, you may take up watercolor painting. Supporting human rights and fighting the subjugation of the human spirit might "click" for you. Or your mission in life might, for a while, be the repair of an overgrown cemetery, organizing a retreat, or making pottery.

Some may have transcendental experiences, or experience a religious calling, all of which may go a long way toward settling their individual crisis of meaning.

But for the rest of us, who share bemusement and uncertainty, *it's the search that matters*. And in today's multi-option world, the hunt for life's meaning is eclectic.

The search might be nothing more glamorous than slowing down to 33 after living for years at a breathless 78. That's what happened to florist Jane Roe, who said, "I was spending my whole life in that store and it was beginning to feel like a little box. I thought, I can't spend the rest of my life looking at these four walls. I have a chance to think now, to reflect."

And for others, work never did hold deep meaning, anyway. John Bell in Tennessee, whose job involved troubleshooting machines used to build airplane parts, expresses a simple wisdom: "Some people build their life around their job, and if they lose their job, it's just like they lose their identity. I enjoyed what I did. But that wasn't my main goal in life, you know. I guess my main goal in life is to first of all be a Christian. I'd like to be a good deacon, I'd like to be a good father, a good husband, a good grandfather. There are no guarantees on any job. So . . . seeking that satisfaction, I think, is false."

IT'S A TRIP—ONE YOU CAN'T NECESSARILY MAP OUT BEFORE YOU START.

One thing's for sure: People are searching. In mid-2004, the *Wall Street Journal* featured a lengthy front-page article, "The Second Midlife Crisis," about men and women past the age of 60 who are trying to "find themselves," again. Teresa Pool, a career coach from Texas, says the path many of her executive clients take toward planning the second half of their life is rather circuitous. For most, moving directly into retirement is too much of a culture shock. She says, "My initial focus with these leaders and executives is typically helping them rediscover their passion for their work. Their passion had been to climb up the ladder. Once they get near the top it gets kind of boring. Most of the time—I'd say fifty to sixty percent of the time—what they're really looking for is a dramatic *transition*. . . . We start working on improved productivity, getting them sharper again, getting them more interested in their current job. After a few months, what we really end up working on is, What is it really that they want to do with the rest of their life?"

The things that commonly provide people with a lasting sense of meaning don't necessarily cost huge sums of money. Caring for a relative. Teaching a child. Enjoying nature. Learning. Creating. Experiencing spirituality. Being with friends and deepening relationships with family. If you're embarked on a search for meaning, there's one thing that's for sure. It's *you* who has to do it. So hop on your bike. *Vroom vroom.*

Resource Guide

The Five People You Meet in Heaven by Mitch Albom (Hyperion, 2003).

Living A Life That Matters by Harold S. Kushner (Alfred A. Knopf, 2001).

Man's Search for Meaning by Viktor E. Frankl (Washington Square Press, 1997).

Prime Time: How Baby Boomers Will Revolutionize Retirement and Transform America by Marc Freedman (PublicAffairs, 2002).

The Progress Paradox: How Life Gets Better While People Feel Worse by Gregg Easterbrook (Random House, 2003).

Stillness Speaks by Eckhart Tolle (New World Library, 2003).

The World According to Mister Rogers: Important Things to Remember by Fred Rogers (Hyperion, 2003).

CHAPTER 8

A Tale of Two (or Two Hundred) Transitions

So you're no longer that union member, that schoolteacher, that executive. With (some) money in the bank and free time on your hands, with thirty years or more invested in life, jobs, and careers and relationships, who are you *now*? For a few months (or even a year) you might feel you're in transition.

Well, it's not ONE transition, truth be told. There are many, especially in the first year. From that paycheck to a no-salary-based income. From squeezing in dates with your spouse or partner on weekends to sharing egg-white omelets every day for lunch. To selling the shop to your employee and then—switcheroo!—working part-time for someone you hired and trained. Everyone's got their own version of The Transition. Yet whether you go through two or two hundred, experiencing some type of transition in THE RETIREMENT ZONE is almost unavoidable.

SEVERAL COMMONLY REPORTED TRANSITIONS INCLUDE:

1) Baby steps: "I didn't think I could retire, I thought it was something I couldn't handle. I'd been working for all my life. But San Diego got bigger and the traffic problems got worse, and finally I decided I didn't need that any longer," recalls Erlene Carter, on moving from San Diego back to her home state of Arkansas. "Still, I wasn't sure enough to quit. I took a leave of absence for a year and at the end of that time, I quit."

2) Cold Turkey: Linda Moore of Colorado tells this story: "I retired suddenly—in fact, over a weekend. I looked at my money and said, 'I don't have to be getting up at five thirty every morning and I am neglecting the things I love to do.' So I went in on Monday and quit."

3) Denial: "I would say for the first five months I was on a well-deserved vacation," says Jane Roe, in New York. "I didn't work over the summer. And it struck me in September when I didn't go back to work—like a kid going back to school—I said, wait a second, I'm not working!"

4) Loss: Horrors! You open your day planner . . . to a completely blank page. As one top corporate officer, Janet Rogenstein, retired director of sales and marketing for the American Stock Exchange, puts it, "What was most fearful to me was the loss of status. I *defined* myself by my job, right or wrong. This is what I *do*. I run this and that and I have my staff . . . and suddenly, nothing. You know, well, I went into mourning. I was saying, 'Who the hell am I, now? And what am I going to do with my time?'"

5) Pinch yourself, you're still alive: "You don't change in retirement from the person you were before," comments Rogenstein. "You may change what you do on a daily basis, but you bring your little red wagon with you. My style is to be a Type A, hyper busy. I would not be happy *not* being hyper busy. So if you think when you retire, you are going to just *sit*, and you're an active person, well that's not going to happen."

Many people discover that their essential "me" is remarkably resilient, irrespective of their work status. The National Institute on Aging's Baltimore Longitudinal Study found just that. After decades of research, they concluded that age and retirement don't transform an individual's personality much, or the kinds of things in which they are interested.

6) Reinvent yourself: After the last retirement-party champagne cork has landed, many people spend months crossing off projects on a mental "to do" list: Fix up the house. See family. Sleep late. Read a lot. Perhaps travel. Get on an exercise regimen. Organize the family photo albums. Clean out the garage. Garden. Take a course. After getting through the initial punch list, they begin to really restructure their lives.

The myth that leaving full-time employment automatically precipitates a depression is based on old data. Public health researchers have recently found that in retirement people are generally *less* stressed, exercise *more*, and have *higher* degrees of life satisfaction than when working. That's especially the case among healthy people with some financial flexibility.

Meanwhile, be good to yourself in this transition. Being in-between can be stressful. Common wisdom holds that oftentimes one door closes before another opens. Some people enjoy the process of change. Others endure it. And many recognize transition as a process that just takes time. As one recently retired entrepreneur put it, "I'm floating. It's uncomfortable, but I believe that's when people change. Retirement is liberating, threatening, satisfying—all at the same time."

A WORD FOR WORKING WOMEN

If you are a woman whose age now hovers near 60, you can easily recall the days when careers were mainly for men. There were male doctors and female nurses; male lawyers and female secretaries; male executives and gal Fridays. Even Superman had his Lois Lane. In the 1950s and early '60s, if women worked at all, it tended to be in retail sales, clerical, teaching, nursing, and other so-called helping professions, along with manufacturing jobs, cooking, and waitressing. Being a stewardess was considered glamorous. Aspiring to be a pilot or CEO of an airline was virtually unheard of.

As recently as 1972, when the oldest of the baby boomers were already a few years out of college, women could expect to be paid half as much as males for doing the same job, legally. That is, if they could get hired in a "man's world" at all.

The path-breaking women now approaching THE RETIREMENT ZONE, or in it, didn't blithely "enter the labor market," as the social scientists like to say. They stumbled, networked, sweat, sued, dressed for, and just plain worked their way in and up. For many it's been a roller coaster, with highs of success and lows of sacrifice. Lacking models for how to simultaneously manage both a job or career and a family, women improvised and juggled. It's an understatement to say that their workplace experience has been distinct from that of their spouses or male colleagues of the same generation. Like flares illuminating a nocturnal landscape, terms such as "glass ceiling," "mommy track," "equal pay," "old boys' club," "consciousness-raising groups," and, yes, "sexist pig" briefly shed light on what's been a decades-long slog along a remarkable road of change.

Like many women who have struggled to develop a professional identity in addition to fulfilling the traditional role of spouse or parent, you may be understandably reluctant to give up working. You might wonder, did I get the balance right? Do I want to keep on working? Will I feel lost without work? And in dual-career couples, of course, one person's decision about retirement can affect both the family finances and the marital dynamic. (Regarding the latter, see page 247.)

As you decide whether to put on your power suit again and build another career, or hop on a Harley and embark on an adventure of a different sort, take this as a point of pride: working women in their 50s and beyond have done yeoman's work in forging real opportunities and a new independence for themselves and future generations. The cultural corset that bound women into the predetermined roles of homemaker and wife has snapped wide open in your lifetime.

Resource Guide

Creating the Work You Love: Courage, Commitment and Career by Rick Jarow (Destiny Books, 1995).

Managing Transitions: Making the Most of Change, 2nd Edition, by William Bridges (DeCapo Press, 2003).

What Should I Do with My Life? The True Story of People Who Answered the Ultimate Question by Po Bronson (Random House, 2002).

LOOK INWARD, ANGEL

Thomas Wolfe's famous novel, *Look Homeward, Angel,* is the quintessential coming-of-age story, about a boy who left home for bigger things. In a sense, you're coming of age again, too (OK, with a few more candles on your birthday cake). If you take the time to listen to your inner signals, you'll enhance your chances of building a later life that's fulfilling. As this guide frequently reminds readers, you've got choices of how to invest your energy and time in THE RETIREMENT ZONE. That's the case whether you decide to go back to work, volunteer, or just sit quietly and "be."

You will learn about different techniques you—or your spouse, friend, or parent—can use to get a grip on the nonfinancial aspects of retirement planning. With just a pencil in hand, you can use the worksheets in this book to find your own way, simply by thinking through your options on your own or with friends or family. Or, after reading about the array of paid services such as coaching and personality testing centers, you might choose to pay a professional to help jump-start your planning for the next phase of your life.

Sure, you're thinking about your *financial* future—maybe even polishing your worry beads over it. But money's not everything. It doesn't buy happiness. And it can't buy you love, either.

So look inward, angel.

CHAPTER 9

Before You Move to Florida: Know Thyself

A WORKBOOK

You're approaching the map-less land of THE RETIREMENT ZONE.

Now what?

This little workbook chapter is meant to help you find your way. Don't plan on using every one of these exercises; just pick a few and see if they help you focus on where you want to go in the next twenty years or so.

You might want to do these exercises sitting under a tree, on your own. Or work with a friend who's also thinking about restructuring his or her life after work.

Whether you are semi-retired or just thinking about it, consider revisiting these exercises again in a few years, as your needs and interests develop.

Before you begin, a word on change. It's healthy. Life *brings* change. But only you can calibrate your own ideal balance between change and continuity.

WHAT DO I WANT FROM THE NEXT PHASE OF MY LIFE?

"Not everybody does the systematic go-to-the-library, get-on-the-Internet," one observer of the post-work transition notes. "I think, a lot of times, it's a feeling— I want change, I want something different. And whether actively or not, you're always sort of seeking out help and ideas." Setting some achievable goals—in terms of money, relationships, and other realms of your life—can also be helpful.

It's worth the effort.

As a 60-something retiree puts it, "I can only tell you that, number one, you never lose much by trying to follow your dreams. And particularly when you get to be at the age that I am, you have to realize that you are on the downhill slope, meaning not feeling old and decrepit, but a slope toward the end rather than the beginning of your life. And so you need to take advantage of the time as much as possible. And that ultimately, you can achieve what you set out to achieve."

Take a look at the holistic, big picture.

1) The Ol' Pie Chart Approach

HOW I SPEND MY TIME

Step 1: Use pie chart 1 to draw how you currently allocate your time during an average week, using categories such as "sleep," "social life," "exercise," "work," "volunteer," "hobbies" (be specific), and other things you do. (This is going to be harder than you think!)

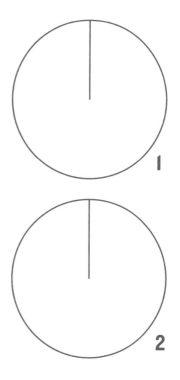

HOW I WANT TO SPEND MY TIME

Step 2: Use pie chart 2 to draw how you would ideally allocate your time during an average week, using the same categories as above, or new ones. (For instance, you might delete "work" and substitute "family time.")

Step 3: Compare the two pie charts and write down a reminder to yourself of what you want to do more of and what you want to do less of. Post the reminder on the refrigerator or bathroom mirror.

I want to spend more time _____

I want to spend less time _____

Your goal is to eventually have the two pie charts look very similar.
Repeat this exercise in a few weeks to see how you're progressing.

WHO AM I, NOW?

If you feel like your identity is evaporating and you are struggling to reinvent yourself, here are two sets of exercises to help you get clear. If you're an extrovert, focus on the first five ideas. If you're an introvert, check out page 75.

2) Ways to Get in Touch with Yourself

LISTEN TO YOURSELF TALK. If you're not sure what you might like to do in THE RETIREMENT ZONE, the easiest way to sound yourself out might be to talk about it. Yak it up with your spouse or significant other, your children and friends, your poker or golfing buddies. It's not really that you need to listen to their advice (though you might). The point is to hear *yourself* think—out loud. Jot down some ideas.

Before you start, prompt your partner to ask you, "Tell me about your ideal day . . . life . . . career . . . relationship. . . . "

Note to Self: _____

_____

LISTEN TO OTHERS TALK. Put your antennae up! When you're receptive, you can learn a lot. "I was in my apartment-building elevator one day when a neighbor told me about the Institute for Learning in Retirement—so I went, and I love it," recalls a man in his 80s. Another bored retiree's story led to paid work: "On the golf course, an acquaintance says to me, 'What are you doing with yourself these days?' so I said, 'Not much, to tell you the truth.' So he says, 'So come work for me part time.' I did. And now, at 68, after owning my own business, I'm a salesman for California Closets."

Note to Self: _____

_____

GET OUT 'N' ABOUT. One woman who was leaving a high-stress corporate environment and using consulting as a way to transition to THE RETIREMENT ZONE sought a lot of advice from colleagues. Her best tip? "Try to schedule your day and not get in the habit of being by yourself. . . . Go pick up the paper. Get out. Go schedule lunches with people. Because one of the things you miss when you try to do something by yourself is a chance to bounce ideas off people."

Note to Self: _____

_____

BE A SHAMELESS COPYCAT. Do you know someone who seems to be doing great things in THE RETIREMENT ZONE that you could see yourself doing, too? Be a shameless copycat. (Be kind to yourself, don't pick a billionaire to emulate.) If you're green with envy at the way the Joneses launched an Internet-based business, join in community service projects, or sail on weekends, then try it yourself.

Note to Self: _____

_____

MAKE IT A SOCIAL THING. Join a support group. An 82-year-old retired engineer recalls, "I had no expectation of what retirement would be. I retired rather suddenly from my last job. I quit. The next thing I did was call up a couple of friends who had retired a couple of years ago and told them, I'll take you to lunch if you tell me how to retire."

You could talk to some friends. Or you might organize a dedicated support group to help you through the rite of passage after your formal work life is over, with the specific agenda of talking about this transition: hopes, fears, what you all are doing and discovering. *Focus on more than just the financial dimension of your life in* THE RETIREMENT ZONE.

Given the millions of people in the baby-boom generation, you'll hardly be alone in whatever ups and downs you might face. Log onto any of the retirement

Web sites for ideas and other people's experiences, or join a chat room. There, in sublime anonymity, let it all hang out, everything from dealing with your spouse to finding fulfilling part-time work to planning leisure activities.

Note to Self: _____

_____

3) Special Ideas for Non-extroverts

If baring your soul to strangers, joining a support group, or discussing future plans with relatives is about as appealing to you as a dancing naked in Times Square, here are more suitable ways to look inward, for the already introspective.

KEEP AN "IDEA LOG." Creative people do this all the time: Keep an idea notebook or a sketchbook. Here's how it works. You are watching *Oprah* or listening to National Public Radio and something strikes you as very cool, or very interesting, or something that you identify with. Jot it down.

And before you lose that scrap paper, transfer the idea into a file—either on your computer, binder, file drawer, or shoebox along with your tax receipts.

Toss into this file every silly or not-so-silly idea you have about what you'd like to do in the future. If you clip newspaper articles, and you see something that catches your fancy, toss that in too. It makes no difference if the ideas are hand scribbled snippets such as "learn to belly dance" or nine-page letters from an old friend raving about Baja. Don't evaluate every idea as it comes along. Save your random ideas for a few months, long enough to forget what's really in there. Then one dark and scary night, open it up. You may decide to follow one of those leads.

Note to Self: _____

_____

SIT DOWN AND WRITE YOURSELF A LETTER. Don't worry about punctuation or whether your prose flows like Tom Wolfe's. Just be 15 years old again, writing in a diary. Go ahead, spill your guts about where you are going next, what you like to do, and what longings still need to be addressed. Cancel that negative inner voice that says, "Nah, you can't. . . . " Think broadly! Be brave! And write!

Primal scream therapy. Go ahead. Scream for relief. For confusion. For joy. Give voice to your inner transitional animal!

CAN DREAMS COME TRUE?

Here are a couple of ways to sort through the possibilities.

4) Ways to Discover What You Want out of Life

List all the things you want to do for the next five or ten years. Include the good, the bad, and the naughty; the possible and impossible, the friendly and hostile desires. If that's too steep a climb, just try the four questions that follow.

What have you always dreamed of doing?
a) *sailing around the world with a debonair man/woman*
b) *acting in a play*
c) _____

What are the one, two, or three top wishes you'd like to see come true in the next phase of your life?
a) *writing a mystery novel*
b) *training pedigree dogs*
c) _____

What did you want to do as a child, that you haven't yet done?
a) *learn to read Latin and live for a year in India*
b) *play basketball*
c) _____

What is your ideal day? Describe.
a) *sleep till eight, great exercise class, lunch with friend, creative work in afternoon, phone call with kids, early dinner, and a movie out.*
b) *go to airport, get on plane to somewhere fabulous for two weeks.*
c) _____

5) Scenario Writing

When architects design a new skyscraper, or NASA designs a new spacecraft, they build a 3-D model and then tinker with it until it's right. You can build a two-dimensional model on paper of a three-dimensional life in THE RETIREMENT ZONE that suits you. Just for fun, here are some suggestions for getting started on your "model" life.

The Hawaii Model—a change of venue, have fun and relax
The Columbus Model—traveling and discovering "what's out there"
The Steady State Model—no significant change, because you keep working
The New York Model—you're incredibly busy, incredibly overbooked, intense
The Mañana Model—day-to-day life is fine. You'll worry about it tomorrow
The Little Engine That Could **Model**—a change of career or avocation. "I think I can, I think I can." And you can!

Note to Self: _____

_____

IS THERE LIFE AFTER WORK?

If your head/heart/identity is completely enmeshed in the world of work, you might find it helpful to deconstruct what it is you love, hate, and ignore about your life as a working person. (Your ultimate goal, of course, is to skim what's best and leave the hassles behind.)

For executives, work can provide logistical support in the form of secretaries, travel services, insurance departments, and a myriad of other services. For small-business owners, work is a jack-of-all-trades job that calls on many skills. Workers, managers, teachers, and many others engage in a huge number of social interactions, some superficial, some close, in the course of a work week. Unless you work alone, being employed automatically gives a person a reason to say "we." We won the contract—or lost it. We are having a picnic. We hate the boss's husband. We are the best company in our business. The list could go on and on.

What will you miss from your working life? Do the exercises that follow, and seek ways to compensate in THE RETIREMENT ZONE.

6) The Transition from Work

STEP ONE: What You'll Miss—and Not

Answer the following questions:

1) What do you miss about work? Or, if you're still working: what do you expect to miss about work?

   For instance: *The paycheck, the challenge, having somewhere to go in the morning, and all the gossip. Yes, paid vacation, too.*

   _____

   _____

2) When you were working, what were your fantasies about life without this job? If you're still working: what fantasies do you have about life without this job?

   For instance: *Exercising more, learning the guitar, movies in the middle of the day, long, lazy days at the beach, reading all those books on the dresser top, finally organizing the kids' photo albums, fixing up the downstairs bathroom, taking a class, planting some new roses, lunching with friends, having time to visit Mom in Chicago.*

   _____

   _____

3) What are/will you be thoroughly glad to be rid of, thank you very much, when you've left work?

   For instance: *The sales meetings! Crabby clients! You-know-who and her endless stories. The lousy lunches. The stress—especially in busy times. Having to rush everywhere, all the time. Sitting at the computer eight hours a day.*

   _____

   _____

4) What do you consider your biggest accomplishments in your work life? And what would you still like to accomplish now that work is over, or if you are still working, before you leave?

   For instance: *Biggest accomplishment was getting promotions. Yet to do: Increase sales.*

   _____

   _____

STEP TWO: Compensate for What You'll Miss.

Review your answers to step one. For each thing you miss or expect to miss about work, list three options for making it happen:

1) the obvious choice,

2) something you have thought about but not investigated, and

3) the far-out best-case-scenario, wild-idea option.

The sample chart that follows shows how you can set goals in many areas of your life.

	OBVIOUS	POSSIBLE	FAR-OUT
Work	*Work part-time at old job*	*Freelance or consult*	*Do something new: sell antiques on eBay*
Exercise	*Do more of what I already do*	*Join a gym and start training*	*Go for the black belt or run a marathon*
Movies	*So, go!*	*Go with a group of pals once a month*	*Volunteer in the film collection at the library*
Guitar	*Buy a book and teach myself*	*Enroll in an inexpensive group course*	*Get serious lessons with a professional guitarist; have a jam session with friends (Awful Amateurs Night, for laughs)*
Lose weight	*A good diet— for real!*	*Diet plus exercise*	*Learn to hate chocolate, form a weight loss group*

PRACTICAL TIP: Left your social life along with the water cooler at the office? It's time to reconstruct and think ahead.

For instance, if you love to do a particular activity—travel, play ice hockey, dance—but don't anymore because you don't have a partner, don't deny yourself. By participating in something you love, you may find a new friend with a similar interest.

HOW'M I DOIN'?

In the 1980s, residents of New York City were frequently treated to hearing their garrulous mayor, Ed Koch, asking "How'm I doin'?" You don't have to be walking down Broadway in the Macy's Thanksgiving Day Parade to be wondering the same.

Jokes aside, the factors listed in this ad-hoc quiz are well-established elements in life satisfaction among older Americans. What works for your neighbor might not satisfy you. But generally speaking, these are the main categories of experience that make or break how people feel about their life in THE RETIREMENT ZONE.

7) Am I Satisfied?

STEP ONE: Take inventory. Am I satisfied with my life in terms of

Activities you enjoy?	___ yes	___ no	___ maybe
A place you like to call home?	___ yes	___ no	___ maybe
Body stuff (physical health, enough exercise)?	___ yes	___ no	___ maybe
Cheery outlook?	___ yes	___ no	___ maybe
Direction (sense of purpose and meaning)?	___ yes	___ no	___ maybe
Enough money to not worry too much?	___ yes	___ no	___ maybe
Intellectual challenges?	___ yes	___ no	___ maybe
Relationships?	___ yes	___ no	___ maybe

STEP TWO: List some other things I care about or like to do. Am I satisfied with my life in terms of

(e.g., gardening)	___ yes	___ no	___ maybe
_____	___ yes	___ no	___ maybe
_____	___ yes	___ no	___ maybe
_____	___ yes	___ no	___ maybe

STEP THREE: Analyze your strengths and weaknesses. Get a few dozen file cards. Look at your answers to Step One and write out a card for each. Put the question on one side of the card and your answer on the flip side. Organize the cards into "yes," "no," and "maybe" stacks.

Congratulate yourself on the "yes" stack and mentally tie those up with a nice red ribbon. On those dimensions, you're doing fine.

Write each of your "maybe" and "no" items at the top of a blank piece of paper.

STEP FOUR: Consider your options. Take the "maybes" and the "nos" and start writing or drawing or doodling on those pieces of paper. Think like an optimist (even if you aren't one yet). Start jotting down ideas. If this exercise seems hard, pretend you are a friend looking at someone else's life. How would you help them make things better?

So your social life isn't adequate? Okay, admitting that is half the battle. So what's ideal? What would you like to be doing—perhaps going out salsa dancing three nights a week? Please be honest and realistic. ("I want to win the lottery" or "I want to look like Twiggy" aren't all that helpful.)

STEP FIVE: Make a plan. Write down three changes you'll try:

1) _____

2) _____

3) _____

Change is hard work! Congratulations for even trying. Work on this as long as you can stand it. Then put it away and tackle it again—very soon, perhaps tomorrow.

8) Food for Thought

Open a computer file or designate a special notebook to answer these questions. You may wish to come back to them from time to time.

1) How can I make the most successful transition into a life where work is no longer what organizes my days and weeks? How can I do this in a way that "works" for my spouse/partner, too?

2) What am I hoping the next phase of my life involves? Or not?

3) What am I worried about (or looking forward to) in THE RETIREMENT ZONE?

4) What relationships will be most important to me, looking ahead?

5) Do I hope or need to earn income in THE RETIREMENT ZONE? How much?

6) Is "being productive" high on my priority list, and if so, what do I mean by that? Do I want to "give back to society," and if so, how?

7) Are there things I'd like to accomplish in THE RETIREMENT ZONE? Specific goals I'd like to achieve?

8) How do I feel about relocating from my current home? Community? Where would I like to go? What would a move mean for me?

> **If you're reading this book for a spouse, friend, or parent . . .** you might want to select some exercises to do together, for fun. Encourage him or her to take responsibility and do a few on his or her own. Remember, you can help the person identify goals, or prioritize the things they want to do, or calm anxieties—but in terms of setting directions, it's their life, after all.

Resource Guide

The Artist's Way: A Spiritual Path to Higher Creativity by Julia Cameron (Jeremy P. Tarcher/Putnam, 2002).

Feel the Fear and Do It Anyway by Susan Jeffers, PhD (Fawcett Book Group, 1996).

I Don't Know What I Want, but I Know It's Not This: A Step-by-Step Guide to Finding Gratifying Work by Julie Jansen (Penguin Books, 2003).

What Do You Want to Do When You Grow Up? Starting the Next Chapter of Your Life by Dorothy Cantor with Andrea Thompson (Little Brown & Company, 2001).

CHAPTER 10

More Ways to Know Thyself

TESTS, COACHES, AND PROFESSIONAL GUIDANCE

This chapter scopes out the landscape of paid-for services that can help people in transition figure out what's next in their lives. People do sometimes get confused or feel a bit lost. The period right before leaving work and the first transitional years are sometimes the hardest, when people may miss their work identity and on-the-job relationships. After all, many people have invested more time working than anything else. Many have spent more time with their coworkers than their families.

The following story isn't unusual: "I go to someone's house for dinner and when they ask casually, 'What do you do?' I flush red and want to run away," says a former editor of a local newspaper who retired before she turned 60. "And when I say I'm retired, they wander away, assuming that I have nothing interesting to say. It's like I disappeared. It makes me wonder, Okay, I *was* that editor, Who am I *now?*"

Sometimes professional input can help you focus on your next steps. "What?" you shriek. "A consultant?" Sure. Using one of the services outlined below isn't any weirder than using a travel agent to help you plan a big trip.

LIFE REVIEW AND GUIDED AUTOBIOGRAPHY

You may hear the term "life review" or "guided autobiography." What are they?

The idea is that people can gain perspective on their own lives by writing their life story. And many folks, experts say, benefit enormously by recalling, organizing, and sharing their life experiences in a structured group, like a class.

A participant might be asked to write about questions such as, "What is the first thing you remember about your life? How would you describe your childhood? Your adulthood? Your family?" The process isn't simple; and as any storyteller knows, your audience can affect your story. And you might forget significant things one day that pop out at you the next. But the very process of dredging up, ordering, and accepting your own life lets you move on to the next phase.

James Birren, PhD, associate director of the UCLA Center on Aging, an octogenarian and one of the founders of this method, has himself retired "oh, four or five times," he says. In his method, participants meet in a small group on a weekly basis for ten weeks. They are given an assignment about a specific topic, such as early life, parents, money, love, and work, and asked to write several pages about their own experiences. Workshop members read and comment on one another's work—and in the process amazing things happen.

You dig into your own experience, beyond a simple resume, and past random reminiscence. You find words to describe how you've navigated your own life, coloring in feelings about important moments and people. In class, there's feedback you didn't expect. Perfect strangers hearing snippets of your life story may surprise you with a "Wow! You did that?" or "My, that was really hard." The whole process can be rejuvenating, like a fresh breeze through a musty closet of memories. It's a great tool for people facing transition.

GETTING HELP AT CAREER CENTERS

If you're the type of person who needs to talk it all through with someone who's in the know, a career center or counselor may be right for you. Career-center professionals can help you discover things to do that would be right for you.

Transition Counseling and Career Centers at Universities and Colleges

Most career centers affiliated with schools or colleges offer services to the general public, from testing and individual counseling to classes, workshops, and weekends. These can be utilized by folks at any age. Don't be fooled: Just because "retirement" isn't in the title of some of the course offerings doesn't mean they won't be right for you.

Many career centers also offer a battery of tests with individual counseling sessions as a package. The sessions are a dialogue, where you, the client, do most of the talking. "Self-assessment is the starting place for everything," says one experienced counselor who works in a university. After administering either or both of the Myers-Briggs and the Strong Interest Inventory, counselors talk through the results, usually over three sessions. The point is to turn the results into a plan of action or a set of goals—to make it practical: "The testing is helpful. It gets that person talking about who he/she is, really. The counselor's job is to help a person see and articulate what really matters to them." You could come out with new ideas for volunteering, part-time jobs, or other activities.

Career centers often have bulletin boards with local activities and mini-libraries with resources on transitions (including retirement). Some sponsor brown-bag lunch talks on various topics, which offer an opportunity for networking and discussion.

PERSONALITY TESTS

Personality assessments date back to the age of Hippocrates, who categorized his countrymen by their dominant "humors"—blood, yellow bile, phlegm, and black bile. The humors have long since disappeared from the daily vernacular, but nearly 2500 years later, personality assessments still abound. The mainstays of vocational counselors include the Myers-Briggs Type Indicator, the Strong

Interest Inventory, the Self-Directed Search, and the DISC (which stands for dominance, influence, steadiness, and conscientiousness). Many people have taken these through a school guidance counselor, at a college career center, through professional career counseling, or just for fun.

The Retirement Success Profile is geared specifically for people heading for retirement. Individuals rate simple statements on a scale of 1 to 10—things such as: How well do you get along with your spouse? How important is it for your peers to prepare for retirement? How well do you like your current leisure activities? After 120 questions (administered online), the RSP program offers a 20-plus-page personal interpretive report, which reveals things about your expectations (E) and your present behavior (PB).

The assessment is meant to be used *with* a trained counselor who can help someone develop a "personal retirement mission statement" and "retirement strategy plan." Assessments don't function like a crystal ball, and they do not diagnose problems, either. At best, assessments can give someone who's not sure about their next step a structured way to look at their choices. You have to take the results and ask, "What does this mean for me?"

GETTING HELP FROM COACHES

The last decade has seen the profession of personal "coaching" spring into full bloom. Coachville.com, a professional coaching network, boasts more than 33,000 members in 120 countries worldwide. CoachInc.com, through its two training schools, says it trains over a thousand coaches a year; students are from all over the United States and dozens of countries. They've also launched the International Coaches; dial 1-800-48COACH or visit www.findacoach.com.

Coaches are a hybrid: part career counselor, part enthusiastic friend-for-hire, part partner in crime. And coaching comes without the sometimes perceived stigma of "therapy" or "counseling." "Men don't want counselors," says one career counseling professional of the coaching phenomenon. "They want coaches." For some people, "counseling" suggests a problem orientation; "coaching" denotes competition, teamwork, and opportunity.

There are various breeds of coaches—aggressive executive types, holistic life-healers, cheerleaders, you name it. In choosing a coach, however, the difference in title matters less than the chemistry between coach and client.

Career and Executive Coaches

Career coaches help you figure out where you want to be and what you want to do—whether it's golfing in Tempe or developing a consulting business that lets you work half time—and then help you draw the map that gets you there.

Career coaches contract with corporations to do seminars on such topics as productivity, employee relations, and high-stress transitions such as mergers. They often have a background in human resources; quite a few have gotten their start doing outplacement. Some have advanced degrees related to business psychology or counseling. Many of these corporate coaches also work with individuals.

While career coaches may not advertise themselves as retirement coaches, per se, the issues faced by their clientele—by and large professionals between 40 and 65—invariably include retirement, or in some cases, a reluctance to retire. Teresa Pool, an executive coach from Texas, says retirement is an unavoidable topic: "It's like, here we go again—let's talk about retirement."

If you've worked in government positions and want to seek full- or part-time paid employment in the private or voluntary sectors, you'd be advised to consult a career coach in your target industry. That's because sometimes it's important to "translate" experience from one sector to another so that prospective employers get a clear idea of your capabilities.

Life Coaches

Unlike career coaches, who tend to focus on the key issues of work, and money, life coaches embrace all the messiness of life, from clearing the clutter from your desk to talking to your kids about the will to living the life you've always wanted to live. That last one is the heart and soul of life coaching. One of the most common opening lines is, "Describe your ideal career . . . relationship. . . ."

Some life coaches are former social workers, have advanced degrees in counseling, or trained at one of the coaching "universities."

"Artful questions—that's very key with any client who's being coached," says June Hershey, a life coach from Washington State. "We have to ask questions that are going to get them to dig deep down inside themselves and think." They also utilize a whole array of tools to help them leapfrog past the getting-to-know-you stage into the nitty-gritty of helping someone change their life. Mari Craig, a life coach from the DC-Metro area, even blends her clinical background in social work with tai chi, meditation, deep breathing practices, imagery work, and hypnosis. "I deal with the whole person," says Craig, "mentally, physically, spiritually, and emotionally."

GETTING HELP IN GROUPS: WORKSHOPS AND WEEKENDS

If one-on-one counseling isn't for you, consider a group approach. A mini-industry of seminars, workshops, and weekends is developing around life transitions, including semi-retirement, reskilling for another career in retirement, financial planning before and during retirement. They are marketed under various names, such as Career and Life Planning Workshops, Creative Retirement, and Life Transitions. Check your local college or university for starters, as well as publications and Web sites geared for the mature market. Elderhostel runs some educational programs on transitions, including post-work possibilities. And you can find programs at centers located in Sandy Hills, South Carolina; Manitoba, Canada; and Seattle, Washington.

At New York University's Center for Career, Education and Life Planning, classes like Loosening Your Grip on Your Old Career and the ever-popular Mid-Career Change consistently draw individuals who have retirement on the brain.

If you want to mix the business of planning your future with the pleasure of a weekend getaway, the University of North Carolina at Asheville's Center for Creative Retirement sponsors a Creative Retirement Exploration Weekend, typically held over the Memorial Day weekend. Seminars and topics run the gamut from Deciding to Move—or Not, Choosing a New Lifestyle, Retirement Issues for Singles, How Moving Impacts Taxes, and Health Care Quality and Availability, with an accent on what Asheville has to offer.

WHAT'S ONLINE?

Have fun with online assessments, but take them with a grain of salt unless they are associated with a valid vendor. Many free online personality tests are *not* statistically reliable or valid.

Combination book/online programs are available as well. Purchase of books associated with the Gallup Organization, for instance, will enable you to obtain a code to go online to access a tool called the Strengthsfinder, advertised as Gallup's "online assessment tool that reveals your Signature Themes—your five greatest areas of talent." What's unique about this tool is that it was designed using Gallup's extensive database, developed over 25 years. Here's the link: www.gallup.com/publications/strengths.asp.

O*NET, accessible at http://online.onetcenter.org, is an online service offered free to the public by the Department of Labor. Unlike personality or career assessments that evaluate a pattern of answers to reveal something about you as a person, O*NET lets you account for your own skills and simply shows you what's out there, job-wise. It lists nearly a thousand occupational categories, with descriptions of the knowledge, skills, abilities, interests, preparation, contexts, and tasks involved in each. It's not fast, but it's free, and you might enjoy it. More important: It might give you some ideas.

 ## YOUR MONEY MATTERS

Shop around and know what you are getting for your investment. There's a range of expertise available. Some career guidance services offer trained counselors—people with advanced degrees in counseling or psychology. At centers where the staff is not professionally trained, costs are lower—but the counseling may not be as skilled. Coaching is a new and unregulated profession, though professional associations and training organizations do exist, with attendant standards of conduct and ethics. Check Coach University (www.coachu.com), International Coach Federation (www.coachfederation.org), and Coachville (www.coachville.com).

Obviously, counselors and coaches differ in training and experience, and a few quick questions can get you to the bottom of those facts. The true test of a good counselor or coach is simply chemistry: It's there or it's not.

Retirement counseling and career center services run from $40 to $300, depending on whether the staff is professionally trained.

Coaches typically charge $100 to $150 per session or $400 to $600 per month, including the sessions, e-mail contact, and the use of certain tools. Personality assessments are usually extra. Ask for a complimentary session.

Classes and weekends can run from free courses at local community colleges to affordable fees for Elderhostel trips to several thousand dollars.

Personality tests range from free to the $100 range. Again, ask at community centers or local colleges. Full-blown assessments and counseling can cost in the hundreds of dollars.

If you're reading this book for a spouse, friend, or parent . . . you might do a little homework in your own city or community to identify available post-career planning resources, and get references of people who have used them.

Career Coach is Catalyst for Sassy Senior

At 57, Leah Thayer left the high-powered, high-stress realm of commercial real estate in Houston to return to the Virginia horse country of her childhood and to a long-forgotten dream of acting and doing voice-overs. Thayer's dramatic life change was enabled, in part, by a life/career coach in Middleburg, Virginia. She's now poised to start a radio show about people over 55 who are doing amazing things in their lives, called *Sassy Seniors.*

"For thirty years I'd been in the business of developing shopping centers. For sixteen years, I was an officer of a major international real-estate company, in charge of, among other things, negotiating the deals with major clients, such as Neiman Marcus and Saks Fifth Avenue and Macy's.

"It was high pressure. I was constantly on the go. I'd thought for a while that I might want to do something less frenetic. I no longer wanted to log three hundred fifty thousand miles per year and wake up at three a.m. wondering if we were going to make the next hurdle for the lender. I enjoyed the business. But I also wanted to move from Texas back to Virginia and do something different.

"A couple things happened to make the changes possible. My only child graduated from law school, got married, and moved to Washington. Then my company decided to sell off its retail portfolio. That was my department.

"At first, it was sort of a devastating blow. You think about what you've been building up in a company. Then it is about to no longer be there. I was only fifty-seven. I had not thought about retiring—and certainly not before sixty-five. 'Retirement' is a word that I don't completely identify with, because I want to be very active.

"I had a horrible identity crisis initially. My whole identity for thirty years was wrapped up in the profession, being a VP of this company, living that role, and everything that went with it. It was a big adjustment, at first, to lose that identity. I had always been under the protection of a very large corporate umbrella. Suddenly, I was willing to fold up the umbrella. Eventually I saw it was an opportunity.

"I moved to Virginia. I continued to consult to the real-estate profession, but I was sort of languishing, thinking, 'Well, maybe I could do this, or maybe I could do that.' My business is not the challenge it was twenty-five years ago. I was looking for something creative that would make me want to get up in the morning. But I don't paint. I'm not a dress designer or a sculptor.

"Meeting a career coach was luck. I would like to say that I went on this great research project. But I met her at a party. Through a half dozen sessions, she saw my specific talents and how they might be used. What occupations, careers, professional involvement would be harmonious with the talents that she saw. She uses a wheel to represent various slices of your life—what your goals are professionally, personally, relationship-wise. The theory is that you can't isolate one part of your life and not have the other parts affected. She also administers the Myers-Briggs test. I'd done that before in a corporate situation, but it was used to help us get along with coworkers. This time, the test was strictly about how aspects of my personality could be used positively towards my goals.

"She asked, 'Have you done anything creative?' I was a drama minor in college and I did a little summer stock and two voice-overs in my early twenties. I've always missed that. I've made many presentations as a corporate executive, so I've used some of those skills. She suggested some training courses. I've since taken a voice-over workshop and an on-camera training workshop. I have come up with a concept for a radio talk show called Sassy Seniors, featuring people fifty-five and over who have realized that they don't have to be put out to pasture after they retire—they can do fun and exciting things. A local radio show has expressed interest in picking it up. I've since done a couple of radio gigs, a lot of improv, and acting training. I'm going to start doing auditions again.

"This coach makes you set goals. You have to tape them up on the wall! Really focus on what you're doing. You come up with a date by which you'll *have each goal accomplished. The coach encourages you, which is helpful. You tend to have doubts when you're my age and about to do something entirely new. Some people figure a coach will say, 'Here are all the reasons you should be a fireman.' But you arrive at the concept of what you're going to be. It's not handed to you on a platter.*

"Retirement is changing for lots of people in this country. I'm not alone. We want to do something different with our lives. But we don't, certainly, want to sit out on the dock and fish."

Resource Guide

PUBLICATIONS

Do What You Are: Discover the Perfect Career for You Through the Secrets of Personality Type by Paul D. Tieger and Barbara Barron-Tieger (Little Brown & Company, 2001).

Telling the Stories of Life Through Guided Autobiography Groups by James E. Birren and Kathryn N. Cochran (Johns Hopkins University Press, 2001).

ORGANIZATION AND WEB SITES

Coach University: www.coachu.com

CoachVille: www.cvcommunity.com

Gallup Organization's StrengthsFinder: www.strengthsfinder.com

International Coach Federation (ICF): www.coachfederation.org

North Carolina Center for Creative Retirement in Asheville (NCCCR): www.unca.edu/ncccr

US Department of Labor O*NET OnLine: www.online.onetcenter.org

PART III

Anchor Activities:

GROWING, DOING, AND JUST BEING

Ahoy!

Take a peek through your binoculars to that distant shore of THE RETIREMENT ZONE. You'll see people of all ages teaching school, starting Internet businesses, playing with grandchildren, discovering their family genealogy, running marathons, getting political, doing upside-down yoga postures, and yes, just smelling the roses. They are discovering old passions, new loves, and contributing to make this a better world now and for future generations. They're napping, daydreaming, and thinking about life. They're growing, doing—and just *being*.

They've dropped new anchors in their lives.

As Popeye or any self-respecting sailor knows, an anchor's essential to keeping a boat from drifting aimlessly with the currents. And depending on changing circumstances, sometimes you need one anchor, sometimes two. An anchor activity could be holding sick babies at the hospital, participating in a book club, or doing pro bono accounting work.

ALTRUISM AND WORK

It probably wasn't a Freudian slip when Sigmund himself purportedly said, "Love and work are the cornerstones of our humanness." If it were being advertised in the Sunday paper, this thing called work could be marketed as a heck of a great package deal combining a half dozen life essentials in one neat bundle: a place to belong, other folks to interact with, money, challenges and responsibilities, and, well, a job to do. Wow!

So no wonder many in THE RETIREMENT ZONE maintain their life-long work habit. Some get paid. Others transfer their work ethic into altruism and work—often very hard!—for a good cause.

There's a world of difference between working because you have to and working because you choose to. In this section, meet the people who work for pay, love, or altruistic reasons. Hard-core cases are often up with the morning birds and zoom around all day until they collapse into bed at night, plotting and scheming about their tomorrow. They love being busy. Typically, their calendars are full. Instead of "gone fishing," the sign on their front door might well read:

RUNNING OUT FOR A MEETING...BACK SOON...LET'S TALK!

Working for Pay (and Fun)

It's an Alice in Wonderland world. Older seems to be getting younger. And it's not at all clear, not in the slightest, whether "work" is now part of "retirement." Or is "retirement" just a phase of "work"? (Yes, things were once simpler, back when old was old and work was work, and retirement was the end of the line.) And when, oh when, did we ever fall down this rabbit hole anyway?

Connie Acton retired at 62 from administrative positions in education, and within a month was working again. Fascinated by computers, she'd learned about them on her own and kept up her skills. "I teach computers to seniors two or three days a week," says Connie, now in her early 70s.

Retired from his photo shop, Beal's Photography in Salt Lake City, Bill Beal is learning the ropes of the freelance world. His photos sell in several shops in five states. Spurred by his recent success placing photo-journalism pieces about rural Iowa in three national magazines, he has big ideas for the future. His throttle is set at full steam ahead. Bill is 79.

To set the record straight: historically, most people have not worked during retirement. According to government data, in 2002, fewer than one in seven Americans over 65 were in the workforce. Yet we keep hearing media reports that work is increasingly a part of "retirement." There are, in fact, cross-currents. Some people are working longer, while others are retiring earlier. Many surveys find that baby boomers claim that they intend to continue working. For instance, a 2003 survey by Milwaukee-based Strong Retirement Plan Services found that one third of respondents planned on retiring early, by age 60, with the average expected retirement age being 61.3 years. Half of those surveyed expected to continue some sort of paid employment during retirement, and three in five of those anticipated working at least twenty hours per week.

What these respondents will actually *do*, of course, may be an entirely different matter. Much depends upon the economy.

Jeff Taylor, founder of Monster.com, says, "People have short memories. In the period from about 1997 to 2000, people were set on retiring, or 'graduating,' as I call it, in their late forties and early fifties. That view was pervasive. And after the 2001 to 2003 market, everyone's mutual funds are a shadow of what they were. Some people are out of work and using their savings. They think they will have to work until they are a hundred. But people have short memories as we go through recovery and boom cycles. We've had a consistent cycle for the last four decades. My prediction is that by 2008, everyone who was thinking they would have to work until they're a hundred will be retiring at age sixty-eight instead of sixty-seven."

It remains to be seen whether continuity or change will characterize the relationship between older Americans and their work. Surely, it is hard to argue with long-established historical patterns. On the other hand, there's reason to believe that new combination lifestyles are evolving as baby boomers approach THE RETIREMENT ZONE.

NEW RETIREMENT PATTERNS:
Simultaneously Retired and Working

Retirees today barely bother to blink at the contradictory notion of being simultaneously retired and employed. Every year, more men and women—from those who took early retirement to those who retired at 65—find themselves trying to weave paid work back into their lives, one way or another, perhaps consulting, selling in a retail store, or working part-time at home instead of commuting to a grueling 50- or 60-plus-hour-a-week job. One impetus: maintaining health insurance benefits. As the chart below shows, a study of 1155 people over 65 years of age conducted by the National Council on the Aging found that one in three people work at least part time, not including homemaking. That's higher than census data suggests.

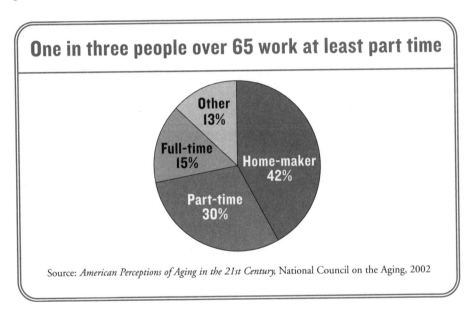

One in three people over 65 work at least part time

Other 13%
Full-time 15%
Home-maker 42%
Part-time 30%

Source: *American Perceptions of Aging in the 21st Century*, National Council on the Aging, 2002

Working in retirement has long been the norm in some sectors of our society. For instance, the U.S. armed services, like municipal police and fire departments, offer retirement benefits at a relatively early age.

Take the case of "Buzz" Buse, who has been director of Officer Placement for the Military Officers Association of America since 1996. He's a retired Marine Corps colonel who served in the infantry throughout his 25-year career. After retiring from the military, he worked for Deloitte Touche as the director of office services, and then as a branch office administrator in a major mid-Atlantic law firm. He joined the Military Officers Association of America (MOAA) in 1994, and now Buzz helps guide others into new post-retirement lives. He runs MOAA's job transition and career counseling services for a membership consisting of over 350,000 active-duty, former, and retired officers and warrant officers from uniformed services, the National Guard, and reserves.

"We have had people who are doctors and dentists who don't want to practice medicine," says Buse. "After twenty or more years of active duty, their interests cut the swath. One dentist became a paralegal. An Air Force pilot was director of a zoo. Some buy a franchise and run their own business. Some do Department of Defense contracting and jobs related to the military. We have people who've sold real estate. A lot have gone into teaching in classrooms in every level, and administrative positions. Many become managers in a wide variety of corporate businesses, and many get into the not-for-profit arena."

Although retired military officers are different from civilians in significant ways—they retire young, with full pensions, and enjoy a strong network of contacts—the fact that they can roll their training and skills into totally new fields should be encouraging to anyone looking to start a new career in THE RETIREMENT ZONE.

WHY WORK IN RETIREMENT? THE FIVE COLORS OF WORK

If this is retirement, why work? There's a spectrum of answers, including the notion that work is what makes life interesting. New Yorker Milton Zlotkin says, "You can only enjoy leisure when it's something that you get from hard work, and relaxation as a result of what you're doing, but if it's a full-time job, it's not leisure anymore. It's boredom."

Color me . . . green. Green's the color of money, of course. Middle-aged and mature people stand at an intersection of spiraling health costs, increasing longevity, a national hunger for credit, products and services, and economic uncertainty—and even the unknowns, now, of a world with terrorist threats. That stew of uncertainties can increase one's appetite for a regular paycheck.

Often pensions don't stretch as far as you might expect. Unanticipated costs erode the nest egg. Grown children may need financial help to finance graduate school or start a business. Some companies are cutting retiree health benefits.

Health care costs, even for people with insurance, send early retirees back to the labor force, seeking better coverage. And investments might not meet expectations, especially if your assumptions were pie-in-the-sky optimistic, or the stock market has a sustained dive.

Two thirds of respondents in the Strong Retirement Study said they will work during retirement due to financial necessity or a combination of financial necessity and a desire to continue to work.

"No one is talking to me about retiring," says Nancy Hutter of White Plains, New York, president and founding partner of Executive Career Strategies. "They're all talking to me about working–either becoming an entrepreneur, buying a business, buying a franchise, being a consultant, or continuing a career. When they reach a certain age, people are finding it harder to get another position in a corporation, so they look for alternatives."

Color me . . . red. Red's a heart color. Some people work because they love to. Especially for those who are used to a high degree of autonomy, such as entrepreneurs, artists, and writers, work is simply what they do. At 72, Jack Hobbs of Morristown, New Jersey, still consults extensively. "It's a marvelous feeling of independence. I can pick and choose whom I want to work for and I can ignore those I don't want to work for, or with. I can call my own shots. I happen to like to work hard, so I'm one of those crazy people," he happily admits.

Work can be a calling, a passion, and a lifestyle. It's all three for Helmut Friedlaender, who was the investment advisor for a wealthy family for about 40 years, and then retired at age 75. With ample income and an active social life, he had his 90th birthday bash at London's Kensington Palace. He still works, managing his own family's finances. "On Monday morning I got to bed at six A.M.," he reports cheerfully, "because I was working on a bag of papers to send to the office. I can generate more work than anybody can handle," he almost gloats. (His two full-time secretaries would agree.)

Color me . . . blue. According to color marketing psychologists, blue suggests continuity, tranquility, and confidence. That may be how some workaholics feel about working past 60, 65, or 70. For them, work is an important anchor activity. Other seniors who have to work for income might just, well, feel blue.

Color me . . . black. One person's pleasure can be another's lack of hobbies. Psychologists note that people who work day and night emerge into retirement like moles blinded by the light; they'd rather just go back in and work some more than face adjusting to a different lifestyle.

Color me . . . yellow. Gregarious and chipper, like the color yellow, social life and work life are closely intertwined. At 78, Estelle Ravage loves running her Bridgeport, Connecticut, arts and crafts gallery. It's a social hub and also a way for her to be involved in the world of art. With the assurance born of experience, she says, "When you do something you like, you don't want to retire from it."

RETIREMENT PACKAGES IN ALL SIZES AND SHAPES LURE YOU BACK TO WORK

Two different trends—deferred and early-retirement packages—can end up keeping people in the work force beyond age 60. Clearly, deferred retirement plans are designed to do just that, by offering employees the opportunity to work fewer hours per week over a longer number of years. But early retirement packages also afford people the chance to find another job or career.

Different Packages

DEFERRED OR DELAYED RETIREMENT: The employee delays the point at which he or she will stop working. The decision is usually made by the employee based on personal financial considerations. The employer may or may not be able to/want to accommodate this wish; if not, the employee seeks a different job.

PHASED OR GRADUAL RETIREMENT: The 2001 Retirement Risk Survey, released by the Society of Actuaries, found that there is significant acceptance of the idea of a gradual retirement. The employee moves from full-time to part-time work with the same employer. Adjustments are made in the pension and reimbursement plans; the shift to part-time work may be more difficult in executive and management positions. Phased retirement represents an effort on the employer's part to keep workers in the workforce past normal retirement age.

Instead of stopping work all at once, almost one in five retirees say they reduced their working hours as they retired. Nearly two in five pre-retirees say they are very interested in gradual retirement, if they can collect part of their pension as they cut back.

EARLY RETIREMENT: The employer seeks to terminate the employee before standard retirement age and offers a compensation package as an incentive, including health benefits, because the retiree will not be eligible for Medicare until 65. Early retirement is one cost-containment strategy used by employers.

In 2003, major companies offered early retirement packages to targeted groups of employees—those in corporate areas identified for downsizing. As a result, a new crop of early retirees is taking the money—sometimes an appealing package of severance cash, retirement pension, and importantly, health benefits—and running straight back into the job market. Some are as young as their forties or fifties. It's a gamble in an uncertain job market. But downsizing pressures are such that, for many, it feels safer to take a really good package than wait and worry about being laid off in a year or two, with less money and fewer benefits.

WHERE THE FULL-TIME JOBS ARE

Will the people seeking salaried employment actually be able to find jobs? Some economists predict that with so many baby boomers coming into retirement age, huge vacuums in the workforce will be created, opening up other opportunities for those seeking employment. For instance, certain professions now happen to have a large number of older workers. Teaching, nursing, home health care, and government white-collar work are all areas predicted to witness a huge exodus in the next decade or so. As millions retire, opportunities will arise.

One leader in the job placement field predicts, "It won't be cycling you individually to better opportunity or perfect match . . . but there will be a mathematical shortage, which will be filled from a global talent pool as well as aged workers, career changers, and grads."

It's worthwhile to scope out the large-scale changes that experts predict will occur in the job market. The U.S. Department of Labor has a user-friendly Web site called Career Voyages that lists "What's Hot." As of this writing, "what's hot" for people with a four-year college degree or more are computer software engineers, and network and computer systems administrators. "What's hot" for people with some college are computer support, medical assistants, and social and human service assistants.

Other job categories that are predicted to grow by 2012 include customer service reps (expect on-the-job training); computer system analysts and computer support specialists; medical assistants; home health aides; physical and occupational therapists; fitness trainers; sales managers; convention and meeting planners; desktop publishers; workers in cable and pay television service; business services; and management and public relations. Keep track of this as the economy evolves, by logging on at www.CareerVoyages.gov/whichindustriesaregrowing.cfm.

The chart below, based on U.S. Department of Labor data, shows the top industries that are expected to add the most jobs. In first place is the software publishers industry. It's expected to grow by 5.3 percent in terms of jobs by the year 2012. This is followed closely by management, scientific, and technical consulting services; community care facilities for the elderly and residential care facilities; computer systems design; and employment services industries. Job growth for these industries is expected to be 4 to 5 percent by the year 2012.

Job Projections for 2012

INDUSTRY	2002 total (in thousands)	2012 projected (in thousands)	Increase (in thousands)	Growth Rate %
Software publishers	256	429	173,700	67.9%
Management, scientific, and technical consulting services	731	1,137	405,600	55.4%
Community care facilities for the elderly and residential care facilities	695	1,077	382,300	55.0%
Computer systems design and related services	1,162	1,797	635,000	54.6%
Employment services supply services	3,248	5,012	1,763,500	54.3%

Source: U.S. Department of Labor, www.careervoyages.gov

According to projections, the economy will continue generating jobs for workers at all levels of education and training, although growth rates are projected to be faster for occupations requiring a postsecondary award (a vocational certificate or other award or an associate or higher degree) than for occupations requiring less education or training. Most new jobs, however, will be created in occupations that require only work-related training (on-the-job training or work experience in a related occupation).

WILL THERE BE PART-TIME WORK?

If most people entering THE RETIREMENT ZONE would like to work, but less than 40 hours a week, what's the likelihood of finding part-time employment? That's anyone's guess. Cornell University's Professor Robert Hutchens, PhD, says, "There's nothing in the recent trends to suggest an increase in part-time jobs." However, there is a growing trend toward freelance and contract work. "People who are capable knowledge workers yet are getting older can work as consultants or as contract executives, for instance, a contract marketing director. You decide the hours that you work," says Jeff Taylor of Monster.com. Of course, under that scenario, the employee is essentially a freelancer, responsible for their own health and other forms of insurance.

Your best bet for part-time work might be staring you right in the face the next time you go to talk with your boss, according to a 2003 *Cornell Study of Employer Phased Retirement Policies*. Their study of 950 employers found that part-time work policies are largely informal (and not advertised). Other findings:

1) **It may be easier to find part-time work by staying right where you are, with your current employer.** Three in four establishments would permit an older employee to reduce hours before official retirement, but few report that this is part of a formal policy. Most employers prefer that hour reductions occur before official retirement.

2) **Certain industries are more amenable than others** to employees shifting to part-time work. Professor Hutchens says, "Employers in health and education tend to be more open, for instance, than those in government organizations, prisons, police and tax collection offices, where there's a large bureaucracy. It's more workable in the retail trade and service-sector businesses."

3) **Benefits change.** The Cornell study finds, "Of those establishments that permit an older employee to reduce hours before official retirement, 26 percent

would not alter health insurance benefits, and 40 percent would permit the employee to draw pension benefits."

The study also found that those organizations that tended to be more open to these arrangements were smaller, in the service sector, and growing (rather than contracting), and that they tended to have a largely female workforce. Most of the companies that allowed phased retirement did not try to "fill in" the extra hours by organizing a job-sharing system.

CONSULTING AND FREELANCING: Working for Yourself

People dream about being self-employed. The fantasy might include working in sweats all day. Not having to wear those annoying stockings, or for men, ties. No boss. Just the work and the world's quickest commute, from the bedroom to the home office. Freedom! Or is it?

What's it like?

Freelancing is no different at age 65 than at 35. Without office support staff, you're doing the billing, travel booking, bookkeeping, mailings, and callbacks yourself, not to mention paying your own health insurance. Friends still shackled to office jobs are jealous, certain you're leading the life of Riley. It's hard to turn any reasonable job down, so scheduling can be tight. You're simultaneously *doing* the work and marketing yourself to *get* the work. Often, assignments arrive in feast-or-famine spurts. Still, you have an exciting chance to "shape your own life." Sort of.

Unlike many freelancers, finding work doesn't seem to be a problem for Harry Moody, PhD. At age 56, he took an early retirement package from his position as executive director of the Brookdale Center on Aging at Hunter College. Moody knows better than most what the challenges of retirement are. He's an intellectual polymath with expertise in ethics, philosophy, and gerontology—and he's also a senior associate at New York's International Longevity Center, not to mention chairman of the board of Elderhostel. "I am a workaholic," he says somewhat ruefully, "I am writing articles, working on two or three books, and constantly traveling around the country, doing a lot of things. I work as consultant and speaker. I never stopped working."

He likes the flexibility of his new life, compared to his previous 9-to-5 job as a teacher and administrator. But there are trade-offs. "You have to reshape yourself and become a free agent," he says. "You are always thinking about the next thing." He's experienced a new undercurrent of uncertainty. "How do you know what is coming in the door next year? Or even next month?" he says. "You have to learn to live with unpredictability. Networking becomes very important."

Moody's moving at a fast pace, but like others in the freelance game, he's ambivalent. As an expert in the academic study of aging, he recognizes in others what he calls the I'm-so-busy-in-retirement syndrome. "People end up, sometimes, working *too* much," he observes. "I think it would be worthwhile to look critically at that. Why are you so busy, what do you get out of being busy? People need to ask themselves how much is enough and to what extent am I refusing a lifestyle that is more paced and leisurely. Sometimes, it's denial." As for his own appetite for work? He loves what he does, but, Moody admits, "I just don't know if I wish I weren't working so hard. . . ."

It remains to be seen whether self-employment becomes a huge trend as some have predicted. There are advantages in terms of time flexibility, and being one's own boss. *Self-Employment and the 50+ Population,* a study released in 2004 by the AARP Public Policy Institute found that the self-employed are more likely to be working part time and to have family-owned businesses or spouses who are also self-employed than salaried workers. Among the self-employed aged 51 and above, nearly half are working part time, compared to about one in four of their wage and salary counterparts. Not surprising, managerial, executive, and professional occupations lend themselves more to self-employment. They found that among workers aged 50 and older, 16.4 percent—5.6 million workers—are self-employed, substantially more than the 10 percent of the overall workforce. And about one in three of those workers made the transition to self-employment after age 50.

Generally speaking, the self-employed are older; are more likely to be male, white, married, and college educated; and are more likely to be healthier but to have a health condition that limits their work, than salaried people. Fifteen percent of the self-employed age 51 and older report a work-limiting health condition compared with eight percent of salaried workers in the same age group.

Consider the upfront costs of starting and marketing a new business if you go that route. First scope out all the costs and issues, including office rental or home-office setup, hiring, accounting, taxes, and any relevant costs such as licensing, professional association membership, incorporation, and insurance before hanging out your shingle. Determine whether you can write off your home office, car, or communications equipment such as computer and cell phone as legitimate business expenses. Lastly, dream up a backup plan in case you fall short of your goals.

When starting out, one perplexing question is what rates to charge. In 2004, average hourly rates nationwide hovered between $50 to $60 for graphic design, desktop publishing, and digital photography, with slightly higher rates paid for multimedia services and slightly lower rates for data processing. Current fees for writing, editing, scanning, graphic design, DTP, prepress, multimedia, web services, virtual assistance, and more are available from Brenner Books, at www.brenner-books.com.

For information on starting your own business, consulting, or freelance career, consult the myriad of resources available through the Small Business Administration (www.sba.gov), the public library, or local bookstore. *Entrepreneur* magazine's Web site has a section dedicated to home business information, with a "Top 40" listing of current resources (www.entrepreneur.com).

Lastly, consider health insurance if you are younger than age 65, the age at which one becomes Medicare eligible. The good news is that if your spouse works and gets health insurance benefits, you may have decent coverage too (but check it out). Also, low-cost group health-care plans are available for freelancers in certain fields, such as information technology, arts, media and publishing, entertainment, and banks and finance.

The bad news is that many independent workers risk being uninsured or under-insured for health-care costs. It can be close to impossible for freelancers, temps, continent workers, day laborers, contract workers, part-time workers, and others not tied to full-time employers to afford individual rates. (One study found that residents of New York City must earn over $100,000 a year to afford an average HMO plan on the individual market.)

Sara Horowitz, founder of the nonprofit organization Working Today, says, "There is a pressing need to address the concerns of the independent worker. More workers are forced into what we call 'permalance' or contract positions. As a result, these professionals are forced to give up the benefits and security associated with long-term employment." To meet this challenge, Working Today has created the Freelancers Union, which offers affordable health benefits and other union-like supports for white-collar freelance workers in the service sectors in the New York area, in a pilot project that may expand in the future (www.working today.org). Before you go it alone, investigate your health insurance options.

OPPORTUNITY KNOCKS:
Making Money in the "Mature Market"

Whether you're an entrepreneur, self-employed, or looking for a salaried job, a new market may be opening up: yours. In the next decade, a new universe of jobs will be created for people over 50 who are providing services and products to THE RETIREMENT ZONE market itself.

A fit, energetic 67-year-old Phyllis Rogers of Marietta, Georgia, works full time teaching strength-training classes in homes for senior citizens. The retired computer ad designer says, "I know what I'm supposed to do when I grow up. It took me this long to find it. I liked what I did before, but this is a *calling.*"

Don Schmitz, who grew up on a farm in Dundas, Minnesota, says, "We had pigs, chickens, cows, cats, and dogs. My father thought I was to be the next farmer." Instead he became a teacher. After decades in the classroom, he started a business called GrandkidsandMe that helps bring grandparents and grandchildren together in a fun, educational environment.

Yvonne Wheeler was barely retired when she embarked on a new career. In 1996, she codeveloped the Institute for Learning in Retirement, in Denver, for older learners. Its acronym is VIVA!, "vibrant, intelligent, vigorous adults."

Known as the "egg lady," who promotes eggs on TV for an industry trade association, 67-year-old Jo Manhart of Columbia, Missouri, founded an employment agency for seniors within six months of losing her full-time job in a merger. Called Available Jones (www.availablejones.com) after the Li'l Abner cartoon character (who was always available), her employment agency has placed people in positions as diverse as handyman, office manager, painter, and in such areas as auditing, executive, clerical, accounting, inventory, fleet maintenance, interpreting, greeting, retail sales, invalid care, software, and state fair retail.

Manhart says employers see the benefits of experience: "They say, 'I'm sick of these young people, they don't show up the next day, they take off, they don't take it seriously, they don't follow through, they don't know how to handle people.' Many employers realize there are advantages to using older people." A drawback is that some don't command their previous hourly wage or salary level, she adds. She's also created a free manual so that others can start similar senior-focused services in their own communities. Jo says, "I've got a perfect deal here, with the fun of being the egg lady on television again and starting something that, without exception, everyone says, 'What a great idea!'"

It's common sense that mature people have a feel for what their peers want, like, and do. After all, today's teenagers enjoy working in retail shops that sell rap, techno, and urban gear. And the baby boomers fueled industry after industry—from the explosion of blue jeans into a billion-dollar fashion industry to music, adventure travel, health foods and alternative medicine, and more. Each age cohort represents a mini-universe of consumers, products, service needs, and so on.

Practical Tips:
9 TIDBITS ABOUT WORKING IN THE RETIREMENT ZONE

1) **Consider asking about part-time before retiring:** "If you are thinking of retiring, one of the things that maybe you should consider is discussing the topic with your present employer, to find out, would they be receptive to some kind of part-time arrangement or job-sharing," notes Jon Sargent, economist with the Federal Bureau of Labor Statistics.

2) **Leapfrog:** If you can, leapfrog over the transition. Try to get your next job or career before you leave the first one. It's easier said than done. But if you can, moonlight and start your home-based business, or map out the strategy for renovating that old farmhouse into a marvelous inn. The more you put into it early on, the easier the transition will be—and the clearer your future costs and challenges.

3) **Use the Internet to help snag a job:** If you don't know how to use the Internet, try to learn. You can get a book on the topic, take a class at a local university job center or library, or ask your grandchildren!

4) **Update your skills/get educated:** Taking a few months to re-tool your credentials. Taking a formal computer course, for example, adds another skill to your resume. If you want to shift into a new career, such as selling real estate, you'll need to study and pass a broker's licensing exam.

5) **If you relocate:** If you're relocating for retirement, but want to continue to work, get adequate information first about the kinds of jobs or consulting opportunities available, including local rates of pay. Check Web sites such as the U.S. Department of Labor's Career Voyages (www.CareerVoyages.gov) for state-by-state lists of growth industries, costs of living, and other useful information.

6) **Polish up your resume:** Don't just recycle that old resume. Overhaul it. Read the trade press in your industry or profession to see what's new and what employers are looking for. Do multiple resumes, targeted to different kinds of jobs you're interested in. Decide whether to make an asset of your age or to obscure chronological facts. As always, your resume is your personal emissary, so make sure it's had a shave and a shine.

7) **Circulate!** The best way to get a job is through personal contacts. Often you can hear about a job just being out among people.

8) **Stay competitive:** Attitude and self-presentation can make a difference. "We encourage folks to act young, think young, and dress young. Keep yourself fit. Don't walk around like an old dried-up sock, looking disheveled. Have some energy and spark and life," says Buzz Buse, who administers a job transition program.

9) **Find the silver lining in your gray hair:** Experience is marketable. In some settings, older people are sought after for reliability, judgment—and good looks!

There's no real magic to getting a job. And the process isn't much different if you are 35 or 55. Networking is always important. Knowing what you want, and can do, is essential. References, self-presentation, persistence, and flexibility are key. Talent certainly helps. And experience—well, that's your strong suit.

RETRAINING, RE-SKILLING, RECYCLING YOURSELF

Back in the 20th century, a retiree might "pick up some work." Now, you retrain and reskill.

COMPUTER LITERACY IS KEY. In a fast-changing technology environment, here's an important ingredient in the skills arsenal: computer literacy at a level that's required for the position you are seeking. If you keep up with your skills, you can keep up in the workplace. "There are people over sixty embracing technology, e-mailing with four generations, and downloading music for their computers. And others who ignore it completely. If you can't meet the one-hundred-level challenges, you can't go to the two-hundred challenges. If you don't use a computer, for instance, for sure you can't work in a retail store in the mall," comments Jeff Taylor, founder of Monster.com.

Noting that "training drops off within firms as people age, as does their participation in outside job-related courses, Cornell professor Robert Hutchens, PhD, points to a common problem. "If a person's skills erode as they get older, they ultimately aren't competitive anymore. At the moment, very little job retraining effort is targeted to older workers—you have to do this on your own," he notes. "A lot of people in their fifties are losing jobs because of displacement in large corporations; maintaining their skills is essential to getting a new one." Which specific skills depends on the person and the field they are in, but generally, "computer skills are part of this story."

EDUCATION WITH A JOB IN MIND. Is the cost of going back to school, either online or in a classroom, worth it to help a 50- or 60-something reenter the work world? The answer depends on your career aspirations and the job market in your community. These courses may either boost your current career or give you an advantage in pursuing a second career. Here are some specifics:

Teaching: You can earn a teaching credential online. The nation faces a teacher shortage for specialists, such as teachers of English as a Second Language.

Information technology: You'll find numerous short certificate courses in specific computer information technologies, with dozens of exams leading to specific credentials and certifications. And you can study Web design, among other specializations. With computer literacy, the more you learn, the easier it gets. So stick with it.

Health: Some larger universities offer four-course online sequences in health professions, and there are many local opportunities to train and get credentialed for specific health service jobs.

Leisure: Education might open doors in areas you might not have thought of, such as getting a part-time job in a resort or upscale retirement community. Take, for instance, nationwide educator Phoenix Online's (http://degrees.uofphx.info) course in turf-grass management, which prepares you for an outdoor job that's important in the competitive business of golf. Phoenix also offers a certificate in hospitality.

Professional degrees: People in their 70s are getting certificates in gerontology and degrees in law. You can even get an MBA online. Dozens of colleges and universities have instituted online MBA programs, as does the for-profit company, University of Phoenix Online. Duke University's Fuqua School of Business (www.fuqua.duke.edu/admin/gemba) has a combination online and classroom MBA program that is designed for older professionals, not full-time students. In 2002, the Web site for *Peterson's Guides* listed the Wayne Huizenga Graduate School of Business and Entrepreneurship at Nova Southeastern University in Ft. Lauderdale, Florida, and Worcester Polytechnic Institute as "cool picks" for MBA students.

 ## HEALTHVIEWS

How does working while retired impact your health?

Going *back* to work when you've already retired can either increase or decrease stress. Of course, it depends on the circumstances of that post-retirement job; if it's stimulating, it could be a positive experience. Bagging groceries to make some extra change might not be fun. If you've been a manager and used to making decisions and controlling a department, it can be hard to scale back to being a staff-less employee. On the other hand, not having to take work home, work long hours, and commute may add to the "plus" side of the equation. And then, there's health insurance.

 ## YOUR MONEY MATTERS

Look at your overall personal financial picture: Look at your overall costs and compare them to the benefits of working in your retirement years. Consider how your new job or consulting practice will impact your overall financial situation, taking into account expenses, income, and investments such as IRAs, taxes, and eligibility for benefits such as Social Security. Don't forget to factor in emergency situations, such as providing or paying for home care for a frail relative. Know what salary you need, too. (See Chapter 21, Paying for Retirement.)

THE BIG PICTURE:
Europeans Redefine Work/Life Balance

"Moving beyond your own personal situation for a minute, step back and look at these pushes and pulls in the workplace. That's what the European Commission has done, in trying to figure out a more humane, sensible way to organize work in the future. Specifically, they've invited a rethinking of the way in which periods of work, leisure, learning, and caring are distributed over the life cycle," begins the 2003 report, *A New Organisation Of Time Over Working Life,* by the Dublin-based European Foundation for the Improvement of Living and Working Conditions. In the European Union, there's considerable discussion about "rebalancing work and life." Work, as most of us know it, is based on the idea that life progresses along in neat stages, from 1) education to 2) work to 3) retirement. European policy makers are thinking about a radically new paradigm of work in which these three stages happen at variable times, with mid-life sabbaticals and time off for caregiving balanced by working until later in life. This is being forged by new realities: the shrinking and aging of the workforce, simultaneous with increase in life expectancy.

European solutions include a range of inventive ideas, from incentives for older workers to remain in the workforce (such as gradual retirement packages, or raising the eligibility age for Social Security) to an overhaul of the entire system to allow more sabbaticals, time off for caregiving for elderly relatives and raising children, and retraining periods.

Now, that's food for thought.

(For more information, check the section Population and Society on www.eurofound.eu.int. Or to read the study yourself, see www.eurofound.eu.int/publications/EF0336.htm.)

If you're reading this book for a spouse, friend, or parent . . . expect to be supportive during transitions. People of any age have complex feelings about both work and money. So regardless of which way the work transition is going (e.g., your loved one is leaving work, starting a new job, shifting to part-time work, continuing to work when they want to quit), there could be rough patches. For instance, small-business owners often have trouble selling or letting go of their enterprise. Professionals like doctors and lawyers can feel acutely the shift of status and position if they go from a high-prestige job in a medical center to, say, part-time work in a clinic. Accepting lower pay or fewer benefits can rankle. Job changes can be stressful at *any* point in life.

Work Trade-offs for Health

Some people retire on Friday and start a new job on Monday. That's what 64-year-old George Fox of Princeton, New Jersey, did when he took a retirement package from IBM a few years after suffering a heart attack in 1997. His daughter Susannah recalls, "Before my dad got handed the commemorative clock from IBM, he landed a retirement job as a programmer at a start-up company. He'd been an IBM executive for twenty-five years, a white-collar guy wearing a suit. But at night after dinner you'd find him reading a C-Plus Plus handbook. He *loves* programming. So it was a great thing in retirement for him to become a programmer in a cubicle. And he really likes the new company's golf league."

Analytical, competitive, and talented, George now works closer to home, putting in 40 to 50 hours a week. Even more than the paycheck, he enjoys the challenge of his fast-paced retirement job.

"This is not lifetime dancing lessons. The company is making choices all the time, like, should we go offshore. People left and right are being asked to leave. It's a somewhat pressured environment—if you can't keep up, you don't stay long. When I was forty, I was working for a fifty-four-year-old, and he seemed ancient. And I am now working with peers who are my kids' ages or younger. I am active and vigorous and I've had my share of, 'You don't act like sixty-four years old.'

"I don't have 100 people reporting to me now, so I don't have that pressure of being responsible for other people's livelihood, and deciding who gets jobs or bonuses. I miss the excitement of making a decision that's not so obvious but that's right, and taking on something really tough that nobody thinks is possible—and making it happen. That's all very stressful and my heart can't take it. I am careful about the scope of what I agree to do now."

Working in the Wonderful World of Older Learners

In 1989, 50-year-old Yvonne Wheeler started thinking about demographics and the growing population of older people. She had directed a corporate foundation for a major bank. She wanted to start something that she could move into and grow with, so with a colleague she started VIVA!, the Institute for Learning in Retirement in Denver for older learners.

"It's an incredible group. There are 350 people in the program, all retired. Ninety-nine percent are college educated. They're very vibrant. VIVA! is an acronym for "vibrant, intelligent, vigorous adults." It really fits. They come from all walks of life, including many professionals and businesspeople. We meet in a church in central Denver, where it's easily accessible.

"What I love is being open and receptive to the ideas that people have. The job's creative: Anything goes, I tell them. Last term they had a line-dance class of 40 people—doctors, lawyers, bank presidents—all doing country, swing, line dances. We've got people going out in the park and painting, a Monday morning class for people who want to learn how to play pool. I organize monthly "Hot Topic" lectures on global issues. It's hugely popular.

"There's a gold mine of intelligence here. We have a retired doctor who was always interested in astronomy. He has spent time researching, researching, and researching more. He loves the topic. He is now teaching an astronomy class. People love him, he's that good. There's story after story after story like that.

"I've learned that the differences among people are not by age, but attitude. We have some very young 80-year-olds and some old fogies who are in their 50s. Our most popular classes are current affairs, music, and international issues. Very few people in our organization are not on e-mail. These people are curious. Most don't want to go back to the classics and retake Shakespeare. They want to be up with what is going on. It's all attitude.

"I'm also president of NorthStar Institute, started in 1992. NorthStar runs weeklong programs for people over 50 in resort areas like Vail, Colorado, Santa Fe, New Mexico, and Italy. The curriculum combines history, literature, music, painting, photography, gourmet cooking, writing, hikes after classes, and field trips.

"My work? I'm thrilled with what I do!"

Resource Guide

PUBLICATIONS

The Age Advantage: Making the Most of Your Midlife Career Transition by Jean Erickson Walker, EdD (Berkeley Books, 2000).

Career Change: Everything You Need to Know to Meet New Challenges and Take Control of Your Career, 2nd Edition by Dr. David P. Helfand (VGM Career Horizons, 1999).

Changing Careers for Dummies by Carol L. McClelland, PhD (Hungry Minds, 2001).

Don't Stop the Career Clock: Rejecting the Myths of Aging for a New Way to Work in the 21st Century by Helen Harkness (Davies-Black, 1999).

Free to Succeed: Designing the Life You Want in the New Free Agent Economy by Barbara B. Reinhold (Plume, 2001).

Getting Started in Consulting, 2nd Edition by Alan Weiss, PhD (John Wiley & Sons, 2003).

I Could Do Anything If I Only Knew What It Was: How to Discover What You Really Want and How to Get It by Barbara Sher with Barbara Smith (Delacorte Press, 1994).

Monster Careers: How to Land the Job of Your Life by Jeff Taylor with Doug Hardy (Penguin Books, 2004).

What Can You Do with a Law Degree? A Lawyer's Guide to Career Alternatives Inside, Outside & Around the Law by Deborah Arron, (Decision Books, 2003).

What Color is Your Parachute? by Richard Nelson Bolles (Ten Speed Press, 1971-2004, published annually).

ORGANIZATIONS AND WEB SITES

America's Job Bank: www.ajb.org

Career Voyages, collaboration between U.S. Department of Labor and U.S. Department of Education: www.CareerVoyages.gov

Monster, online global careers network: www.monster.com

O*NET Center, the Occupational Information Network: online.onetcenter.org

CHAPTER 12

A Volunteering Primer

In this chapter, you'll find background on volunteering and how to connect with a position that works for you. In the next chapter, called Volunteering Guide: 10 Ways to Pitch in, from Animals to Politics, there's an overview of many different volunteer opportunities.

Like certain vegetables, volunteering has a bad reputation among those who don't partake. "I was thinking of volunteering for a hospital or something—but I'm afraid it might depress me," says a 67-year-old retired computer programmer who competes for fun in bicycle races—and wins. Wrinkling up his nose, he adds, "Not for nothing would I go to the local hospital and say, 'Here I am,' and carry books around." But this athlete's on the wrong track. Just as "veggies" can mean anything from carrots to kale, "volunteering" can mean choices far beyond the standard fare of hospital and soup-kitchen jobs.

Take, for example, political activist Clifton Arrington, who in retirement maintains his decades-long involvement in social issues affecting minority communities. He works on problems ranging from police brutality to racial profiling to domestic violence. "There's a real need for effective change," he says. "If there's going to be any change at all, you have to be involved. For me it's not a labor of love; it's more a labor of need."

Others find themselves gravitating toward volunteer jobs that draw on skills for which they were once paid. Ken Brown, an engineer who worked at construction oversight during the restoration of the Ellis Island National Immigration Museum in the 1970s now works as a part-time volunteer at the same place, helping to solve maintenance-engineering problems. They've welcomed him with open arms.

And people sometimes invent curious yet fulfilling niches. An 80-year-old Bostonian, an avid Zionist, joined the Israeli Army reserves in her 60s and flew to Israel once a year for a decade, to serve. One couple ("We're over 80 chronologically, but only twenty years old in spirit") volunteer together at a small zoo library. He's a retired medical school professor of anatomy and helps out cataloging both books and bones; she's a retired schoolteacher. It's a perfect fit.

Use your imagination if you really want to "give back." You've got training, skills, and life experience. Dozens of worthy causes would benefit from your talent, verve, and intelligence. It's natural to experiment. As Ted Couch in Denver recounts, "I went through a bunch of volunteer activities, teaching first aid and tutoring at the county jail and then tutoring welfare mothers for the GED program."

If you've already got the habit, that's great. But if you don't, try a few new things—and take a nibble before you bite. It all goes down better if you realize you've got choices, like broccoli instead of brussels sprouts. You can coach kids to race bikes, instead of hauling that book cart through the hospital.

THE PARALLEL UNIVERSE OF UNPAID WORK

Alongside the workaday world of jobs and paychecks, there's a parallel universe of unpaid volunteer work.

The nonprofit sector is *huge*. The largest component is hospitals and other health care institutions. Together with arts, educational, cultural, and religious institutions, nonprofit organizations had revenues of $875 billion and, in addition to assimilating the work of 84 million volunteers, employed 11.7 million workers in the United States in 2001.

Despite the enormity of the sector, individual volunteer contributions of time do make a difference. *The New Nonprofit Almanac and Desk Reference* notes, "Giving and volunteering are the lifeblood of independent sector organizations. A major component of giving is donating one's time."

There's a nonprofit version of just about every kind of paid job imaginable. There are volunteer slots ranging from the board of directors to door-to-door canvassing. In between, there are management, finance, labor relations, mergers, e-commerce, strategic programming, solicitation, event planning, and other positions similar to what's found in small- to medium-size businesses and larger companies. As in the paid-work world, management styles vary. Some bosses are likeable, others loathsome. As in the paid-work world, big is not always better, and image can be deceptive. Volunteers might have negative experiences in high-profile, household-name nonprofits, and find more excitement working for a start-up organization that's low on resources but high on vision. Finally, as in the paid-work world, different "benefits" come with different jobs: free tickets to events or classes, hats and T-shirts, free memberships, discounts on lunch, occasional volunteer recognition ceremonies, and even, sometimes, promotion to the next level of (unpaid) responsibility. Once in a rare while, a volunteer opportunity becomes a paid position.

RETIREMENT ZONE TRENDS:
1 in 9 Americans over 55 Volunteer

Hearts of gold.

It's hard to imagine an army numbering 14 million, the size of the part-time older volunteer workforce in the United States (see chart). That's more people than the entire population of Pennsylvania.

Let's take a closer look at what goes on in THE RETIREMENT ZONE. If you're a volunteer over age 55, there's one of you for every nine people in the U.S. workforce. Of people over 55, about one in four volunteers. Both men and women volunteer.

On average, volunteers in the 55-plus age group give 2 hours a week, or 96 hours a year, according to the U.S. Bureau of Labor Statistics. About one in every ten volunteers over the age of 65 gives 500 hours or more annually (that's the equivalent of about one full week every month). Most volunteers concentrate their efforts on one commitment. But nationally, about three quarters of a million people over 55 volunteer with at least four nonprofit organizations. Over a hundred thousand Americans over 55 are committed to five or more volunteer jobs.

What kind of work do volunteers do? More people do the very basic work of calling, soliciting, arranging, and generally just helping with special events than any other kind of volunteer work. One in ten volunteers over age 65—about 70,000 people—provides transportation for others. About one in every five volunteers is involved in a managerial capacity, either as a board member or in a neighborhood association, on a part-time basis. About 150,000 volunteers do construction and maintenance.

A Bird's-eye View of Volunteering in America, 2002

A LOOK AT THOSE WHO VOLUNTEER	55-64	over 65
Total volunteers *(in thousands)*	7,146	7,492
Where They Volunteer	**55-64**	**over 65**
Religious	41%	45%
Social/community service	13%	18%
Hospital/health	10%	10%
Civic, professional, international	9%	8%
Educational/youth services	13%	7%
Other	8%	7%
Sports, hobby, cultural, arts	4%	4%
Environmental	2%	1%
How They Got Involved	**55-64**	**over 65**
Were approached by the organization	43%	40%
Approached the organization	41%	43%

Source: Volunteering in the United States, U.S. Bureau of Labor Statistics, Dec. 2002.

8 REASONS WHY PEOPLE VOLUNTEER

Fourteen million Americans over age 55 volunteer. Why? It's certainly not the pay. Here are reasons a range of people gave for their commitment to volunteering:

Reason #1: It broadens your vision.

Reason #2: It can be empowering.

Reason #3: It's rewarding.

Reason #4: It can be social.

Reason #5: It can be expanding, and even therapeutic.

Reason #6: It's a substitute for a job.

Reason #7: It's important work.

Reason #8: It connects you to a spiritual source.

You might be surprised by what you discover about yourself. Connie Douglas, volunteer coordinator at the Memphis Zoo, recalls, "I have friends who said, 'We're not sure we'd like to work at a hospital.' Then they investigated volunteer opportunities. And it turns out they have a gift for working with children in the hospital that they never imagined that they had. I'd say not to be afraid to try things out. That's especially so for people who have had a lifestyle change, not just retiring, but perhaps who have had a loss in their life, a spouse, for instance. Sometimes volunteering is the thing that brings you back. . . ."

Keeping involved with things you love to do is a motivation for volunteering. Marvin Mausner says, "My wife and I are both musicians, and we play in a chamber orchestra and sing in a choir that performs in public places and at senior residences. We're involved in a million other things such as sleeping in homeless shelters as hosts."

Eldon Murray of Milwaukee, and founder of the Gay People's Union, one of the first gay liberation groups in the country, explains the motivation for his volunteer work: "Older gays and lesbians not only have to swim against the current of ageism found by all older people, but they must also swim against a second current of prejudice and ignorance because of their sexual orientation."

In Los Angeles, Ann Reiss Lane, 73, expresses a kind of gratitude for the opportunity to serve. Given her six decades of community and civic service, one would think others would be thanking her. She was the first (and only) woman president of the L.A. Fire Commission and subsequently served on the L.A.

Police Commission, both highly visible positions in L.A. city government. Her decade-long career as the founder and unpaid head of an education and advocacy group, Women Against Gun Violence, came about as an answer to a call. This was not a spiritual "call." It was literally a telephone call from Betty Friedan asking Ann's help in countering NRA marketing campaigns targeting women. Working with victims' families, running an organization on a shoestring, and encouraging the passage of stricter gun laws hasn't been easy. She nonetheless counts herself lucky for her life of activism.

Reality Check: Nothing's Perfect

Volunteering sounds virtuous. It can also be personally rewarding—but not always. With no salary involved, interpersonal relationships and getting recognition might seem more important; petty grievances can loom larger. Retirees complain that rigid scheduling can cause conflicts with volunteers' doctors' appointments and other responsibilities. Sometimes, they say, host organizations (and their younger staff) aren't respectful and don't bother to find out what volunteers can do. Awkward tensions with paid staff sometimes surface, too.

"I happen to like the places I'm volunteering now, which is unusual," admits one volunteer, who chose to remain anonymous. "I've done other volunteer work. I know it can be hard to do. I've sometimes been miserable."

MONEY MUSINGS

It would be an understatement to say that in the nonprofit world, people have a lot of feelings about money.

Some people couldn't, and wouldn't be paid to do this work. "A salary *obligates* you," is what people often say. One woman, a retired real-estate agent, tutors English as second language. She has a teaching license, but prefers, she says, to retire and use her free time as she likes: "Right now I don't want to earn money at a job. I don't want the structure of having to follow somebody else's rules. I feel like a free spirit. The very fact that you're working but not for money means you're not shackled to the job."

Volunteers sometimes wonder if their value is diminished because they aren't paid. How is volunteer time valued? According to Independent Sector (www.independentsector.org), a coalition representing 700 national nonprofit organizations, on average, volunteer time was valued at $17.19 an hour in 2003.

Many volunteers also donate money. When the recipient organization is somehow near and dear to a donor's heart, this can be a memorable and rewarding experience. Nearly 80, Jean Andrews has been a collector of ethnic textiles for over five decades.

"I don't do volunteering like hospital visits," she said. "But since 1982, I've spent a lot of time in Costa Rica, where I helped to start an artisan's cooperative in a mountain village. They do sewing and painting and that sort of stuff. I helped them build a building and get better training. I can't go there now because there is no oxygen equipment and it's a distance to the nearest hospital. I used to go at least once every year for twenty years, and often take other teachers down there. They asked why did I do this. And I told them, I have no grandchildren. So the next time I came, the whole village had balloons out with signs saying, 'We love you, Grandmother,' in Spanish. They call me their grandmother. And *that* was my volunteering."

The Irresistible Charm of Unpaid Labor

From a business perspective, the prospect of people working for absolutely nothing has a certain allure. American volunteers contribute an estimated $240 billion annually in donated services, according to Independent Sector. Put in perspective, the dollar value of their unpaid labor equaled the value of the entire U.S. transportation sector in 2002.

And in truth, many organizations dedicated to wonderful causes have appetites far bigger than their budgets can serve. Often, the constituencies they serve—for instance, homeless people—have multiple interrelated problems.

The dollar value of volunteer labor has not been lost on society's leaders. Consider the following developments:

- Farsighted nonprofits have their eye on "capturing" the participation (and financial contributions) of a huge new generation of "giver backers." In 2003, the report *Experience at Work: Volunteering and Giving Among Americans 50 and Over*, by the nonprofit organization Independent Sector (www.independentsector.org), heralded the boomer generation as "the largest untapped pool of potential volunteers for the nonprofit community in recent history."

- Policy advocates have recently exhorted the older non-working population to shoulder more civic responsibility. Organizations from the secular Experience Corps to faith-based programs seek to harness the intellectual and professional power of the boomer and Eisenhower generations toward lofty social goals, such as providing social services to those who are impoverished.

- The actual job of *managing* volunteers in nonprofit organizations is slowly becoming professionalized. The growing stature of volunteers as a valuable asset may be measured by the job title for the person shepherding them: "volunteer resource manager." The job "is similar to a human resource professional who is responsible for paid staff," according to the Virginia-based Association for Volunteer Administration (www.avaintl.org).

- Lastly, opportunities are opening up for virtual volunteering, harnessing the ability of wired seniors to pitch in on a volunteer basis via cyberspace without ever going to an office.

Of course, nobody wants to be doing a job that *should* be salaried. If you're volunteering for an organization and you think their volunteers are being inappropriately deployed, do inquire—or find a different, more clearly philanthropically minded organization.

INSIDER'S GUIDE: How Not to Get Stuck Stuffing Envelopes

The secret to a happy volunteering experience is finding a position that suits your time and needs in a cause that you find inspiring.

1) FOLLOW YOUR OWN LIGHTS. Say "yes" to what you want to do. One elderly man described himself as happily situated in retirement. He was very clear: "I am enjoying myself too much. I'm certainly not going to go to a domestic violence shelter or homeless shelter, no, I just don't want to. I DID that kind of thing for years. I volunteer at the library now because I want to do something that meets my needs. I go every week. . . ."

You're entitled to say no! As one 65-year-old college administrator said on the cusp of leaving her decades-long job, "I have to be careful not to be pulled into every organization, the church, and every do-good group in town. Opportunities for volunteerism? There are too many in this town . . . and I'm a sitting duck."

2) KNOW YOUR LIMITS. Be honest with yourself about your physical stamina. Don't volunteer for a job that's going to knock you out. "Until about a year ago I worked delivering meals to AIDS patients," explained one fellow, born in 1922. "I'd be there at six A.M. one day every week and work for three hours. But I have foot and back problems. I had to give it up."

The last thing you need is for your volunteer work to create health problems. Think it through before you sign up.

3) REMEMBER, YOUR TIME IS YOUR OWN (OR IS IT?). There's so much that needs doing in the world that you could spend your entire life working as a volunteer. As one volunteer joked, "When I worked, I worked a five-day week. Now, it's a seven-day week!" Start by volunteering about two hours a week, which is the average amount of time that most Americans over 55 give.

4) DIFFERENT STROKES FOR DIFFERENT FOLKS. You are likely to have a very different experience if you work for a large national organization, a small community start-up, or a local affiliate of a large organization.

Large nonprofit organizations with local chapters, such as the YMCA, Meals on Wheels, or the American Cancer Society, usually have programs, annual campaigns, and materials that are orchestrated from the national headquarters, and might provide more structure and direction to volunteers.

At small local groups things might be more ad hoc, and you may have a greater opportunity to work more closely with staff or contribute ideas.

Not all nonprofits are set up to manage volunteers. The head of one national environmental think tank said ruefully, "Sometimes someone calls from out of state because they've read a newspaper article about our work and they are eager to help. But it's really hard to figure out what they could do, no matter how good they are."

5) NIBBLE BEFORE YOU BITE. The local United Way has lists of many community-based organizations, and you can call the United Way in your community to identify volunteer opportunities. You can scan volunteer opportunities offered by over a hundred organizations by logging onto a Web site called Ask a Friend organized by Senior Corps (www.volunteerfriends.org). Or you can access a state-by-state Volunteer Center Directory of organizations and resources from the Points of Light Foundation and Volunteer Center National Network in Washington, D.C. (www.pointsoflight.org).

Many national organizations can now help you find a local volunteer group with just a few clicks of the mouse. Log on at the Web sites of your favorite nonprofit organizations to see what programs they might run in your community.

Also, a new 2-1-1 telephone service may soon be coming to your town. It enables people to volunteer in their community and call for assistance, from finding an after-school program to securing adequate care for a child or an aging parent. The system is now available statewide in Connecticut, Hawaii, Minnesota, and Idaho, and in communities in 25 states, serving over 80 million people. Visit www.211.org.

Some trade and professional associations encourage retirees to become involved in volunteering. For instance, the National Education Association (NEA), which has a membership of nearly two and a half million educators, has a special division that offers support and opportunities for volunteering (mostly in education and areas related to young people) to its members.

6) WHAT TO ASK. Once you connect with an organization, here are some things to ask:
- Who funds the organization?
- Is there a job description for volunteers?
- Is there a volunteer coordinator?
- What are the organization's overall goals and what programs would a volunteer be working on?
- How many volunteers do you have? What, in general, are their jobs? What skills and background do they have?
- Are the hours flexible? How much time must a volunteer commit?
- How long does a volunteer commitment generally last?
- What are the working conditions? If I have special needs, will they be honored?
- Are there any times when volunteers get together to discuss the work they are doing?
- Can the organization send information? Do they have a Web site?
- Can the organization place prospective volunteers in contact with someone who has already been a volunteer there?
- When relevant: are volunteers covered by the organization's liability insurance?

If you're reading this book for a spouse, friend, or parent . . . the volunteer experience can be very gratifying—or feel like a waste of time. But it's such a potentially valuable anchor activity in later years that it's worthwhile searching for the right opportunity. You may need to lend an encouraging word, however!

Just the Facts, Ma'am: The Who, What, Why, Where, and When of Volunteering

Here's a checklist of things to help you decide where to volunteer.

1) MY TIME AVAILABILITY

_____ I'd like to do volunteer work on a regular weekly basis for

_____ 1-2 hours _____ 3-5 hours _____ 6-10 hours _____ more

_____ I'd like to volunteer, but just occasionally, such as around the holidays

_____ I'd like to volunteer for a specific, time-limited project

_____ I'm flexible

2) MY INTERESTS

The areas I'm interested in working in are (list as many as you like)

_____

_____

I've always wanted to work in an environment where

_____

_____

I'd like to work in an organization that deals with (check as many as you like)

_____ community service

_____ education

_____ social change/social and economic justice/politics

_____ religious community

_____ children

_____ animals

_____ environment

_____ politics

other (write in): _____

3) THE WORK ITSELF

_____ I want to use my work skills (e.g., editing, bookkeeping)

_____ I'd like to do something new

Here's a list of tasks I can perform for a nonprofit organization

_____

_____

4) LOCATION

The ideal volunteer job for me would be located

____ in my home

____ within walking distance of home

____ within _____ miles driving distance of home

____ outside my community

(such as Habitat for Humanity or an international program)

other: _____

5) ENVIRONMENT

I'd like to help out (check as many as apply)

____ in an office

____ in an institution (library, hospital, museum, national park, etc.)

____ outdoors

I'd prefer to work in a

____ big organization

____ small organization

____ one-on-one

____ with a group

____ alone

6) TRAINING

____ I'd like on-the-job training (in_____)

____ I'm willing to get training on my own time

(in_____)

7) BUILDING YOUR OWN RESUME

Is there something you'd like to get out of volunteering (e.g., attend concerts or plays for free, do some gardening in a public space, or gain skills, such as Web site design)? List here:

_____

_____

_____

_____

HEALTHVIEWS

According to nearly a dozen medical studies published in peer review journals from 1999 to 2000, giving back is good preventive medicine. Among the apparent health benefits are increased happiness, life satisfaction, self-esteem, sense of control over your own life, better physical health, and even living longer. The benefits accrue especially when a person makes a real *commitment* to something.

If one of your concerns about quitting work in THE RETIREMENT ZONE is missing all the social hubbub at work, here's good news: Volunteering also serves as an antidote to social isolation, so it can be a good way to fend off depression. A study published in the May 2003 *Journal of Gerontology: Social Sciences* found that older adults who volunteer and who engage in more hours of volunteering report higher levels of emotional and physical well-being. Those findings held steady, regardless of gender, the number or types of organizations the person volunteered for, or the extent to which the volunteer thought the work really made an impact on others.

Giving might be better than receiving, from a health perspective. Some research suggests that people who volunteer live longer, on average. A five-year study published in the July 2003 issue of *Journal of Gerontology: Psychological Science* found that those individuals who reported providing "instrumental" support—such as shopping, cooking, and doing household tasks—to friends, relatives, and neighbors, and individuals who reported providing emotional support to their spouse lived longer than others. Conversely, *receiving* support had no effect on mortality. (This pattern held true, even controlling for other factors, such as demographic, personality, health, mental health, and marital-relationship variables).

It apparently doesn't make much difference, from a health perspective, what you volunteer for. It's the doing that counts. And the benefits show up quickly. As for how much time you have to spend to reap these benefits, well, that's unclear. One study found positive benefits of as little as 40 hours a year—less than an hour per week on average. Some studies suggest that the health benefits increase with the amount of time volunteered.

YOUR MONEY MATTERS

As one retiree put it, "I don't have a problem with volunteering to do free work, but it costs money to drive across town to work at the hospital free for two hours. If you're there for half a day, then you've got to buy lunch. There are expenses involved."

Just because you're doing something good for society, doesn't mean you have to go broke doing it. Many volunteers shell out for extras: supplies, gifts for people they work with, even arts and crafts materials to make signs or posters. There are ways to write off these deeds and contributions to charity on your tax return, which sweetens the endeavor even more.

GIFTS: As long as the organization that you've donated to is a registered not-for-profit with a 501(c)(3) designation from the IRS, you should have no trouble deducting the full amount of your cash gift. You can even give non-cash gifts and receive a deduction. Clothing, automobiles, and toys all get the IRS's nod for deductions, so save receipts for these things. You can also give away your investments and get a tax break. For example, if you give a charity one of your stocks that's appreciated, you get to write off the full amount of the donation, yet you won't have to pay the capital gains tax you would have if you had sold it.

TRAVEL: Travel expenses incurred on behalf of volunteer work are tax deductible—hotel, airfare, meals—as long as a majority of the trip was for the purpose of volunteering.

MISCELLANEOUS: Laundering or dry cleaning uniforms used for volunteer activities is a legitimate deduction, as long as the uniform can't be worn for any purpose other than volunteering. (In other words, it's okay to deduct the dry cleaning of a hospital uniform, but not for dark slacks worn to serve meals at a soup kitchen.) You may write off any entertaining you do on behalf of a charitable organization, like wining and dining a potential contributor. The cost of your own entertainment in this pursuit is not deductible.

The Case of the Dancing Preacher: Electric Slide, Boogie, and Applejack

Born in 1926, Rev. Howard Breedy lives in the Bronx and says now that he's retired he's busier than when he was working. He spends about a third of his time teaching classes, delivering weekly sermons, and officiating weddings, funerals, and christenings related to a small church and school that he runs. The rest of his time is mostly taken up with volunteer activities, including the 60+ Swingers Dance Group at a senior center in the Bronx. One day, while helping set up tables at the Center, he recounts,

"They asked me would I join, because I sat with them for a while. I choreographed a couple of dances for them, and they liked the dances. Now I choreograph dances specifically for senior citizens, and if they have a hip replacement or foot injury or something, I create dances that will help them to exercise as well as look good.

"I can hear a piece, a selection, and sit in a chair, and do the movements sitting in a chair. Then I write it all down and give it a name, and go out and I show you how to do it. No problem. I've got about ten to twelve dances here that I could show you that are mine. They're dances that you don't have to have a partner for . . . a line dance, for example . . . We did them years ago: Apple Jack. Boogie. Stuff like that. You didn't need a partner. Besides, everywhere you go now, you see more women than men dancing on the floor. We do the advanced Electric Slide, for people who are well and active. And we have some modified dances for people who can't do things like that.

"How do we get them to dance? I can go somewhere and start playing the music and get up and dance. They see I'm not a young person either, and I'll say, 'Just try this.' It's not hard to convince them.

"Dance for senior citizens helps them exercise where sometimes they wouldn't even walk. If they hear the music and they see the steps, they want to get involved. That's what I do—try to get them involved."

On Stage, Off Stage

Sixty-six-year-old Joe Lamb discovered a way to apply his skills as an actor at the International Center, where he is a star teacher of English as a second language. At the Center, Joe says he has "found what I always wanted:" a way to use his acting talents to teach and mentor people. He initiated a program for Tibetan asylum seekers and others referred from the Survivors of Torture program run by Bellevue Hospital. His self-described "acting as teacher" method is effective; Joe captures even these students' attention with his performance in the classroom. So rewarding is this volunteer work that Joe has stuck with it for 17 years.

"I have five classes a week, I'm really not exactly teaching. I'm acting. And what I'm acting is the part of a teacher. My class is a kind of performance. I improvise, and everyone has to participate all the time.

"There are several thousand members of the center, foreign people who come to learn English. I meet extraordinary people from all over the world, from Russia, Tibet, Africa. Some are refugees who don't get any real attention from anyone here. My theory is that even a small amount of attention at the right moment can be extremely valuable to people. I see that work, I see it every day. Many students have told me that their first conversation in English was with me, and that they'll never forget it.

"One wonderful thing is what happens to me here. Because of this work I've become a much nicer and more thoughtful person. If you're alone too much, then you think of yourself, you know—me, me, me and what am I going to do and what's going to happen to me? It is thrilling to make connections with people through humor, or when you give a wonderful performance; it's exhilarating.

"The second greatest thrill is meeting people from other countries. Yesterday I talked to a young man from Mongolia. How many people know Turkish people or people from Sierra Leone or Burma or Mali? It's a rare experience. In my class maybe I'll have people from thirty different countries, sometimes even countries that are enemies. But in class, it's like an embrace of all these people."

You Could Spend Your Day Painting Watercolors

Stuart Stein is a retired CPA who moved to North Carolina and was looking for a meaningful volunteer activity.

"I volunteer as a Guardian Ad Litem, which is a court-appointed child advocate. We act as the advocates for children who are involved in the juvenile court system due to abuse and/or neglect.

"I'd been looking around for volunteer work, other than something related to financial matters, something that would be meaningful and challenging in a new way. I didn't want to go into an office and do clerical work. The local newspaper publishes a weekly list of volunteer opportunities, and I kept seeing the name Guardian Ad Litem appear each week. Coincidentally, I met someone who was already an active Guardian Ad Litem volunteer and was very enthusiastic about it, so I filed an application. I had to provide six personal references, including people with whom I'd been associated professionally. There was a personal interview and they also checked to see if I had any criminal record. I then had to take a thirty-hour training course. Probably half the people in my class were grandparents. The professional staff were happy with that, as the children we are dealing with range in age from infants to age eighteen.

"Our job is to independently investigate the entire case. By North Carolina statutes, we are empowered to review all the records and interview anyone who has involvement in the case. We and the Guardian Ad Litem advocate attorney are the sole representatives for the children. The parents and Social Services have their own attorneys. When a petition is filed with the court alleging the children are abused or neglected, we have sixty days to investigate and prepare a report to be presented to the judge at a hearing where all parties are present. We must report all the facts and then make recommendations as to what services are needed by the children and what actions are necessary on the part of the parents and the services that are to be provided to the children. As the case continues, we have to visit the children once a month to see what is happening with them and also follow up with the parents to see if they have complied with anything the judge has ordered them to do. There are usually monthly team meetings, involving the parents,

therapists, teachers, social workers, case managers, and myself, at which time the case progress is discussed. Every three months, there is a court hearing at which time reports are submitted to the judge with further recommendations.

"The initial goal of all this work is to try to reunify the children with their parents. As time progresses, it is often found that the parents are unable to care for their children and so other arrangements must be made. There may be other family members who could take over the care, or if all else fails, adoption.

"I am now a Guardian Ad Litem in two cases, overseeing the care of three children. One case is with a twelve-year-old child who was removed from an abusive home weeks before I was assigned to the case. He has emotional and behavioral problems and has been moved from one residence to another. After one and a half years on this case, it is still uncertain what the outcome will be. The other case is close to one year old, and different facts are still emerging due to the complex family situation. One child is in foster care and the other is residing with a relative.

"Of course, one could spend the day painting watercolors. But we read too much about child neglect. I knew I needed to make a difference in at least a few lives. It is important to save as many children as possible from these dangerous situations.

"My advice to people who want to volunteer in retirement: Try to do something that challenges your intelligence and ingenuity and gives you some heartfelt satisfaction."

Please see the Resource Guide at the end of Chapter 13, page 162.

Volunteering Guide

10 WAYS TO PITCH IN, FROM ANIMALS TO POLITICS

This chapter outlines ten different portals of opportunity for giving back and reinventing yourself through volunteering. The ten categories are art and culture; community; criminal justice; education; great outdoors and environment; health; homelessness and hunger; political campaigns; public policy advocacy and international issues; and zoos and animals. For each, you will find a list of pleasures, perks, and freebies—and, because volunteering is a form of work, a job description.

ART AND CULTURE

The world of arts and culture can provide some incredibly enriching opportunities for volunteering in organizations such as museums, operas, ballets, orchestras, plays, and many other venues. Just a few are outlined here.

General job description: You could find yourself working as a docent at a museum or staffing the gift shop. You might do: fundraising, organizing special events, staffing exhibits. In the performing arts: planning performances, raising funds and doing publicity, sewing costumes, painting scenery, and handing out programs. In a library: literacy programs, fundraising, organizing special events, staffing book sales and displays.

Pleasures and perks: Enjoy special classes, previews of special exhibits, and a fun and intellectually stimulating environment!

Freebies: Entrance to exhibits, tours, lectures.

Museums

Count 'em. According to the American Association of Museums (www.aam-us.org), the United States boasts almost 16,000 museums, covering art, history, science, military and maritime, as well as youth museums, historic sites, and science and technology centers.

If you live in a major city, you have the opportunity to volunteer in a world-class museum. And yet sometimes the smaller the institution, the more fun you can have. The Isabel Miller Museum in Sitka, Alaska, traces the history of the Tlingits nation, and a little-known chapter of Russian-American relations. In Oregon, the Warm Springs Reservation houses an extraordinary Native American museum. In Utica, Mississippi, treasures of immigration history are stored at the Museum of the Southern Jewish Experience.

Most museums operate on a budgetary shoestring. That means they *need* volunteers. For instance, you might want to become a docent. A volunteer docent is a teacher who acts as a guide or instructor at zoos, aquariums, museums, and other cultural institutions. Be prepared to speak loudly, stand on your feet, and answer the most unlikely questions (including "Where is the rest room?" in multiple languages). Docent volunteers often receive training and in some cases must take a test.

Some of the nation's biggest museums

Boston's Museum of Fine Arts; Art Institute of Chicago; Cleveland Museum of Art; Detroit Institute of Arts; Indianapolis Museum of Art; in Los Angeles, J. Paul Getty Museum and Los Angeles County Museum of Art; Milwaukee Public Museum; New York's Metropolitan Museum of Art, American Museum of Natural History, Museum of Modern Art, Brooklyn Museum of Art, the Whitney Museum of American Art, the Guggenheim Museum, and Ellis Island Immigration Museum; Philadelphia Museum of Art; Pittsburgh's Carnegie Science Center; Fine Arts Museums of San Francisco, and in Washington, D.C., over a dozen Smithsonian Museums and the National Gallery of Art.

Beyond Broadway

Ta da! The world of live performance is hopping, from community theater to comedy clubs, dance festivals, and musical venues. There are choruses, *a cappella* groups, local orchestras, jazz groups, drumming circles, and rock bands.

For instance, do you love classical music? Well, the number of symphony concerts has hit an all-time high. In the 2000–2001 season, America's 1,200 orchestras gave 36,437 concerts—45 percent more than in 1990, according to the American Symphony Orchestra League (www.symphony.org).

Film festivals are popping up in almost every major city. One retired dentist in his 70s regularly volunteers at the Sundance Film Festival in Park City, Utah, in exchange for free tickets and invitations to some of the special events and parties with celebrities. "He'll serve food, take tickets, give directions to people, whatever needs doing," says Susan Lee Strauss-Bearson, a festival volunteer coordinator.

Whether you're working in the back office, selling tickets and ads, or moving props around backstage, getting involved in creative performance can be fun.

Libraries

Other than your furry bedroom slippers, what's always cozy, warm, and welcoming? Your local library. There, you can log onto the Internet, listen to lectures and concerts, enjoy free art displays, and meet your neighbors. Modern libraries multi-task as arts and culture venues, social service organizations, and after-school centers, offering a safe haven and educational programs for the young children of working parents. Volunteers help with fund-raising, literacy campaigns, and other events. Public libraries are one of the nation's great institutions. No wonder giants of industry from Andrew Carnegie to Steve Jobs have invested in them. And as a taxpayer, so have you. They're yours, so love them.

Oral Histories of Your Generation

Your grandchildren may not want to hear your war stories—but the Library of Congress does.

The Veterans History Project covers World War I, World War II, and the Korean, Vietnam, and Persian Gulf wars. It documents the contributions of civilian volunteers, support staff, and war industry workers as well as the experiences of the 19 million living American war veterans. This project, started in 2000 by an act of Congress, falls under the umbrella of the Washington, DC–based American Folklife Center. Veterans can write their war memoirs or have a family member or friend do an audiotape or videotape of their reminiscences. According to one of the project administrators, "If you are a veteran, you possess a valuable resource in your war memories and military knowledge, and we especially encourage you to participate as both an interviewer and an interviewee." You can obtain a "project kit" with ideas of how to start from www.loc.gov/folklife/vets.

Similar projects to preserve the historical memories of different generations are under way at local universities, including a federally funded program called StoryCorps (www.storycorps.net).

COMMUNITY

From neighborhood associations to the office bowling league, most people belong to multiple small "communities."

General job description: Nuts-and-bolts jobs include office work, soup kitchen work, hospice visits, invalid assistance, leafleting, organizing special events, writing and publishing newsletters. Also: mentoring, politics, professional services, church/temple-affiliated volunteering.

Pleasures and perks: Engagement with community, volunteer appreciation, participation in public social events, public recognition.

Freebies: Admission to community events, maybe T-shirts or an occasional meal.

Your Faith Community

You can quickly find lots of direct service opportunities, like serving in a soup kitchen, organizing a winter coat drive, or helping at a local hospice or homeless shelter, through churches, mosques, synagogues, Quaker meetings, Ethical Culture societies, and so on.

Your Alma Mater(s)

Going to your 40th high-school class reunion is one thing. *Organizing* it is quite another. Spending time with fellow alums helps develop fresh relationships, not to mention sharing a few reminiscences about this cranky homeroom teacher or that gorgeous heartthrob. See Web sites such as www.classmates.com and www.classreunionsearch.com.

Your Geographic Community

Most communities face grueling decisions about allocating limited funds, and need smart, capable people. Many cities have centralized clearinghouses for volunteer opportunities. Call the mayor's office or town governing council, or see if the directory at www.pointsoflight.org leads you to a local opportunity. Another approach is to contact your representative in your state legislature or U.S. House of Representatives. (If you're not sure who that might be, inquire at your local library, or log on to www.house.gov/writerep.) Most politicians have staffers who are very well informed and connected to local community activists. Or join a crime-prevention committee or work with your condo, homeowners, or block association.

The national Senior Corps is an umbrella for several programs that can help you plug in. The Retired and Senior Volunteer Program (RSVP) (www.senior corps.org/joining/rsvp) places volunteers age 55 and over in nonprofit organizations, public agencies, and faith-based groups. They mentor at-risk youth, organize neighborhood watch programs, test drinking water for contaminants, teach English to immigrants, and lend their business skills to community groups that provide critical social services.

Your Ethnic Community

If you are in touch with your family's ethnic heritage, be it Hispanic, Asian, Irish, Canadian, Polish, or any number of others, you might enjoy helping plan an ethnic cultural event. There's an organization, or several, representing every ethnic group in our nation, it seems. For example, the National Italian American Foundation (www.niaf.org) offers an Italian language camp, scholarships, and a travel program. Teach a cooking class if you know how to make the best pastille this side of the Mississippi. And if you still speak the language of your immigrant ancestors, *mamma mia!*, you have wonderful opportunities to pass along your language to others. There are folk dances and festivals, oral history projects, exhibits, and trips to the old country. On the more serious side, most ethnic associations sponsor outreach to others who are sick, impoverished, or in the case of political unrest in the home country, persecuted. Other such organizations include, for instance, the American Irish Historical Society (www.aihs.org); Organization of Chinese Americans (www.ocanatl.org); the American Council for Polish Culture (www.polishcultureacpc.org); and American-Scandinavian Foundation (www.amscan.org).

Your Professional or Business Community

So you spent years getting really good at what you do—*did*, that is. And you want to keep doing it, but don't want to bother with the bosses, the schedules, the pressures. Good news: You can keep working—if you don't mind doing it for free.

If you're a professional or businessperson with knowledge that might be useful to start-up businesses or nonprofit organizations, consider consulting for free at an organization such as SCORE (www.score.org). SCORE's network of 10,500 retired and working volunteers provide free business counseling and advice as a public service to all types of businesses, in all stages of development. SCORE is a resource partner with the U.S. Small Business Administration.

Fellow Consumers

Americans *shop*. We are consummate consumers. And for many people who are watching their budgets in THE RETIREMENT ZONE, comparing price and quality of potential purchases, from a can of tomatoes to the cost of long-term health insurance, becomes a way of life.

So why waste all that expertise? If you're passionate about getting a fair deal, then get involved in the consumer movement. The Consumer Federation of America (www.consumerfed.org) works with a network of state and local consumer groups; locate one near you. Consumers Union (www.consumersunion.org), publisher of *Consumer Reports* magazine, has an e-mail advocacy program that tackles consumer issues relating to product and food safety, finance, health, and telecommunications. You can get CU's free monthly electronic newsletter on consumer topics, share stories of your experiences online, and also receive their e-action alerts asking you to send e-mail to legislators. Sign up at www.consumersunion.org. U.S. Public Interest Research Group (www.uspirg.org) and a bevy of small single-issue groups concentrate on concerns such as product labeling, toy safety, and genetic engineering of food.

Environmentally minded consumers also can use the power of their individual dollar. The Center for a New American Dream, a nonprofit organization that promotes socially responsible consumption, found that at least three in five American consumers would like access to socially and environmentally responsible products. Check out the Takoma Park, Maryland–based group's Conscious Consumer Web site (www.newdream.org/consumer). It is packed with information about online and local sources for goods and services that are better for the planet.

Seniors in Your Community

Do unto others. More and more people in their 50s and 60s are providing direct service to needy senior citizens, whether by guiding them to the wonders of the Internet, providing a lift to the supermarket, or serving hot meals. Certainly, there's plenty of need; there are enough impoverished senior citizens in the United States (5.6 million age 55 and over, according to the U.S. Census Bureau) to populate Missouri or Arizona. This work is guaranteed to make you feel as young as a spring chicken.

By hooking up with groups such as the Gray Panthers (www.graypanthers.org) and AARP (www.aarp.org) you can engage in political issues affecting the older American: Medicare and Medicaid coverage, ageism, regulation of the managed care industry, corporate pension reform, and Social Security, among other programs.

Several universities, including Wayne State University (www.iog.wayne.edu/iog), the University of Texas (www.gerotexas.org), and the University of Denver (www.du.edu/gssw/gerontology/gerontol.htm) offer certificates of gerontology. One, the Gerontology Institute at the University of Massachusetts in Boston, seeks to empower older people to be advocates in local government and state legislatures, working for improved services to the older population. Graduates of their Frank J. Manning Certificate Program in Gerontology, named in honor of a longtime advocate for elder issues, have found jobs in city and state agencies on aging, in nursing homes, as aides, and as visitors in elderly people's homes. Visit www.geront.umb.edu.

To find out what's going on regarding senior issues in your local area, one good place to start is your local Area Agency on Aging. You can find the one nearest you by contacting the umbrella organization, the National Association of Area Agencies on Aging (www.n4a.org), that links more than 650 such programs. Their mission is to provide such services as information, home-delivered and congregate meals, transportation, employment services, and support for senior centers and adult day care—in order to enable older individuals to remain in their homes, thereby preserving their independence and dignity.

CRIMINAL JUSTICE ISSUES

People volunteer to work in the criminal justice arena for many reasons: compassion, politics, belief (or not) in the system, and religious faith, among others.

General job description: Volunteers may work on an array of criminal justice issues, such as the death penalty, alternative sentencing for juveniles, health care, isolation, the privatization of prisons, and the treatment of juveniles in the prison system. There also are literacy programs.

Pleasures and perks: This can be challenging work, but when you feel you've reached someone, or helped a person in trouble, the rewards can be enormous.

Freebies: You'll get an education, and a chance to help people who've experienced trouble in their lives.

Court Guardian

Stories of child abuse are heart wrenching. You can do something about abuse and neglect by applying to serve as a special child advocate in the court system. An estimated 70,000 men and women do so, through a national entity called the Court

Appointed Social Advocate program (CASA). Study one child's case, get to know the child and his/her circumstances, deal with attorneys and caseworkers, and advocate to the court on behalf of the child. Follow up to make sure the outcome serves the child's best interests. The position is by application only and requires multiple references. Volunteers receive training and support.

CASA, also known as the Volunteer Guardian Ad Litem program, works with the U.S. Department of Justice's Office of Juvenile Justice and Delinquency Prevention, and has been endorsed by the American Bar Association, among others. With over 900 CASA programs in operation, the chances are good that you can connect with one near home. (See profile of Stuart Stein, page 132).

Prison-related Work

The growth of both prisons and the prison population has caused public debate over a wide range of issues, from inequities in the courts' sentencing system to prison conditions. Over half of incarcerated adults have dependent children at home, raising additional concerns outside the prison itself.

How to get involved? Some volunteers work one-on-one with prisoners, often as teachers or pastoral counselors, or help people reintegrate into society. Many participate in religious training and education. The experience of working with a prisoner's family members may be quite different from helping navigate the social bureaucracy on behalf of an ex-offender who is trying to build a new life after prison. And the universe of prisoners includes special-needs cases, such as women prisoners, juvenile offenders, and prisoners with special medical conditions.

Retirees with professional training, for instance in such fields as health care or social work, may find opportunities by contacting their professional organization's local chapter. You can ask your local church, diocese or the national organization representing your faith community what programs exist to support prisoners and their families. For instance, the National Baptist Convention Prison Ministry and Criminal Justice Commission (www.nationalbaptist.com) supports prison ministry programs. Texas-based Champions for Life claims to be the nation's largest front-line envangelistic prison ministry (www.lifechampions.org). The Quakers' American Friends Service Committee (www.afsc.org) may provide information on prison-related programs. An institution of religious education nearby, such as a Bible college or school of theology or ministry, might also organize such outreach efforts. Or call your local department of corrections and ask them to direct you to community organizations that are currently running programs for prisoners and ex-offenders.

Prison Ministry

"I've been active with Prison Ministry now, a good twenty-five years," explains Gwynne Tomlan-Santiago. "I have made time for this, no matter what. I really feel that it's critical." Working with the ministry program, she's helped conduct worship services in prisons. Recently, she and her husband helped form a bilingual family advocacy group, comprised mostly of mothers, to help ex-offenders and family members.

"We meet every first Friday in the month. We do things like write and ask politicians to help them transfer the children to prisons closer to home, because some (of the mothers) travel eight hours back and forth to visit. Parents have other concerns, too, like getting books into prisons for their children, so we help them. They also work on issues of prison-guard brutality. One woman's son who was mentally ill, died, and was buried while in prison, and they never notified her, and we helped her address that."

As for prisoners' readjustment to society, she adds, "Some people come back out and don't know how to use a cell phone or the first thing about going online to get any information. They don't even know where to begin. They are really isolated, and that can make it hard to become the better person that they want to be. They need help, and the system doesn't provide it."

EDUCATION

Many Americans are passionate about education. It's what has made the American Dream a reality for many of our parents, grandparents, and ancestors. **General job description:** Visit a classroom and read out loud, or work one-on-one with a child in need of special attention. Organize special events, chaperone trips, work in an office and make photocopies, help fund-raise, staff book fairs, and whatever else you can bring to the party. Some large urban school systems have established formal volunteer programs. Volunteers with special skills—if you're a tennis player, woodworker, chef, or calligrapher—have also got something to teach, but may need to look outside conventional school-based opportunities.

Pleasures and perks: The joy of seeing the lightbulb go on when your students "get it." Working with kids, which keeps you young! In adult education programs: helping adults improve their chances in life.

Freebies: A doughnut once in awhile; transportation and admission to chaperoned, school-related trips; and maybe a volunteer recognition event.

Your Local School

From densely populated Millburn, New Jersey, to the sprawling rural area covered by the school district of Bastrop, Texas, thousands of older volunteers help out at the local schools. The value of the unpaid labor of volunteers in private, parochial, and public schools is in the millions of dollars.

Adult Literacy

Volunteers teach English as a second language or work in adult literacy efforts. In the United States, one in four adults functions at the lowest literacy level. America's Literacy Directory, a Web-based directory developed by the National Institutes of Learning, a federal program, helps you find local literacy providers in every state (www.literacydirectory.org).

The "Digital Divide"

If you have some basic computer knowledge, you can contribute by teaching computer skills to people of all ages, from the very young child who has no access to computers to middle-aged, low-income people who need these skills for employment, and to senior citizens. One good place to start is at the Benton Foundation–funded network called the DigitalDivide (www.digitaldivide.org).

Lastly, if you have some special talent or skill, for instance music or dance, don't overlook the fun of sharing it with others. And, volunteers are always welcome to work on fund-raisers whether helping support a scholarship, extracurricular programs, the college office, or a new scoreboard for the football field.

THE GREAT OUTDOORS AND THE ENVIRONMENT

Hankering for a little quiet time with Mother Nature? It sounds corny, but one of your options in THE RETIREMENT ZONE is to get some fresh air and contribute to what Lady Bird Johnson dubbed "Beautification" programs.

General job description: You can sweep and clean up a park, do shrub care, paint benches, and even work with groups of school children to beautify public gardens and parks. Of course, you can do office work and staff the occasional special event. Many larger urban parks have a volunteer coordinator and volunteer orientation sessions. In environmental education projects, you might find yourself building models, working with students on a wetlands preservation project, or helping to orchestrate a computer-printer cartridge recycling campaign.

Pleasures and perks: Working with nature (as well as people) can help provide a healthy lifestyle; the satisfaction of knowing you are helping the environment.

Freebies: Possibly classes/training, T-shirts.

Gardens, Local Parks, and Environmental Education

Tuck in a tulip bulb, yank some weeds, rake a huge pile of leaves. If there's a botanical garden within easy reach, you can participate in year-round education and tour-guide programs, or do site maintenance. Many local parks have "friends of the park" programs or environmental education for children. You can contact the local parks department or mayor's office for starters. You can volunteer at many state parks, too, and maybe even barter your volunteer work in exchange for a free campsite for a few days.

National Parks

About one third of those who volunteer in the National Park Service system work as guides, and another one in five do resource management or maintenance. To get a taste of the available opportunities, log onto the National Park Service Volunteer Web site (www.nps.gov/volunteer). You will find an application form with a list of dozens of categories of volunteer interests, including everything from archeology and educational programs to hydrology and backcountry maintenance. Or, if you plan to visit a specific park or state, call the park itself well in advance of your trip to explore possibilities.

Volunteer jobs may differ from season to season, but you might be surprised at what's available (to name just a few such openings as we go to press):

- At the Statue of Liberty or Ellis Island in New York, volunteers provide information and visitor services, or work in administration with the museum collection, archives, library, and oral histories.
- At Harpers Ferry National Historical Park on the Appalachian Trail—which is located in West Virginia, Maryland, and Virginia—you can volunteer for information services, historian, archeologist, curator and library assistant, or gardener.
- In Nevada's Ely District, a 12-million-acre area in the Great Basin and the Mojave Desert area, you can assist Bureau of Land Management archeologists with field documentation (mapping and photography) of rock art or prepare scale photos and measured drawings of rock art panels.

Volunteering with Government Programs and Parks

"Volunteers are essential to the national park experience," according to Jim Maddy, president of the National Park Foundation. There are over 300 different volunteer programs through the National Park Service, which is responsible for 388 National Park System areas covering more than 84 million acres. More than 125,000 volunteers contributed in 2002 to the National Park Service at an estimated value of $72 million.

Sometimes a job is one of a kind. Administrators at South Dakota's Badlands National Park were grateful to a retiree who "did a lot of work writing letters, getting information, and preparing grant letters for us." They'd been seeking funding for an improved transportation system linking their park with Minuteman Missile National Historic Site (a Cold War–era nuclear missile silo) just a few miles away.

Another volunteer dedicated over 2,800 hours to maintaining a 10-acre tidal wetland adjacent to Fort McHenry National Monument and Historic Shrine in Baltimore. Volunteering six days a week (and single-handedly over a two-year period of time), he removed over 50,000 pounds of debris, developed an interpretive trail, and conducted guided walks all year. Laura E. Joss, superintendent of Fort McHenry, describes this 70-year-old volunteer as having "the enthusiasm and fortitude of someone half his age."

OTHER FEDERAL GOVERNMENT PROGRAMS Uncle Sam has a lot of projects going on that could use a little volunteer assistance. Eight major government organizations have joined forces in creating a Web site at www.volunteer.gov/gov that advertises volunteer opportunities.

In some cases, prior knowledge is essential. A project in Nevada's Moapa Valley National Wildlife Refuge seeks to restore a habitat area. Volunteers would need to know how to monitor species or conduct surveys: "Enumerate wildlife populations, vegetative habitats, and routine baseline monitoring of air and water quality. May include inventory and monitoring procedures, development of species lists, qualitative and quantitative surveys, special cooperative surveys, habitat classification and monitoring including development and use of GIS, survey planning, data collection, analysis and reporting." Other jobs are more generic.

Environmental Protection

Is our lovely planet in jeopardy? Millions of Americans are profoundly interested and committed to environmental issues, from clean air and water to overpopulation to global warming and urban sprawl to alternative energy sources.

It's easy to get involved. Most of the larger organizations have Web sites with state contacts. The Sierra Club (www.sierraclub.org), founded in 1892, boasts 700,000 members and is the nation's oldest environmental organization. In addition to education and advocacy, they offer trips. The Audubon Society (www.audubon.org) also has a full program, including publications, campaigns, and even a summer camp for nature lovers of all ages. Like the Audubon Society and Sierra Club, U.S. PIRG (www.uspirg.org) also has a broad-based grassroots network. Other national organizations that lead the environmental charge include the National Wildlife Federation (www.nwf.org), Environmental Defense (www.environmentaldefense.org), Friends of the Earth (www.foe.org), and the Natural Resources Defense Council (www.nrdc.org). Or get in touch with organizations such as the Cousteau Society (www.cousteau.org), Nature Conservancy (www.nature.org), and Save the Whales campaign (www.savethewhales.org).

"At the extreme end, if you are really moved by an issue, you can hang off a building with Greenpeace," jokes a longtime environmental researcher. "But the way things often really get changed is at the local level." Groups such as RiverKeepers, Ducks Unlimited, and Trout Unlimited have wonderful community campaigns, too.

> **PRACTICAL TIP:** Dedicate a rainy afternoon to surfing the Web and checking out the mission statements of the different groups. You might find yourself getting quite an education about the environmental hazards that we humans present to the animal and vegetable kingdom—and to each other!

HEALTH

There are many ways to help alleviate the suffering and everyday challenges of people, both young and old, who are hospitalized or fighting serious illness.

General job description: You might act as a "friendly visitor" to people who are sick and alone, reading to them or playing a game of cards. You might even build up a regular visiting schedule and establish a relationship with a hospital or hospice inpatient. Some volunteers help with child care, such as holding and playing with hospital boarder babies. Also: office work; staffing special events; organizing fund-raisers; and helping in public education campaigns.

Pleasures and perks: It's better to give than to receive.

Freebies: An insider's look at the U.S. health-care system; the occasional cup of coffee; some hospitals give cafeteria vouchers to volunteers who ask.

The classic approach to helping those who are sick is, of course, visiting patients in a hospital, nursing home, or mental institution. You might also be asked to sit at the information desk, translate, work in the library or gift shop, or provide assistance/information to visitors. You can also opt to volunteer for an organization that is specifically concerned with a single disease, such as schizophrenia, blindness, cancer, or AIDS.

It's understood that there are limitations to what you might do, based on patient privacy, licensing, and other requirements. Still, opportunities abound, especially if you take the initiative. For instance, at the Long Island College Hospital in New York, one woman in her 50s who had always wanted to be a nurse midwife became a *doula* (a birth coach). She volunteers to assist indigent or troubled young women who are alone when they are giving birth. Another woman who lost loved ones to cancer volunteered to provide grooming services to "perk up" female patients. She spends five hours a week at the Cancer Center doing hair, makeup, and nails. Ms. Zipporah Dvash, director of public affairs, advises, "You can volunteer through the hospital volunteer department, which runs ongoing programs. Or if you have a desire to help with a specific need, contact the departmental administrator."

Beyond Hospital and Nursing Home

Providing emotional support to family members of patients with incurable diseases such as Parkinson's or Alzheimer's is an important service, particularly if you've "been there" yourself. As the population ages, more people will find themselves concerned about, or caring for, older relatives with these conditions.

Volunteers are the backbone of many local hospice programs, which seek to provide comfort care to the terminally ill person at the end of life, and to support family members (visit www. americanhospice.org for information). Often, people who have shepherded a loved one through a hospice program feel they'd like to do the same good turn for another family. Visit the National Hospice and Palliative Care Organization at www.nhpco.org.

Combine Working Out with Helping Out

Join in fund-raising walkathons, bike races, and even dance-a-thons. There's no rush (it's not a race); you can have fun, and with sponsorship from some friends, make a contribution to the March of Dimes (www.modimes.org), American Cancer Society (www.cancer.org), and similar organizations. If you start participating when you are 55 and walk every year with $5,000 in sponsorships, then by the time you are a healthy 75 you will have contributed $100,000! These are big, popular events: upwards of 40,000 people participated in the AIDS walk to benefit the Gay Men's Health Crisis (www.gmhc.org) in New York City in 2002.

Love Animals as Much as People?

A new approach to cheering up inpatients is called pet therapy. Volunteers bring a trained pet to a hospital, nursing home, hospice, adult day care center, or retirement home.

Various organizations do this work. Perhaps the best known is the Delta Society (www.deltasociety.org). The nonprofit organization trains thousands of volunteers and their pets through hands-on workshops and home-study courses. Registered pets include dogs and cats, but also guinea pigs, rabbits, horses, goats, llamas, donkeys, potbellied pigs, cockatoos, African gray parrots, and chickens. Before visiting facilities, the pets are independently tested for skills and aptitude by Delta-licensed animal evaluators. Not only do the animals enhance comforting, nurturing environments, but patients who have had the opportunity to have them visit have shown both physical and mental improvement.

Specific Diseases and Conditions

For almost every diagnosis, there's a support group and a disease-specific organization dedicated to research, better prevention, and treatment. Susan King of the League for the Hard of Hearing (www.lhh.org), which provides hearing health services to over 30,000 infants, children, and adults each year, notes, "We welcome over a hundred volunteers annually. Most work on an interim basis, lending support to special projects and fundraising activities."

To help enhance public awareness or get political action on a given health issue, contact your state's chapter of the American Public Health Association (www.apha.org), American Hospital Association (www.aha.org), or the national office of a specific illness of concern to you, such as the Alzheimer's Association, Inc. (www.alz.org) or the National Alliance for the Mentally Ill (www.nami.org). The reference book *Gale's Encyclopedia of Associations* is a treasure chest of information; you can find it in most public libraries.

Breast cancer or prostate cancer support groups sometimes invite outside speakers who can discuss their own experiences; clinical departments in hospitals often run these programs.

And when no advocacy organization exists—in cases where the disorder is rare, which the NIH defines as affecting fewer than 200,000 people—often family members of a person with the condition start their own advocacy group to raise funds for research. It is helpful to obtain guidance from a qualified medical researcher or medical research organization working on the disorder, whether in regard to prevention or treatment. If fundraising is involved, it may be necessary to establish a separate nonprofit corporation.

These efforts can make a *huge* difference. For instance, since it was founded in 1970 by parents of children with the disease, the Juvenile Diabetes Research Foundation International (www.jdrf.org) has raised more than $600 million for diabetes research, and advances are being made toward a cure.

Addiction and Substance Abuse

Working with substance abusers takes energy and focus. If you know something about this field, you might already be familiar with the network of services, such as halfway houses, residential centers, and adolescent prevention programs. Contact your local faith-based organization, or Volunteers of America's Substance Abuse Services (www.volunteersofamerica.org), which organizes intervention programs and educational opportunities. For more information, visit Join Together Online, a Boston University–based pioneer in using the Internet to support people working on substance abuse at www.jointtogether.org.

THE HOMELESS AND HUNGRY

The intertwined social problems of homelessness, hunger, and poverty—and the faces of the people who suffer from them—stand out in stark contrast to the general affluence of our society.

General job description: Work with services that pick up extra food from restaurants to deliver to shelters. Volunteer to sleep as a monitor at a local homeless shelter. Collect and distribute clothing or canned goods. Counsel people in need. Help find emergency housing for abuse victims. Lobby the city and state government for better social policies and write letters to the editor of your local newspaper. Collect and send books to schools serving underprivileged students, whose libraries are usually lacking. Contribute your time during the winter holidays to collect, wrap, and deliver gifts. The list is almost endless.

Pleasures and perks: The pleasure of helping those in need; the perk of seeing the world through another's lens; and the blessing of cleaning out your closets!

Freebies: A bite to eat while you are serving free lunches to others; invitations to the local charity holiday event you helped plan.

An estimated three million people in the United States are homeless each year. Among them are people who simply cannot find affordable housing. About one in three homeless are families with dependent children, and another fifth are military veterans. About one in five, according to the U.S. Conference of Mayors, are among the working poor, who have jobs.

As with any social issue, you can throw yourself into it either by working on a personal one-on-one basis or approaching it politically and lobbying, writing letters, and demanding a change of public policies affecting the homeless. Some of the best direct-service organizations may be located right in your hometown, starting with your local faith and civic organizations.

About 23.3 million Americans are served each year by the America's Second Harvest network (www.secondharvest.org), the largest hunger-relief program in the United States. Of their clients served, 39 percent are from households with working individuals; nearly half (47 percent) live in rural or suburban areas; 39 percent are children (17 and under); and 11 percent are seniors (over 65). There are over 200 food banks in the United States, designed to collect unused food from manufacturers and bring it to the needy. There's even a "Pantry University" (modeled after corporate franchising operations) helping to streamline the operations of organizations like the Greater Chicago Food Depository, a food bank that feeds over 300,000 people annually.

America's Second Harvest's network distributes food and grocery products to approximately 50,000 local food pantries, soup kitchens, and women's shelters, plus community kitchens, and other organizations that provide emergency food assistance.

POLITICAL CAMPAIGNS

You might enjoy getting close to the rough and tumble of democracy in action. One of the advantages of participating in a political campaign is that it's eventually over, so you are not making a perpetual commitment.

General job description: There are a million jobs to be done in the world of political organizing. Leafleting on street corners, clerical, making presentations to other groups, writing letters to the editor, lobbying at the city government or state legislature levels or, of course, raising funds. Also: organizing rallies, conferences, and special events.

Pleasures and perks: The pleasure of participating in a democracy, meeting others with similar concerns and perspectives, an opportunity to use your skills.

Freebies: Fabulous T-shirts, buttons, and stickers; and if you're lucky, a victory celebration.

Take it from a seasoned organizer: "Campaigns are all set up to use your talents, whatever they may be. If you have talents, they will recognize them and put them to work. You can put in as many or as few hours as you want. Plus, you can do something at every skill level, from the proverbial stuffing of envelopes and making phone calls to writing the position papers for the campaign and arranging press conferences for the candidates. It's especially the case in local politics; you can organize meetings at your house, and if you are good at it, you will soon find that you are organizing other people to stuff the envelopes, finding other people to get the refreshments. There's an infinite amount of work to be done. It's fun and social."

Internet advocacy is a powerful political tool. If you have moved to some gorgeous rural setting and don't want to drive to meetings, log on to your favorite cyber campaign. For the Democratic Party, visit www.democrats.org. For the Republican Party, visit www.rnc.org.

If partisan politics is not your cup of tea, consider volunteering for a voter registration drive or working with a group such as the League of Women Voters (www.lwv.org). After all, the right to vote is a privilege all Americans enjoy.

PUBLIC POLICY ADVOCACY, PEACE, AND INTERNATIONAL ISSUES

If you are hardwired for the big picture, your time in THE RETIREMENT ZONE affords you a tremendous opportunity to weigh in on globalization, social and economic issues, the environment, church-state boundaries, tax and tort reform, national health policy, discrimination, education, consumerism, women's issues, abortion versus right to life, labor issues, and so on.

General job description: See above job description for political organizing. In disaster relief operations: organize fund-raising or collection drives, transport goods, staff phone banks and Internet fund-raising campaigns.

Pleasures and perks: The challenge of getting your message across and of trying to make change; the rush of conquering logistical and strategy challenges; political access; networking.

Freebies: Sometimes participation in meetings or special events.

Public Policy Advocacy

Whether you are passionate or p.o.'d about Medicare or American foreign policy, you can find a like-minded organization pushing your agenda. Advocacy organizations often have a strong presence in Washington, D.C., and in state capitals. They range from AARP to the Christian Coalition. Most unions offer opportunities to stay active in the advocacy arena, particularly in regard to issues relating to health coverage and benefits for retirees.

If you are thinking of adopting a new advocacy issue, here's a tip: try to attend an annual meeting of the major nonprofit organizations dedicated to that issue. A day or two of meetings will give you a year's worth of connections, information, and perspective on who's who.

Civil Liberties

Many issues fall under the umbrella of civil liberties. The passage of the USA Patriot Act just 45 days after the attacks of September 11, 2001 has opened up a new territory of concern. Numerous organizations around the United States have called for the rollback of some of the act's provisions, including the government's ability to search an individual's library records, Internet activity, and bookstore purchases, without probable cause or individualized suspicion. "Several of the provisions in the USA Patriot Act go too far . . . removing traditional checks and balances on law enforcement and oversight powers from the judiciary," says Dorothy Ehrlich, executive director of the ACLU of Northern California.

If you are concerned about protecting free speech and civil liberties, one nerve center of activity you can contact to learn more about both issues and campaigns is your local office of the American Civil Liberties Union (ACLU). Visit them at www.aclu.org.

War and Peace

To support the men and women of the armed forces, their families, and veterans, contact your local American Legion (www.legion.org) or Veterans of Foreign Wars (www.vfw.org). Through these organizations, you can learn how to send an online message, donate blood, or help welcome home returning soldiers. Each branch of the military also has a family support council, for instance the Army Reserve and National Guard Family Support Council (www.nmfa.org/family resources). You may wish to volunteer at a Veteran's Health Administration hospital (you can find a map and listing of hospital locations at www.va.gov/directory/guide/division_flsh.asp?divisionld-1).

A number of peace organizations seek to do public education and grassroots organizing as well. Prominent groups include Peace Action (www.peace-action.org), Interfaith Alliance (www.interfaithalliance.org), United for Peace and Justice (www.unitedforpeace.org), and the Iraq-invasion era group Not in Our Name (www.notinourname.net). Formed in 2003, the Clergy Leadership Network (www.clnnlc.org), under the leadership of such prominent activists as Rev. William Sloane Coffin, plans a national grassroots peace effort.

Homeland Security

Since September 11, 2001, the federal government has begun a broad public debate over civilian participation in homeland security.

In 2003, the White House launched the USA Freedom Corps (www.usafree-domcorps.gov), which subsumes two existing organizations—the Peace Corps and the Corporation for National and Community Service—and added the newly established Citizen Corps (www.usafreedomcorps.gov/content/programs/citizencorps/indez.asp). The Citizen Corps includes four programs: Neighborhood Watch, Medical Reserve Corps, Community Emergency Response Teams, and Volunteers in Police Service. Citizens are invited to volunteer to help local police departments, mostly through community outreach, telephone work, research, and other administrative tasks through the Volunteers in Police Service.

Medical Emergency Preparedness

Open only to qualified health care professionals, the Medical Reserve Corps is charged with coordinating physicians, nurses, health professionals, and other volunteers during emergencies. Their responsibilities may include emergency medical care and triage, logistic or backup support for trauma units and hospitals in the event of a disaster, immunization campaigns, and public health awareness efforts.

The general public has limited opportunities in this area. You can fund-raise. For instance, in 2001, a community-based effort raised $50,000 for the Long Island College Hospital emergency room, enabling the purchase of special Hazmat suits and antidotes to chemical exposures. Contact your local hospital or public health department to make a contribution of either money or time.

International Causes

As the world shrinks, the number of global concerns that demand attention expands. Among them are international human rights violations; poverty and illiteracy; social injustice; war zones; child soldiers; international trafficking of small arms and the spread of nuclear weapons and landmines; humanitarian relief through clean water, emergency food, and clothing supplies; international trade issues; the rights of women in third world countries; the dwindling rain forest; global warming; threats to whale and other wildlfe endangered species.

Major relief organizations include the International Committee for the Red Cross (www.icrc.org) and a number of faith-based organizations such as Catholic Relief Services (www.catholicrelief.org), American Friends Service Committee (www.afsc.org), CARE (www.careusa.org), Save the Children (www.savethechildren.org), and Amnesty International (www.amnestyusa.org).

Opportunities for foreign service include both faith-based missions and a handful of nonprofit organizations that generally seek people with specific qualifications. People who are serious about volunteering abroad may need to train. The director of a well-regarded intensive summer language program recalls one 78-year-old physician who completed both an undergraduate and graduate degree in Spanish, and then relocated to Guatemala to volunteer his medical services!

ZOO ANIMALS, PETS, AND WILDLIFE

The human-animal bond is ancient. It's no surprise then that some people look like their pets, pamper their pets, and even love their pets.

General job description: You can work with animals, either at the zoo, a petting zoo, or a local farm, or at services such as the ASPCA and animal foundling hospitals. Also: dealing with policy issues, writing letters, staffing protests, and mounting public relations campaigns to get the word out.

Pleasures and perks: The pleasure of working with animals and sometimes being outdoors; learning about environmental issues and animals.

Freebies: Free admission to the zoo, lectures, and volunteer recognition events.

Wildlife Preservation

Want to know where to buy a buffalo? Or what to do if you find a baby bird? Ask the United States Fish and Wildlife Service (http://refuges.fws.gov). More than 30,000 Americans volunteer annually with this federal agency, working in such diverse settings as national wildlife refuges, fish hatcheries, and wetland management districts, and performing educational as well as ecological services. Volunteers might conduct fish and wildlife population surveys, lead tours, and assist with laboratory research and special projects, such as bird banding or reestablishing native plants to a riverbank. Generally, no special skills are required to volunteer, which you can do online (www.volunteer.gov/gov).

You may discover local options too, such as counting species of birds at sanctuaries during migration season. Seaside communities often hold beach cleanups, in part to prevent litter such as the plastic rings for soda cans from ending up in the wrong beaks. You can obtain information on local wildlife protection campaigns from national organizations such as the National Audubon Society (www.audubon.org) or the Sierra Club (www.sierraclub.org).

With increased interest in domestic travel, and with record numbers of visitors to America's national parks and other natural settings, casual travelers often don't realize that littering is hazardous to wildlife. Some members of the generation that grew up with Smokey the Bear may want to become volunteer educators with the nonprofit organization Leave No Trace, Inc. (www.lnt.org). They aim "to educate visitors about the nature of their recreational impacts as well as techniques to prevent and minimize such impacts" for hikers, rafters, kayakers, equestrians, and others. Or, if you're scientifically inclined and have an ample travel budget, check out Earthwatch Institute's expeditions (www.earthwatch.org). They offer opportunities for volunteers to directly assist scientists doing field research, much of it involving wildlife. Trips available in 2004, for instance, included a study of sandhill cranes in Cuba, an exploration of caterpillar defenses as a way to preserve rainforests, and a study of the reproductive biology and nesting ecology of endangered sea turtles in Malaysia.

Lions and Tigers and Bears, Oh My!

If you love animals and want to spend the day watching the elephants and monkeys, well, give the local zoo a call. Most states have laws restricting the handling of "Class one animals"—the dangerous ones—to professionals. Smaller "mini-zoos" featuring tame animals such as rabbits and goats are more likely to allow volunteers to become involved in handling and feeding. But there are lots of other fun and educational ways you can participate. Connie Douglas, volunteer coordinator for the Memphis Zoo, estimates that volunteers contribute $200,000 a year in labor.

"We have about three hundred volunteers, of those, about a hundred are docents, and about forty of the docents are retirement age. They bring life experience.

"Some work in the animal areas, scrubbing and washing feeding dishes. They can be in our hoof stock area, where there are giraffe, zebra, and antelope, and the domestic farm animal area. But most help with staffing tables and helping with crafts, or special events like the Zoo-Boo, our Halloween event.

"A lot of them have traveled and done some fun things like safaris in Africa or India. They tend to stay [here] for years; many have been here eight, ten, twelve years. They are very dedicated. Docents commit sixty hours a year; a majority gives over a hundred hours. Clerical volunteers don't have to commit to a certain number of hours.

"Some older volunteers work with a group of at-risk school children who attend an alternative school and who come to the zoo every week. They become close to some of the children they mentor.

"You'd think our volunteers were in their late fifties to early sixties, but most are in their later sixties to early seventies. They sure act younger. One woman is eightyish, but I thought she was in her late sixties. They have personality and physical ability. We have one eighty-two-year-old gentleman who can't do the walking anymore, but he got a scooter and he goes around the zoo on that."

Pets, TLC, and Other Animal Issues

You can find work in rescue services and organizations such as the ASPCA (www.aspca.org). Or spend a few hours a week petting homeless animals there. Local chapters of the Humane Society of the U.S., which since the 1950s has been dedicated to the protection of all animals, may have some volunteer work slots (www.hsus.org).

Many animal lovers oppose the exploitation of animals, whether through the fur trade, greyhound racing, or the whaling industry. Some animal advocates work to raise public awareness of the use of animals in laboratory experiments, especially product testing. If you're vehemently opposed to genetic engineering of animals, then you might sign up with Organic Consumers Association (www.organicconsumers.org). "You may find opportunities to dress up in a cow suit and protest genetic engineering of animals you eat," said environmental activist Jean Halloran.

In a nutshell, there's plenty to do. And you can make a difference. Connie Douglas of the Memphis Zoo muses, "People don't give themselves credit for how valuable seemingly insignificant jobs are. But we have volunteers who help with things like membership renewals every month. Their two hours a month is extremely valuable to us." You don't have to do surgery on the tiger to make a contribution to the zoo.

The Story of a Pipe-smoking, Retired Kind of Guy

Dick Mooney turned his talents to benefit nonprofit organizations, in his early 60s.

"I'm a pipe-smoking, retired guy. During my career I was an administrator in higher education purchasing and materials management. As it turns out, now I'm doing volunteer work that has great meaning for me and, I hope, helps others.

"If anyone wonders why I'm able bodied and yet have been a writer for the Mutual Amputee Aid Foundation for five years, and why I put up the Western Amputee Support Alliance homepage, I'll tell you. And I'll be mercifully brief. I met Suzi in 1978. She was a wonderfully competent manager and totally self-assured woman—sweet and pretty, too—and we fell in love. We married in 1982. A diabetic since age ten, she started having complications in 1988. As diabetes will do, the disease ravaged almost every part of her body. She ended up losing both legs in 1990 and passed away in 1991—at the age of 41!

"During that last year, Los Angeles's Mutual Amputee Aid Foundation (MAAF) helped us a lot, probably me more than her. After she died, I was burned out and thoroughly demoralized, so I retired from my position as director of materials management at UCLA. For practical reasons it was a good decision, but the emotional cost turned out to be extreme and unanticipated. The bottom line is that I started being a volunteer for MAAF as a way to be busy and regain some contact with human beings, and as a 'payback' for all the help MAAF gave us. As I learned more about amputation-related subjects, I felt more competent to write about them. After a while, I felt like I was pursuing a second career—and others told me I wasn't doing all that badly at it."

Resource Guide

PUBLICATIONS

Prime Time: How Baby Boomers Will Revolutionize Retirement and Transform America by Marc Freedman (PublicAffairs, 1999).

Volunteering: 101 Ways You Can Improve the World and Your Life by Douglas M. Lawson (ALTI, 1998).

ORGANIZATIONS AND WEB SITES

(Note: Due to space constraints, only selected national programs are listed here. You may be able to find programs in your community by contacting these larger organizations which have links to state and local groups.)

Arts and Culture

American Association of Museums
1575 Eye Street NW, Suite 400
Washington, DC 20005
202-289-1818
www.aam-us.org

American Symphony
Orchestra League
33 West 60th Street, 5th Floor
New York, New York 10023-7905
212-262-5161
www.symphony.org

Community/Business

AARP
601 E Street NW
Washington, DC 20049
202-434-2300
www.aarp.org/volunteer

Points of Light Foundation
& Volunteer Center
National Network
1400 I Street NW, Suite 800
Washington, DC 20005-2208
202-729-8000
Volunteer Info: 800-VOLUNTEER
www.pointsoflight.org

Retired Senior Volunteer Program
(RSVP)
Corporation for National and
Community Service Headquarters
1201 New York Avenue NW
Washington, DC 20525
800-424-8867
TTY: 800-833-3722
www.seniorcorps.org/joining/rsvp

SCORE
1110 Vermont Avenue NW, 9th Floor
Washington, DC 20005
800-634-0245
www.score.org

Consumers

Center for a New American Dream
6930 Carroll Avenue, Suite 900
Takoma Park, MD 20912
877-68-DREAM
www.newdream.org/consumer

Consumer Federation of America
1414 16th Street NW, Suite 604
Washington, DC 20036
202-387-6121
www.consumerfed.org

Consumers Union
101 Truman Avenue
Yonkers, NY 10703-1057
914-378-2000
www.consumersunion.org

Criminal Justice

American Civil Liberties Union
(ACLU)
125 Broad Street, 18th Floor
New York, NY 10004
212-549-2500
www.aclu.org

American Friends Service Committee
1501 Cherry Street
Philadelphia, PA 19102
215-241-7000
www.afsc.org

CASA
(Court Appointed Special Advocate)
Volunteer Guardian Ad Litem
    Programs
100 West Harrison, North Tower
Suite 500
Seattle, WA 98119
800-628-3233
www.nationalcasa.org

Champions for Life
PO Box 761101
Dallas, TX 75376-1101
972-298-1101
www.lifechampions.org
(click on "Prison Ministry")

National Baptist Convention
    Prison Ministry
2585 Van Buren Street
Gary Indiana 46407
219-886-2541
www.nationalbaptist.com
(click on "Ministries")

National Institute of Corrections
    Prisons Division
320 First Street NW
Washington, DC 20534
202-307-3106
800-995-6423
www.nicic.org

Environment

Cousteau Society
710 Settlers Landing Road
Hampton, VA 23669
757-722-9300
www.cousteau.org

Ducks Unlimited
One Waterfowl Way
Memphis, TN 38120
800-45DUCKS or 901-758-3825
www.ducks.org

Earthwatch Institute
3 Clock Tower Place, Suite 100
Box 75
Maynard, MA 01754
800-776-0188
www.earthwatch.org

Environmental Defense Fund
257 Park Avenue South
New York, NY 10010
212-505-2100
www.environmentaldefense.org

Friends of the Earth
1717 Massachusetts Avenue NW
Suite 600
Washington, DC 20036-2002
877-843-8687 (toll free)
www.foe.org

Leave No Trace Center
  for Outdoor Ethics
PO Box 997
Boulder, CO 80306
800-332-4100
www.lnt.org

National Audubon Society
700 Broadway
New York, NY 10003
212-979-3000
www.audubon.org

National Wildlife Federation
11100 Wildlife Center Drive
Reston, VA 20190-5362
800-822-9919
www.nwf.org

Natural Resources Defense Council
40 West 20th Street
New York, NY 10011
212-727-2700
www.nrdc.org

North American Nature Photography
  Association
10200 West 44th Avenue, Suite 304
Wheat Ridge, CO 80033-2840
303-422-8527
www.nanpa.org

Save the Whales
1192 Waring Street
Seaside, CA 93955
831-899-9957
www.savethewhales.org

Sierra Club National Headquarters
85 Second Street, 2nd Floor
San Francisco, CA 94105
415-977-5500
www.sierraclub.org

Trout Unlimited
1300 North 17th Street, Suite 500
Arlington, VA 22209-3801
800-834-2419
www.tu.org

U.S. Fish and Wildlife Service
1849 C Street NW, Room 3361
Washington, DC 20240-0001
202-208-4131
http://refuges.fws.gov

U.S. PIRG
218 D Street SE
Washington, DC 20003
202-546-9707
www.uspirg.org

Ethnic Communities

American Council for Polish Culture
c/o AnnaMae Maglaty
35 Fernridge Road
West Hartford, CT 06107
860-521-7621
www.polishcultureacpc.org

American Hellenic Educational
    Progressive Association (AHEPA)
1909 Q Street NW, Suite 500
Washington, DC 20009
202-232-6300
www.ahepa.org

American Irish Historical Society
991 Fifth Avenue
New York, NY 10028
212-288-2263
www.aihs.org

American-Scandinavian Foundation
58 Park Avenue
New York, NY 10016
212-879-9779
www.amscan.org

Chinese American Citizens Alliance
1044 Stockton Street
San Francisco, CA 94108
415-434-2222
www.cacanational.org

Congress of Russian Americans
2460 Sutter Street
San Francisco, CA 94115
415-928-5841
www.russian-americans.org

German-American National Congress
4740 N. Western Avenue, 2nd Floor
Chicago, IL 60625-2097
773-275-1100
www.dank.org

HERMANA, A National Latina
    Organization
1725 K Street NW, Suite 501
Washington, DC 20006
202-833-0060
www.hermana.org

National Council of La Raza
1111 19th Street NW, Suite 1000
Washington, DC 20036
202-785-1670
www.nclr.org

National Italian American Foundation
(NIAF)
1860 19th Street NW
Washington, DC 20009
800-989-NIAF (6423)
www.niaf.org

National Slavic Convention
16 S Patterson Park Avenue
Baltimore, MD 21231
410-276-7676

Organization of Chinese Americans
1001 Connecticut Avenue NW
Suite 601
Washington, DC 20036
202-223-5500
www.ocanatl.org

Faith Community

American Ethical Union (AEU)
2 West 64th Street
New York, NY 10023
212-873-6500
www.aeu.org

American Friends Service Committee
1501 Cherry Street
Philadelphia, PA 19102
215-241-7000
www.afsc.org

B'nai B'rith
2020 K St., NW, 7th Floor
Washington,DC 20006
202-857-6600
www.bnaibrith.org

Catholic Charities USA
1731 King Street
Alexandria, VA 22314
703-549-1390
www.catholiccharitiesusa.org

Islamic American Relief Agency
IARA-USA
P.O. Box 7084
Columbia, MO 65205
800-298-1199
www.iara-usa.org

Salvation Army USA National
615 Slaters Lane
P.O. Box 269
Alexandria, Virginia 22313
703-684-5500
www.salvationarmy.org

Health

Alzheimer's Association
225 North Michigan Avenue,
17th Floor
Chicago, IL 60601-7633
800-272-3900
www.alz.org

American Hospital Association
1 North Franklin
Chicago, IL 60606-3421
312-422-3000
www.aha.org

American Public Health Association
800 I Street NW
Washington, DC 20001
202-777-2742
www.apha.org

National Alliance for the Mentally Ill
Colonial Place Three
2107 Wilson Boulevard, Suite 300
Arlington, VA 22201-3042
800-959-NAMI (6264)
www.nami.org

National Hospice & Palliative Care
  Organization
1700 Diagonal Road, Suite 625
Alexandria, VA 22314
703-837-1500
800-646-6460
www.nhpco.org

Homeland Security
and U.S. Civil Liberties

American Civil Liberties Union
(ACLU)
125 Broad Street, 18th Floor
New York, NY 10004
212-549-2500
www.aclu.org

American Legion
Washington Office
1608 K Street, NW
Washington, DC 20006
202-861-2700
www.legion.org

Clergy Leadership Network
499 South Capitol Street SW
Suite 110
Washington, DC 20003
202-554-2122
www.clnnlc.org

Interfaith Alliance
1331 H Street NW, 11th Floor
Washington, DC 20005
800-510-0969
www.interfaithalliance.org

Not In Our Name
PO Box 20221
Greeley Square Station
New York, NY 10001-0006
212-969-8058
www.notinourname.net

Peace Action
1100 Wayne Avenue, Suite 1020
Silver Spring, MD 20910
301-565-4050
www.peace-action.org

United for Peace and Justice
PO Box 607
Times Square Station
New York, NY 10108
212-868-5545
www.unitedforpeace.org

Veterans of Foreign Wars
National Headquarters
406 West 34th Street
Kansas City, MO 64111
816-756-3390
www.vfw.org

Hunger

Catholic Charities U.S.A.
1731 King Street
Alexandria, VA 22314
703-549-1390
www.catholiccharitiesusa.org

Greater Chicago Food Depository
4501 South Tripp Avenue
Chicago, IL 60632
773-247-FOOD (3663)
www.chicagosfoodbank.org

National Meals on Wheels
    Foundation
PO Box 1727
Iowa City, IA 52244
319-358-9362
www.nationalmealsonwheels.org

United Jewish Communities/
    The Federations of North America
PO Box 30
Old Chelsea Station
New York, NY 10113
212-284-6500
www.ujc.org

International Causes

American Friends Service Committee
1501 Cherry Street
Philadelphia, PA 19102
215-241-7000
www.afsc.org

Amnesty International USA
322 Eighth Avenue
New York, NY 10001
212-807-8400
www.amnestyusa.org

CARE USA
151 Ellis Street
Atlanta, GA 30303
404-681-2552
www.careusa.org

Catholic Relief Services
209 West Fayette Street
Baltimore, MD 20201-3443
800-736-3467
www.catholicrelief.org

ICRC Regional Delegation
    (USA and Canada)
2100 Pennsylvania Avenue NW
Suite 545
Washington, DC 20037
202-293-9430
www.icrc.org

(See also *Combining Travel with
Volunteering*, page 198.)

Oral Histories

Generations United, c/o CWLA
1333 H Street, NW, Suite 500 W
Washington, DC 20005
202-289-3979
www.gu.org

National Center for Creative
Aging/Elders Share the Arts
138 South Oxford Street
Brooklyn, NY 11217
718-398-3870
www.creativeaging.org

StoryCorps
176 Grand Street, 3rd Floor
New York, NY 10013
212-981-5228
www.storycorps.net

Temple University Center for
Intergenerational Learning
1601 North Broad Street, Room 206
Philadelphia, PA 19122
215-204-6970
www.temple.edu/cil

Zoo Animals, Pets, and Wildlife

American Society for the Prevention
of Cruelty to Animals (ASPCA)
424 East 92nd Street
New York, NY 10128-6804
212-876-7700
www.aspca.org

Delta Society
580 Naches Avenue SW, Suite 101
Renton, WA 98055-2297
425-226-7357
www.deltasociety.org

Humane Society of the United States
2100 L Street NW
Washington, DC 20037
202-452-1100
www.hsus.org

National Park Foundation
Volunteers-In-Parks program
Artists-In-Residence program
www.nps.gov/volunteer
(link to online application)

National Wildlife Federation
11100 Wildlife Center Drive
Reston, VA 20190-5362
800-822-9919
www.nwf.org

World Wildlife Fund
1250 24th Street NW
Washington, DC 20037
202-273-4800
www.wwf.org

CHAPTER 14

Social Entrepreneurship

It's all about making a difference.

Even if you never participated in a protest march, wrote a letter to Congress, or burned your bra, the very notion that people with a passion can have an impact on society is as familiar to you as, well, Rice Krispies. Whether you earnestly talked about revolution or held more conservative views, you lived through the social upheavals of the 1960s and 1970s: The civil rights movement, the feminist movement, nuclear freeze movement, Earth Day, and antiwar protests. College kids today study the 1960s and 1970s as a time when people with a passion could, and did, influence the very fabric of our lives.

Of course, the giants of that era are still in our minds and hearts. Every schoolchild in the United States now knows Martin Luther King, Jr.'s historic line, "I have a dream . . ."

DO YOU HAVE A DREAM TOO?

As one founder of an organization put it, "Americans *want* to make things better. We are hopeful that democracy and experiments in science are going to work." Over the years, that's how such organizations as God's Love We Deliver; Big Brother/Sister; Teach America; AARP; and Planned Parenthood got started—by someone, or a small group, with an idea.

Heaven knows there's plenty to be done: Tutoring high-risk children and immigrant adults. Economic development for devastated downtowns. Better home-care support for housebound elderly. Better security around nuclear power plants in densely populated areas. And if you're in THE RETIREMENT ZONE, you may have the skills and time to make a difference.

The job title varies: "Social Entrepreneur," "Activist," "Innovator." Whatever you call them, these are the folks who rise to the challenge. They passionately believe in the possibility of change for the better.

Innovators work on all levels. They might start a campaign to de-pollute a nearby pond. Or organize studio tours of new and emerging artists. Or launch a nationwide effort to help raise research money to seek a cure for a disease. It might involve old-fashioned grassroots organizing, Internet fund-raising, or managing contacts at the highest levels of corporate America.

The majority of people who volunteer tap into programs in existing organizations. These people give and get a lot from their volunteer involvement. However, it is a smaller but very influential group who recognize that they want to innovate, to create something new. It's to these personalities—and their creative impulses—that this chapter is dedicated.

The challenge of a start-up is comparable, in a way, to scaling a mountain. It's risky. You need ambition, a realistic sense of what's ahead, decent preparation, and a workable plan. Inherent in the challenge are unforeseeable circumstances and the real possibility of failure. And while the goal is up ahead, you can only take it one step at a time. A social changer finds solutions, seeks alternative routes, and makes it up as circumstances change.

And although such efforts may seem utterly altruistic, the rewards of "giving back" can be sweet, surprising, and incredibly rich. Like reaching the top of a mountain, trying to coax the world in a certain direction (and succeeding, by however modest a measure) is nothing less than exhilarating.

If you've spent years working, whether in business, the arts, education, politics, or government, you probably have a pretty thorough grasp of how things get done in the world. The problem is, when you're working there's not always *time* to try to make a difference. You may have daydreamed about making the world a better (or more tolerant, or greener, or more musical) place. Now's your chance.

Like Falling in Love, You'll Know if It's for You

Some people have been waiting all their working lives for the chance to work on a given nonprofit project. But for most, it seems to just happen. There's a moment, an interaction, a turning point.

You won't be able to stop thinking about it. You'll find yourself scribbling on the backs of envelopes, working out the finances, trying out slogans, or jotting down the names of people to enlist. In some odd way, these kinds of activities choose their people as much as their people choose them.

Some doers are drawn by the desire to ameliorate a major social problem. Others treat the endeavor as though it were gardening: They plant some seeds, tend the garden, and wait to see what sprouts and flourishes. "I am very interested in identifying a problem and solving it. It's the satisfaction of accomplishing something, of seeing it evolve, worked out. I'm interested in seeing maybe I was right in targeting the lecture series? Is it working?" says 80-something George Warren of Florida, who has initiated several cultural and environmental campaigns in his community.

A certain attitude of cocky defiance plays a part, too. "The more people tell you it can't be done, the more determined you are to make it work," says one experienced community organizer in Brooklyn, New York. "Sheer stubbornness makes me tick."

Are *you* a social entrepreneur? If and when this is you, chances are, you'll know it.

A GENERATIONAL ITCH THAT NEEDS SCRATCHIN'?

The United States has one of the most educated work forces—and therefore, soon will boast one of the most educated older populations—in the world. Count among them legions of lawyers; doctors; educators; engineers; managers; financiers and bankers; nonprofit executives; sales, marketing, and communications professionals; and small-business owners.

All these people—all this talent—collectively spending light years on the golf course? Unlikely! In the decades ahead, there will probably be an explosion of social entrepreneurial activities, as people find their own ways to make the world a better place.

INSIDER'S GUIDE FOR IDEALISTS: 7 Considerations

Some important considerations in starting your own nonprofit, social-minded organization include the following:

I) THE "VISION THING"

The "vision thing," as President George H.W. Bush used to call it, is essential. But as any weary nonprofit director will tell you, vision is only half the story. In addition to vision, you'll need the rest—leadership, management, fund-raising skills, and often just pig headed stubbornness—to get things done.

Think big and start small, so you can build on your successes. As trite as it sounds, when others see that you are making strides, however modest, you'll be more likely to recruit helpers and funding.

2) FINDING TALENT—AND RECOGNIZING YOUR OWN

Unless you're a one-man band, you'll want to find a few other souls to work with as colleagues or board members.

It's likely that within your own immediate circle of colleagues, neighbors, family, and friends you will find some like-minded helpers. Don't be afraid to ask your dentist, your accountant, and your car mechanic for help.

Seventy-eight-year-old Don Illig from Ohio brought years of corporate and consulting experience to the task when in retirement he helped start a service called Management Assistance for Nonprofit Agencies, MANA. It provides free business advice to a potpourri of regional nonprofit organizations, from a county bar association to a cooperatively run company to a community services agency. The launch went smoothly in part because of his start-up team, which included several lawyers, a professor, and several people with PhDs. "It was a darn good group, and we worked well together forming this," recalls Illig.

3) NETWORKING

One of the first pieces of advice for people starting nonprofit organizations is to network, network, and network.

One networking rule of thumb: Make at least one new contact every day, and when you speak with a new person about your project or idea, don't let the conversation end without getting a few new leads.

But a word of warning, too: Some of your best buddies might prefer to go to the racetrack or go shopping rather than kick in. Pursue without pressuring. Not everyone is an activist.

PRACTICAL TIP: You might consider looking for corporate support—not necessarily just money, but, say, used equipment or free services. Some big businesses offer training for nonprofit organizations and also upon your request will include your nonprofit organization on a master database of volunteer opportunities that's accessible to their employees and retirees. For instance, there's no charge to be listed at www.foundation.verizon.com. Contact the corporate communications and/or corporate charities departments of some of the larger companies in your geographic or issue area to see if they might help.

4) DOING THE HOMEWORK

Whether your passion is setting up a small theater company or saving political refugees—or even the native oak trees—there are others who are already engaged in something similar. So before you jump in with both feet, do some research. You might be able to obtain free information, free materials, and certainly free advice from activists working on similar issues.

Remember the popular John Guare play and acclaimed movie adaptation, *Six Degrees of Separation*, which suggested that everyone is connected and is indeed just six contacts apart? The play and the movie are fiction, but there's a nugget of truth in that "six degrees" notion. Networks of issue-specific activists are both plentiful and usually easy to find.

All you need is a bit of determination and decent phone skills (familiarity with the Internet helps, too). With about a dozen well-placed calls, you can tap into some kind of a network of people working in your field of interest. Be persistent.

And you can access assistance from a network of organizations that seek to aid nonprofits, such as the Seattle-based Social Venture Partners program, which has been replicated in over a half dozen major cities. Lastly, many business schools, including those at Case Western Reserve, Columbia, Harvard, Stanford, University of Michigan, and Yale have courses in nonprofit management and social entrepreneurship.

5) PLANNING: THINK LIKE THE IRS

Consider such things as a board of directors, operating bylaws, and your tax and legal status. *Make a plan.* Just because this is a nonprofit endeavor doesn't mean it can survive sloppy thinking or shoddy work.

Early on, if you are engaged in any fund-raising from individuals, foundations, or corporations, you will have to sort out the basic business question of what category of organization you are running. For instance, without a 501c3 nonprofit designation by the Internal Revenue Service, you cannot offer contributors a tax deduction for their contributions.

Administering an independent nonprofit organization can be complicated and expensive. But there are alternatives, including partnering with an existing nonprofit organization to come under their fiscal and legal umbrella, usually for a fee.

Recalling the start-up decisions for MANA, the Management Assistance service, Illig says, "A big question is whether to start your own 501c3 or not. We decided we preferred to be part of an existing 501c3 organization, to take care of liability insurance and billing issues." He and his colleagues approached the local community college and worked out a partnership arrangement. "When we received a foundation grant early on to get started, those funds went to the community college and into our account. It worked out for everyone," he recalls.

6) IMPLEMENTING 24/7

The implementation phase of any brilliant idea is loaded with minutia. Entrepreneurship can sponge up a great deal of your spare time, particularly in the start-up phase. "Remember the song refrain, 'All day and all night, Mary Anne'? That was me," recalls one satisfied (if tired) cofounder of a successful mentoring program. "I recruited everyone I knew. People I'd known for years, decades even, turned the other way when I went down the street." Another quips that his wife "thinks I am part of the computer."

George Warren jokes that he is clinically certified as a "broad-spectrum" kind of person. He's taken on the volunteer job of coordinating a college lecture series for retirees, and meanwhile is also helping coordinate fund-raising to transform a local historical estate into a cultural center. "I have the bad habit of getting all consumed in what I do," he says, cheerily adding, "I happen to be very creative; these things can get you into a lot of trouble."

People who are passionate about moving their agendas forward say their project is never far from their mind, whether they are on vacation, talking to a neighbor, or reading the newspaper.

7) EVALUATE, RETOOL, AND EXPERIMENT

Born in 1927, Joanne Alter still races when she speaks, words and ideas tumbling over one another. The retired Chicago political activist describes meeting a schoolteacher in one of Chicago's most infamous tough neighborhoods, Cabrini Green, in 1990, when her four children were "pretty well grown." After talking with the teacher and seeing tremendous potential—and equal need—Alter heard herself uttering words she'd never said before, "OK, I have some time."

She and others started a program and called it WITS, for "Working In The Schools." Their dream was to enlist working people and retirees to go into inner-city schools to provide one-on-one reading tutoring for children from kindergarten to third grade. One of the barriers, they realized, was that prospective tutors were fearful of the neighborhoods where the target schools were located. Their solution: provide two-way bus transportation from workplaces to the schools.

Alter describes a long process during which she and her colleagues were flexible enough to experiment with different ideas and models, getting feedback, until they crafted and marketed a workable program. But it started small. In the early phases, she says, "I got my husband, and we started going into schools in Cabrini and helped the children read, one on one, ten years ago." Thanks to Alter's organizing genius and a partner's fund-raising expertise, WITS took off. It is now a million-dollar program with widespread corporate support. WITS transports over a thousand volunteers by bus during the day from their corporate jobs to eight different school districts—and then back to work again.

 ## HEALTHVIEWS

It's well known that when people are masters of their own fate, they're happier. Health researchers call this a "high degree of agency." That means you have control over your personal mission and how you spend your time. Being a social entrepreneur certainly offers involvement, a sense of mission, and a chance to be in charge and call the shots. It's also well known that masters of their own fate can run themselves ragged. So in the interests of your health, three reminders:

Assume everything can take twice as long as it should (and that you'll be the one doing it). Most things will take twice as long as you think they should, whether it's getting that first press release written, or finding funding, or getting enough people together to mount an effective leafleting campaign.

As George Warren puts it, "The biggest problem that I find in what I am doing these days, is that I must reduce myself to a detail person—typist, accountant, bookkeeper—and I hate that. I had a hundred fifty-six subordinates in my last job, and I could get anything done by anybody without having to do it myself."

Take a minute (or several) to pat yourself on the back. It's not a problem, it's a *challenge*, remember? If you undertake a big project involving hours of work and meetings, you might find yourself looking out the window wistfully some fine spring day, wondering, "This is what I stopped working for? To work just as hard—for no pay or benefits? What about going fishing? Or to a matinee?"

The impact of some good works is simply hard to measure. Some projects might yield immediate tangible results. (Part of the magic of a program like Habitat for Humanity is that you can literally see the fruits of your labor.) Others might take a decade or more before you can say the proof is in the pudding. You may or may not fully realize your dream. But having tried—that's often well worth the effort.

Activists talk about the ripple effect of social change. You may never know whom you've touched, or changed, or moved. It's worth believing that simply by trying to do something positive you've been an inspiration to others.

Consider an Exit Strategy. Are you willing to make a one-, two-, or five-year commitment? As one retiree joked, "You know what they say: This kind of retirement is when you are doing the things you did before, but back then you got paid for them." Make a plan that will enable you to transition the steering of the organization into another set of hands when you're ready.

 ## YOUR MONEY MATTERS

You might be surprised at both the expenses and time involved in launching a nonprofit campaign, project, or organization.

Starting a project from scratch often means working from home, using your home telephone and computer, your own supplies and postage stamps. If travel is involved, you may find yourself paying for gas and tolls.

Plan ahead. First, guess-timate what your annual financial commitment will be to this start-up and—if you are not organized as a 501c3—whether you can afford to advance funds to the cause on a non-tax-deductible basis. Second, keep receipts for all the small items that you are spending money on, even if it seems silly to account for a ream of paper here or a few long-distance charges there. Things do add up. And you'll want to have receipts to reimburse yourself once you do secure outside funding, or as deductions if you do get 501c3 status.

> **If you're reading this book for a spouse, friend, or parent . . .** Strap on for a bumpy ride; starting something new is always full of surprises. And be prepared to hear a great deal about this grand experiment, even if it's not your field of interest. People with a passion just can't be contained!

Saving Lives

Ed Jenest relocated from the Southwest intending to build his dream house, learn how to play the guitar, and retire. But within a year, he had launched a nonprofit organization that educates people about organ donation in a geographic area desperately in need of community education programs to address the existing donation crisis.

"I worked for Abbott Laboratories for twenty-seven years and retired at age fifty-seven. I didn't have much time to do volunteer work when I was employed, so I was looking for something to do to give back to my new community.

"Before I even moved to this retirement community, someone at the North Carolina Center for Creative Retirement sent me a newspaper article about organ transplantation. I'd been connected to the transplant community through marketing in my job. There's a tremendous need for donors for organ transplantation across the U.S; it is a big problem.

"I called the fellow in the article who's in charge of ethics at the regional hospital and said, 'I am coming to town, let's chat about it.' Over lunch, I asked the hospital contact about what was going on in the region from an educational standpoint. He said, 'There are two people employed with the local organ recovery group who go out and talk, but they can't do it full time, with their other duties.' That piqued my interest. I put this out to him: 'Do you think a grassroots organization would be possible?' The idea was to establish a new volunteer educational organization that could go out and talk, answer questions, and invite people to sign up for organ donation. He thought it was a great idea. I initially traveled across the region to get a sense from the people in local hospitals and in the communities: Would they be interested in it? The goal was to establish small centers of excellence in western North Carolina for organ donation education.

"So in my first year of retirement, I started up a nonprofit, the Western North Carolina Organ and Tissue Initiative. It covers eighteen counties and will serve a population of eight hundred thousand people. We are recruiting volunteers who are organ or tissue recipients, or donor families, as well as health care providers. We set up groups in small, mostly rural communities to educate people about organ, eye, and tissue donation. Then they can make a decision

about whether they want to be a donor, or not. We do outreach through faith communities, civic organizations, and high-school drivers' ed programs.

"It's like a start-up organization. You have nothing, no people. You have to build from the ground up and be patient about it. Although it's different from starting up a dot com or biotech company, it is an entrepreneurial activity. Coming out of a large corporation with rush-rush-rush and everything is due yesterday, I find I am on a slower pace. I went from working sixty to seventy hours to about thirty hours a week. The best part is that you have the opportunity to pick and choose what's important to you and where you think your skills are valuable.

"I was also a member of a work group established to propose a North Carolina State Senate bill to create a statewide donor registry. I worked with about fifteen people from the Department of Motor Vehicles and the Secretary of State's office to eye banks, hospitals, and so on. I was sort of a community representative. That was fun. I got to be involved a little in state government and see how things work. We had an opportunity to meet with two state senators. It was exciting to talk about what we are interested in and determine how they might help us and their constituents.

"I see this as a three- to five-year project. I would like to develop staff and the organization. That way, at some time, I can turn it over and get some new blood into the system, and I will be ready to explore additional opportunities to help others."

We Wanted Young People to Travel

Gaylon Duke and his wife had worked as educators, and more recently had traveled to over one hundred countries for their Santa Fe, New Mexico, import business. When they received a small inheritance when they were in their early sixties, they decided to use it for something special. They camped for a few days high in the mountains and looked at all the possibilities, "just brainstorming," as they put it. The couple had an interest in art and decided to use art as a medium to enable kids to get to know traditional cultures. Because of their travels, they knew where they could run a program that was safe, economical—and different from Santa Fe. They had been to Bali a dozen times over the past 20 years and they knew a lot of people there. They decided to take a small group of kids, who had never traveled, to Bali to learn about that culture.

"The first year, we thought we'd take four kids and pay for the whole thing. We contacted a well-known local high-school art teacher, who said, 'I have just the kids for you.' He showed up for a meeting with seven—not four— kids. In the course of the evening, we invited him, too. But teachers in Santa Fe don't make a lot of money. We started fund-raising, as eight people was beyond what we could spring for.

"That first year, we took seven kids and their teacher to Bali for a month. My wife went to Bali ahead of us and found a perfect hotel at the end of a long lane, isolated and beautiful, at an art center called Ubud. We set up weeklong classes with local teachers in gamelan and dance, painting and batik. The classes were a way of getting into the culture. The kids would learn a dance or song and then go to a performance at a religious site where they would see their teachers playing and dancing. Or we'd attend a cremation, where they would hear music and see the ceremonies. In Bali there are ten-day festivals—every temple has a series of festivals every year. We'd get invited to everything going on in the whole island.

"After that first summer, other people in Santa Fe said, 'Hey, I want to go, too.' So we opened it up to adults for $2,000 for a month and a tax-deductible contribution of $500 to help defray the kids' travel costs. That second year, we took eight or ten kids, and eleven adults. The third year, we took

a dozen kids. A grant fell into our lap, which eased the fund-raising. And each year, the program improved.

"The kids we've chosen are from the public schools. Most have never traveled before. Some were from the Navajo reservation and had not been out of New Mexico. Every year we have about thirty kids interested in going. The students who have participated previously do the interviewing. That's how we put together a compatible group.

"We do about ten language sessions in Indonesian before we go, so they can start a conversation. Often they make friends with Balinese teenagers. Everyone in Bali smiles all the time. You speak to everyone you meet. Our kids are out walking the rice paddies in the morning and talking with people. At the end of the month, we go to a beautiful yoga retreat on the beach. The students write their reflections on the trip. They talk about inner change, how the trip has affected them, and what they got out of it. It is marvelous.

"We have over thirty alumni. They remain close. They may be back from college over the winter holidays, and we will have a big meeting at the house. We'll often discuss how the trip is affecting them now. It's changed a lot of them.

"The kids' trips cost about $1,800 each. We only ask for $2,500 from each foundation so we are not dependent on anybody. We spring for it in the end if we don't raise enough. That way, any kid who's supposed to go is going. The office is in our house. We thought someone would come along and take it over. But because we have so many contacts in Bali, we are not finding anyone else capable of doing it. I work on this every day, even if it's for just an hour. The administration does take more time than we expected.

"Retirement hasn't changed us; we are still doing what we did before: traveling, working with young people, lots of activities. It wasn't like we hit sixty-five and said, 'Now what?' But we did get started because of this gift from a relative, and it has helped in the way we've been able to fund the program.

"We have our wills set up to fund the nonprofit. The executors will be on the board, so there will be money there either for this program or in some way so young people can travel."

Just in case you're still thinking about this, here are two more stories:

In the middle of winter, on February 29, 2000, 90-year-old "Granny D," whose real name is Doris Haddock, completed a walk across America to draw attention to the need for campaign finance reform. The 3,200-mile, fourteen-month walk from Los Angeles to Washington, D.C., was the culmination of a lifetime of activism. She went on to publish a book about the journey, and then, at age 93, published another, entitled, *Granny D: You're Never Too Old to Raise a Little Hell* by Doris Haddock and Dennis Burke (Villard, 2003). It won high praise from, among others, President Carter, who said, "Doris Haddock is a true patriot, and our nation has been blessed by her remarkable life. Her story will entertain, inform, and inspire people of all ages for generations to come." There's now a Web site called Granny D (www.grannyd.com) and a voter registration campaign drawing on her inspiration.

In the mid-1990s, 67-year-old Patsy Clarke of North Carolina, a lifelong Republican, sat down and wrote a long letter to her friend U.S. Senator Jesse Helms recounting the anguished death of her AIDS-afflicted son Mark. Helms held strongly negative and very public views on homosexuality. His harsh reply catapulted Clarke and a friend, Eloise Vaughn, to form a political group called Mothers Against Jesse in Congress (MAJIC). They didn't unseat Helms in the 1996 election, but like Granny D, the two women then wrote a book about their experience called *Keep Singing* (Alyson Books, 2001) detailing their journey from knitting needles to the cover of *People* magazine and the Democratic National Convention.

> "Never doubt that a small group of thoughtful citizens can change the world. Indeed, it's the only thing that ever has."
>
> —Margaret Mead

Resource Guide

PUBLICATIONS

Encouraging the Heart: A Leader's Guide to Rewarding and Recognizing Others by James M. Kouzes and Barry Z. Posner (Jossey-Bass, 2003).

How to Change the World: Social Entrepreneurs and the Power of New Ideas by David Bornstein (Oxford University Press, 2004).

Nonprofit Times (1200 Littleton Road, Suite 120, Parsippany, New Jersey 07054-1803; phone 973-394-1800).

The Tipping Point: How Little Things Can Make a Big Difference by Malcolm Gladwell (Back Bay Books, 2002).

ORGANIZATIONS AND WEB SITES

Alliance for Nonprofit Management
1899 L Street NW, Suite 600
Washington, DC 20036
202-955-8406
www.allianceonline.org

Ashoka U.S.A.
1700 North Moore Street
Suite 2000 (20th Floor)
Arlington, VA 22209
703-527-8300
www.ashoka.org

BoardSource
1828 L Street NW, Suite 900
Washington, DC 20036-5114
800-883-6262
www.boardsource.org

Foundation Center
79 Fifth Avenue
New York, NY 10003-3076
212-620-4230
www.fdncenter.org

Independent Sector
1200 18th Street NW, Suite 200
Washington, DC 20036
202-467-6100
www.independentsector.org

National Center for Charitable
 Statistics
The Urban Institute
2100 M Street NW
Washington, DC 20037
866-518-3874 (toll-free)
nccsdataweb.urban.org/FAQ

National Council of Nonprofit
 Associations
1030 15th Street NW, Suite 870
Washington, DC 20005-1525
202-962-0322
www.ncna.org

TIME FOR FUN, TIME FOR ME

The world's a playground. So why not play? With the gift of extra years of life, people entering THE RETIREMENT ZONE in the 21st century have more time to get a kick out of the world and what it brings them, through travel, hobbies, sweet peas blooming on the fence, a satisfying nap, or a fine sunset.

Meditation and learning to play the clarinet have their own inherent rationale. It's wonderful to seek personal fulfillment in pursuits that have no obvious or quantifiable social value. But because of the American work ethic, people sometimes have a hard time swallowing the idea of not being "productive." Sometimes there's pressure to justify one's existence, or to use "being productive" as a way to try to defy age.

When, if not now, is the time to have these fulfilling experiences? As one psychologist puts it, "I want to take advantage of the next phase of my life, like enjoying my beautiful grandchildren. As we age we become more inner oriented; we start to throw off external pressures of the environment . . ." And, he laughs, "I plan to enjoy my bald head."

CHAPTER 15

Traveling

Maybe you hitched across the country in your youth, or back-packed through Europe. Or just sang along to Bob Dylan's "Highway 51 Blues" or Woody Guthrie's "This Land is Your Land." Perhaps in recent decades you had a work assignment over-seas for a few years. Haven't you had enough travel?

Heck, no!

As one veteran traveler jokes, "My body needs to be at thirty-five thousand feet once a month."

THINK BIG: The World is Your Oyster!

The travel bug comes in different sizes and shapes. For some it's an educational trip; for others it's a two-week summer stint in their RV on the Western flatlands; and for still others it's a three-month home-swap in Portugal.

Boutique travel agents, niche marketing, and special-interest trips have expanded travel options. In just about any social circle, there's likely to be someone who knows a "travel bug"—someone who's been to China five times, taught school in Arabia, been to Antarctica, or just returned from the Galapagos Islands.

Given that people in their 60s are acting like the 40-year-olds of yesteryear, expect to see "mature" travelers doing the following:
- Ballooning in Park City, Utah
- Touring castles in southern England
- Enrolling in a "hands on" program, such as a cooking school in Tuscany or New Mexico
- Volunteering in a Habitat for Humanity home-building program in another state or a foreign country
- Training for physically demanding "adventure" tours, whether it's biking in Scotland or rafting on the Colorado River
- Combining education with travel, such as a "literary tour" that follows the geographic path of a famous author, or a short course in a foreign university

This chapter focuses on just a few kinds of travel that can be both fun and meaningful. However, the travel market is enormous, so the possibilities are almost endless for travel in both the United States and abroad.

INSIDER'S GUIDE:
8 Kinds of Trips, from Adventure to "Roots"

1) Adventure Travel

People of all ages are kayaking, diving, sailing, and fishing in foreign waters. They're hiking, biking, climbing, trekking, and dog sledding across continents.

In fact, older Americans and Europeans are embracing this increasingly popular form of travel in such numbers that several tour companies cater *just* to this market. "They are healthier than anyone at that age has ever been. They're more highly educated, and they have more time and disposable income," says Karl Kannstadter of ElderTreks (www.eldertreks.com), a Toronto-based agency specializing in 40 different small-group expeditions, from circumnavigating Antarctica to riding camels in Morocco to hot-air ballooning over Turkey. The company focuses on travelers over 50. "The people we attract are people with a positive outlook and who are very open-minded. They have a very broad world view," Kannstadter says, adding that adventure travel need not exclude comfort. "At the end of the day, we want to go to a clean hotel with an attached bath and we'd prefer to travel in our own vehicle."

Margaret Green, 70, a former elementary-school office assistant from Stanford, California, has taken several trips with ElderTreks, including Iceland and Mongolia, where she rode camels and yaks and camped in a yurt-like structure called a ger. Green and her husband loved traveling and living in exotic places during his career as a biology professor. When he died five years ago, Green wanted to continue the tradition. So she travels by herself and enjoys meeting new roommates rather than paying for a single supplement. "I decided I didn't want to stay home. I wanted to try to augment the experience we had as a family," she says.

So far, she's been to Mali, Rwanda, Costa Rica, Madagascar, and Antarctica with several different tour operators. "The companies don't want people getting sick," Green says. "So you do stay at nice places."

Many agencies specialize in adventures such as African game drives, SCUBA diving, and bungee-jumping—and invite the over-50 crowd. Dan Lagomarsino, 61, a retired pilot from California, has taken several kayaking trips in Fiji: "My wife and I stay active. We prefer doing things as opposed to looking at things." The couple's latest trip, with the outfitter O.A.R.S. (www.oars.com), included sea and river kayaking, snorkeling, and river rafting.

Robert Leuba, 71, a retired judge from Mystic, Connecticut, traveled through the Indian state of Rajasthan on horseback with Equitours (www.ridingtours.com), a Wyoming-based agency that offers international tours from the Tuscan wine country to the Okavango Delta in Botswana and counts a large percentage of riders in their 60s and 70s. Leuba and his wife have ridden through Spain, France, and the Dominican Republic. Next year, they're going to Kenya. "Horses are ideal. You're on the ground," he says. "You get to see the people of the country rather than riding on a bus and just seeing the tourist attractions." He advises getting to know the tour operator prior to signing up. "You have to research the people who are organizing it. Make sure they've been there before themselves."

Jack Blosky, 67, a former special-education teacher who lives near Philadelphia, learned the hard way. While visiting Brazil for Mardi Gras, he and his wife decided to take a fishing trip on the Amazon River in search of the prized peacock bass. He organized the weeklong trip through his son-in-law's friend. "We went not knowing what we were getting into," he says. The boat broke down and they sat seven hours in the sun waiting for it to be fixed. They slept in a two-person tent on a riverbank with no showers. "We almost got divorced," he says. "It was just a disaster. We didn't catch any fish, and it was hot."

He's since been back to the Amazon several times—by himself—to fish for largemouth bass with Sportventures, a group that organizes sport fishing trips to Mexico and South America (www.sportventures.com). On those trips, Blosky enjoyed his own room with air conditioning and ate in a nice dining area.

No matter how comfortable a tour operator tries to make a trip, however, Green warns that adventure travel is still an adventure, and recommends that the dainty set stay home. "I don't mind if I get dirty. I don't mind if I don't get a shower every day," she says. After taking a long bus ride with open windows in Ethiopia with Elderhostel, she discovered a small sand drift on the bridge of her nose. And in Mali, the best hotel in the area featured toilets without seats and electricity for only three hours a night. She advises travelers to wash their hands frequently, drink plenty of bottled water, and be prepared to fill buckets with water to flush broken toilets. "It's all part of the adventure."

2) Traveling with Your Fellow Alums

Just about every college today offers trips to alumni. The trips can be "educational" in nature, guided by a current or retired professor who has knowledge of the subject or area, or just plain fun. Alumni trips range from one-week low-cost trips to international art jaunts that cross continents.

"People like the educational part," explains Midge Brittingham, a now-retired alumni director of Oberlin College. "The faculty accompanying the trip give three or four lectures during the course of it. Sometimes it's so physically and intellectually demanding, people come back totally exhausted—but exhilarated, too." As these trips don't come cheap, it tends to be both singles and couples in their early 70s. Many sign up for a trip every few years.

Part of the social fun, of course, is the sense of compatibility. Having attended the same college—even if it was a few decades back—adds up to having something in common. Brittingham's files of enthusiastic letters from alumni are packed with comments that it was terrific to be with all these people with a similar "history of intellectual independence" and "sense of humor."

3) Family Travel

With greater time flexibility, you have the opportunity to schedule a family trip around your relatives' busy work and school schedules. (Be aware, however, that school vacations often occur during "high season," when rates are highest.)

Many tour operators and resorts cater to multigenerational family trips, and can offer accommodations that range from simple camplike settings, where you can rent cabin-style accommodations and enjoy natural surroundings, to Club Med's famous multi-activity resorts offering something for everyone, from beachfront yoga to classes in high-wire circus trapeze. Nonprofit organizations, from church groups to museums, also offer package deals for families—with the advantage that you needn't bother with all the reservations and planning. Family reunions and travel seem to go hand in hand, judging by the fact that one in three U.S. adults has traveled to a family reunion at least once every three years, according to polls by the Travel Industry Association of America. With increasing interest in genealogy and trends toward family reunions, taking a trip with the extended family affords lots of opportunities to mix and match and get to know one another. And there are many family biking trips, too. See also Traveling with the Grandkids (page 263).

RVS: FAMILY-FRIENDLY, FLEXIBLE. Just in case you're from another planet: An RV is a "recreational vehicle" that combines transportation and temporary living quarters for travel, recreation, and camping. It's ideal for families. RV trips are becoming a classic activity of THE RETIREMENT ZONE.

Enthusiasts happily tick off a laundry list of advantages. If you keep your RV packed, you can tool off at a moment's notice. (This is especially handy if you're retired or working part time and can travel during the week to avoid traffic.) With an RV, not only can you visit the state park—you can also stay right in it, and wake up to rippling streams and wildlife within camera range. On average, RV campgrounds cost about $20 per night—a fraction of the cost of one motel room. A group of four can easily save at least $30 a day on home-cooked meals instead of eating out. You can make spur-of-the-moment changes in itinerary because you're not locked into airports and hotel reservations. The larger, more expensive units can be outfitted with full kitchenettes, comfortable sleeping arrangements, televisions, and even surround-sound stereos. Kids generally like them, so you can travel with your grandchildren (and their friends, too) and even your pets.

Sales and rentals of motorized recreational vehicles—from the modest folding camping trailer, priced at about $6,500, to the mansion motor home, priced at over $130,000—have soared in recent years. More than 10 percent of people over 55 in the United States already own one, according to a 2001 University of Michigan study. But there are drawbacks, notably that RVs guzzle a lot of gas, and you can't just park them anywhere.

Is the RV lifestyle/culture for you? The best way to find out is to kick the wheels yourself for a weekend. Check the Yellow Pages or the Web site of the Recreation Vehicle Dealers Association, (www.rvda.org) or the Go RVing Web sites (www.rvia.org and www.GoRVing.com) for local dealership listings.

4) Educational Travel and Ecotourism

Pack your notebook, your reading glasses, and camera. Pick a trip, whether with a museum, an environmental organization, your alumni organization, or your local chamber orchestra—and get ready for an educational travel experience of a lifetime. You can choose from a range of options in terms of price, destination, cotravelers (college alums, scientists, etc.) and accommodations, including some that are quite luxurious.

You might like to give the planet a hug while you're traveling and choose an itinerary or tour that will provide some benefits for local conservation. It's called ecotourism. According to the Washington-based International EcoTourism Society (www.ecotourism.org), it's the kind of travel to a natural area that "conserves the environment and improves the well-being of local people."

The nonprofit Elderhostel (www.elderhostel.org) is a pioneer and leader in the educational travel field for people over 55, with over 200,000 participants every year. Trips take you behind the scenes, to theaters, archeological digs, museums, and interesting little corners of the world. You can find at least one or two programs in every state. The trip menu includes creative workshops, intergenerational programs, traditional arts-and-sciences educational programs, birding, performing arts workshops, and service projects where you can participate in volunteer projects, from conservation to tutoring, and weekender programs that cram a lot of learning into three- or four-day courses. "It's a way of life," says one veteran educational traveler.

---

4 Questions to Ask When Choosing an Educational or EcoTourism Trip

1) **What can you expect to learn?** Whether you're traveling to a ski weekend as a beginner, or to Spain to learn Spanish, find out what level the course is. For ecotours, find out what the relationship is between the tour and the local community.

2) **Who are the instructors and fellow students/travelers?** Have your instructors taught this course or been a guide before? Always ask for references. Also, who else has signed up for the trip?

3) **What facilities are available?** Ask what the classroom and hotel accommodations are, whether you'll have access to the Internet, and whether there is an on-premises restaurant, or whatever it is that makes you happy.

4) **What is included and what's not?** Are there meals on weekends or non-course days? Are excursions and special passes (such as to museums) included in the fee? What's available for a spouse or friend traveling with you?

---

5) Tracing Your Roots

You've heard the family tales: How your great-great-grandfather came from Ukraine with nothing in his pockets and made his way . . . or how your grandmother came from Norway and found her cousin in Wisconsin . . . and how things were back in the old country.

"There's something about going to a town and seeing what it looks like," says Peter Robertson, 68, who participated with his wife in a program on genealogical studies run by a small Christian school, Samford University, based in Birmingham, Alabama. Robertson's ancestors came to the United States in the 17th and 18th centuries from England, Scotland, Northern Ireland, and Wales. Although his family had kept careful records over five generations, he was unable to track down any living relatives. However, through local and national archives, he and his wife found the streets where *her* relatives lived in the 19th century. "We walked the cobblestone streets," he says.

Robertson, a retired banker from Seattle, suggests traveling with a program, such as Samford's, with advisors who can help you navigate through records and direct your research. About twenty people go to London for several weeks to visit national archives, churches, and libraries. Armed with whatever information they can find, such as birth, death or census records, participants may branch out on their own to visit their ancestral hometowns. Organizers recommend researching as much of your history as possible beforehand to make the most out of such a trip. The National Genealogical Society (www.ngsgenealogy.org) is a great place to learn about such local groups in your area.

Many programs, which generally range in price from $2,000 to $4,000, offer the option of going as a family or private group. Doris Paulson, 73, a retired production assembler from Wisconsin, traveled to Norway, along with 33 members of her family, with Nordic Co., which specializes in Scandinavian genealogy. They wanted to see the community of Holter, north of Oslo, where their close relatives had lived before moving to the United States in 1908. "I remembered things my grandfather and father talked about," she says. "We had ideas of where to go and what to see." The highlight came when they arrived at the site where her grandparents' farm used to be. The current residents, descendants of the family who owned the farm in 1908, made copies of a stack of letters their grandmother had sent from the States. "The letters were wonderful!"

Thomas Weiss, 69, a retired professor of electrical engineering and computer science at the Massachusetts Institute of Technology, also sought to learn more about his family when he visited the Ukrainian towns of Rozhnyatov and Buchach, where his grandparents once lived. "The Jews were murdered" in this town, says Weiss, explaining that locals turned in their Jewish neighbors during World War II. He says there were "one and a half" Jews left in Buchach and none in Rozhnyatov, but no one remembered his family. Since no records were available, he photographed over 1,500 Hebrew inscriptions of headstones in cemeteries and is posting them on the Internet. "I did get some sense of what my ancestors' lives might have been like once in these small towns, but that way of life no longer exists," he says. He traveled with a program called ShtetlSchleppers, run by Jewish Gen, Inc., which organizes trips to 14 different countries to help Jews connect with their ancestral *shtetlekh*, the Yiddish term for towns.

The reasons for taking these kinds of trips vary as much as the destinations. However, many find themselves returning frequently to learn more about their families, visit new friends, or try to make a personal impact.

Corrie Jones, 72, of Indianapolis, a retiree of Eli Lilly and Company, was born and raised in Oxford, Mississippi. She and her daughter Doris have traveled to many of the 54 countries on the continent of Africa, or the Motherland, as they call it: "There is just a connection that we feel with Africa that cannot always be explained. Our friends in Africa say, 'Welcome home,' and we say, 'We are glad to be back home.'" The Jones family has spent time at Goree Island, one of the major enslavement ports in West Africa. "There is what is called the Door of No Return, where millions of enslaved Africans were shackled and packed like sardines in a ship to leave their homeland forever to be taken to North America and the Caribbean," she explains. Mrs. Jones traveled while employed, but since retirement has traveled to many countries, and makes it a point to go to Africa at least once a year. "Retirement is so sweet," she says.

The agency African American Journeys (www.africanamericanjourneys.com) aims to connect travelers to their African countries of origin by locating genealogical records in secondary countries or organizing naming ceremonies so they can be "reborn" in the African tradition.

Many veterans also want to return to the countries where they served. Military retracing has become a popular and growing travel niche. For example, Military Historical Tours (www.miltours.com) takes about a thousand veterans and their families a year to World War II, Korean, and Vietnamese battlefields. The World War II trips are the most popular, with 30 percent revisiting Iwo Jima.

Dave Thomas, 71, a former deputy sheriff from the Los Angeles area, revisited South Korea as part of the 50th anniversary of the signing of the armistice. While serving as a machine gunner for the 1st Marine division, Dave had been shot in the stomach and sent home. As part of his trip, he went back to the area where his good friend was listed as missing in action. He also wanted to show his 36-year-old daughter how he felt the American military helped the country. "I was wondering if it was all worth it," he says. "It was. The place was a pile of rubble when I was there, and they've made an amazing economic recovery. It was a real eye-opener, and very satisfying."

6) Travel in a Spiritual Direction

Although spirituality is an internal quest, traveling abroad can help you get in touch with your otherworldly self. Whether you want to see the birthplace of a religion, follow the footsteps of a prophet, or simply celebrate your faith with others, spiritual travel aims to help people better understand their place in the world and beyond. "I have heard people say, 'I'm getting ready to meet my maker. I want to check in before my ticket gets pulled,'" says Scott Scherer, president of both Catholic Travel Centre (www.gocatholictravel.com) and Trinity World Tours (www.gotrinitytours.com), which specialize in Catholic and Protestant tours and pilgrimages to countries all over the world. Retirees account for 80 to 90 percent of his business, he says. "People are searching for something more than a tour," adds the owner of a travel agency that also offers Catholic pilgrimages to Europe and the Holy Land. "People are looking for a spiritual experience."

Elizabeth Brunetti, 69, a retired bookkeeper from the San Jose area, wanted to see how Catholicism was practiced in other countries and so traveled to Hungary and Ireland with Catholic Travel Centre. She had taken tourist trips before, but hated the way the guides seemed annoyed whenever she asked about the location of the nearest church. But with a Catholic-themed tour, she enjoyed being with others who shared her faith, including a priest who traveled with the group.

"We sing on the bus. We do Hail Marys and everything," she says, adding that the group gained access to worship services at different cathedrals, abbeys, and churches, including an old Hungarian monastery. "You get a totally different perspective on your religion," says Brunetti. She also gained a new appreciation for the comforts of American Catholicism when she saw the hard wooden benches worshippers use in Ireland. "We don't know how good we have it," she says.

Many Protestant tours specialize in one tradition, such as Presbyterian, Anglican, or Methodist, and explore that branch's history. For example, Betty Meyer, 68, a former homemaker and pastor's spouse from the Tacoma area, took a trip to London to trace the life of John Wesley, founder of the United Methodist Church, on the 300th anniversary of his birth. "I wanted to delve into what made John Wesley tick," she says. "It made me understand the church better and how it came to be." She traveled with Trinity World Tours and visited the rectory where Wesley grew up and the places where he had preached and died. "It made Wesley more real," Meyer says. "I had read about him in books and heard what people had said. It made him more vivid, more alive."

Spiritual travelers should take time to thoroughly research a trip to find out just how much worshipping is involved and whether a member of the clergy will come

along. People who aren't observant may not appreciate a tour in which participants attend services several times a day. On the other hand, those who are seeking spiritual transformation may be disappointed with simply looking at historical sites. For example, although the Wesley tour gave Meyer time for spiritual reflection, she says it was more educational than religious. "It wasn't life changing," she says.

For Mamnoon Marghoob, 71, a semi-retired real estate manager from Queens, New York, his trip to the birthplace of Islam held nothing but spiritual gratification. Marghoob had traveled to Mecca in Saudi Arabia before, to fulfill his Muslim duty of pilgrimage, or *hajj*; but he wanted to re-experience that intense spiritual connection, shared by millions of followers. "It's a vacation which takes you completely away from your connection to this world," he says. "It's closeness to your Creator. Consciousness of God is ever-present in deciding your actions. This is your spiritual growth." Marghoob warns that the trip is strenuous, requiring a three-day journey with long walks, long-awaited bus rides from Mecca to Mena to Arafaat to Muzdalfah to Medina, and sleeping in a tent city. He advises that participants be in good health.

While such spiritual tours offer the chance to celebrate faith, sometimes they can have the opposite effect. Although Ruth Kriegel's parents left Poland after World War I, she lost three uncles and an aunt during the Holocaust. Kriegel, 75, a housewife from the Boston area, and her husband wanted to educate their grandson about his heritage and his family's history as part of his present for his bar mitzvah. "I've always wanted to go back to the land of my parents' birth and see what life was like," she says. On a World Jewish Heritage Tour with the company Ayelet Tours, led by a professor from Union College, they visited historic synagogues and also concentration camps. "You realize how tragic life has been for European Jews," she says, adding that the experience made her less religious.

As you know, spiritual travel isn't always rooted in an established religious tradition. One man traveled to Costa Rica a couple of years ago to practice yoga and meditate for a week just to try a new experience and was surprised at the power of meditation. "The meditation was phenomenal," he said. "The best I can explain it is that your mind shuts down. It was just a blank."

"The act of paying attention to your breath is a deeply spiritual thing. Meditation helps everyone to become closer to the Divine without defining what 'Divine' is," says a teacher who leads these tours.

7) Special Interests

It's fun to pursue special interests when traveling. For instance, about one in five Americans went on a garden tour, visited a botanical garden, attended a gardening show or festival, or participated in some other garden-related activity in the past five years. And gambling trips are hugely popular, of course, with a wide range of accommodations and environments, from Las Vegas to Atlantic City. Industry sources say that trips that include gambling account for 8 percent of all U.S. travel, generating 78.6 million person-trips in 2002.

Some people, when traveling, make a point of contacting others who share their professional or avocational passions. An elderly radiologist makes a point to visit the radiology department of a hospital in another city; an American judge always stops in at a courthouse when she travels to Europe. Ann Reiss Lane of Los Angeles says, "When I was on the L.A. Fire Commission, I used to visit fire departments whenever we'd travel abroad."

Marvin Mausner of New Jersey recounts, "My wife and I belong to the Amateur Chamber Music Players Association. It publishes a book listing amateur musicians all over the world. When we travel, my wife will generally arrange in advance for us to play music with people in the various countries that we visit. We have played chamber music in London; Dublin, Ireland; Edinburgh, Scotland; Haifa, Israel; Budapest, Hungary; Prague, Czechoslovakia; and in Paris and Beijing. In Prague we spent a whole evening playing with people during a period of great ferment in Czechoslovakia. [The president, Alexander Dubcek, had been recently deposed and the Communists had taken over.] We spent a couple of hours of heated political discussion in French, German, and English, since we knew no Czech and our disagreements were eased by the fact that we had just spent an evening playing music together. In China, we were welcomed with open arms by the people with whom we played music. It's been true all over the world. It's a cliché, but music is an international language. It opens the door to getting to know people better."

8) Combining Travel with Volunteering

Americans over 50 are signing up in great numbers to volunteer their time and skills abroad. They're teaching English in China, building homes for the poor in Nicaragua, researching coral reefs in Kenya, running health clinics in India, and caring for orphaned babies in Romania.

Folks in THE RETIREMENT ZONE form a remarkable talent pool. As a group, they possess skills and savvy that volunteer organizations covet. They're doctors, nurses, teachers, scientists, business executives, contractors, and computer experts. Or they're self-starters who can step in and take charge of a project. Men and women who've been factory workers or at-home parents, cooks or counselors, sales clerks or secretaries have life skills—and they may welcome the chance to be involved in something entirely different.

As Peace Corps volunteers in a Bulgarian village with 40 percent unemployment, Robert "Rel" Davis, 66, and wife Edith Sloan, 61, helped find new ways to bring money into the economy. For example, Sloan, a retired school principal, taught quilting classes and set up a women's cooperative to sell handmade goods overseas. And Davis, a former journalist and minister, worked as an economic advisor, setting up a computer system, writing grants, and founding education programs for the local orphanage.

And because many traditional societies revere the wisdom that comes only with age, older volunteers are often embraced and welcomed by communities in ways that idealistic 22-year-olds are not. "We were older and looked up to," says Davis. "They get the best seat in the house!" adds a Peace Corps spokeswoman.

When Frank Braun, 76, a retired professor from Minneapolis, was helping to build a health clinic in Kenya, the villagers asked him to teach an American geography class in the local school. "People smiled and greeted us everywhere we walked," he says of his group from Global Citizens Network (www.global citizens.org), which organizes a dozen volunteer trips abroad each year.

The biggest draws are the rewards of helping the needy and the opportunity to get to know foreign cultures up close. "If I hadn't been there, all I would know about Thailand would be from *The King and I*," says Pamela Jay-Paralikis, 56, a retired computer consultant from Boston. On a trip with Cross-Cultural Solutions (www.crossculturalsolutions.org), which pairs volunteers with development organizations in some 13 countries, Jay-Paralikis did fieldwork in the Northeast and met many Thai people who had never seen Americans—except on television.

Kathleen Ruff, 63, a retired teacher from Boulder, Colorado, would share beers in the evenings with teachers from a Chinese high school where she taught

English for a month through Volunteers For Peace (www.vfp.org), a clearing-house for thousands of volunteer organizations around the world. "I was there as an ordinary fellow worker alongside them and seeing what their everyday life was like," Ruff says. "I thought that was a real privilege. To get an inside opportunity like that was amazing."

Jack Bartlett, 74, a former bank executive from Aurora, Colorado, had traveled abroad on organized tours before, but liked the feeling of making a difference through his work with Habitat for Humanity (www.habitat.org), which builds low-cost homes around the world. "There's a definite high in doing good or imagining that you're doing good," he says. "There's a lot of people who get 'Habitat-itis' after the first build. We become Habitat junkies." Bartlett has participated in nearly two dozen builds in six years.

George Benson, 76, a retired horticulturist from Mill Valley, California, has done everything from studying bees and orchids in Brazil to documenting lion behavior in Kenya to taking water samples in the Gobi Desert on his twelve projects through Earthwatch (www.earthwatch.org), which specializes in environmental volunteerism. "When I get old, I can sit on the beach," he says.

Some volunteers seek as many different experiences as possible; others form attachments to places they've visited. Rita Corcoran, 62, a retired nurse from Chicago, volunteered in a Romanian clinic for orphaned and abandoned babies through Global Volunteers (www.globalvolunteers.org), which runs short-term projects in 18 countries. But after spending three weeks holding and feeding special-needs children in November 2002, she returned three months later to see how her charges were doing. "At that age, they change month to month," she says. "Global sends teams there every month. You realize you're part of that process. And that's a very good and very rewarding thing to know."

While the work is fulfilling, volunteers warn that it can be exhausting and frustrating if community members aren't motivated. And it can be hard to adjust to another culture and language. During her two years in the Peace Corps, Edith Sloan was often homesick. "The commitment we made was worth it," she says. "It was one of the most difficult things we've ever done, but one of the most rewarding."

Volunteer opportunities fall into two categories: long- and short-term. The Peace Corps (www.peacecorps.gov), started by John F. Kennedy in the 1960s to promote peace through international development, is the best-known group when it comes to long-term assignments. Tours run two years, and placements depend on volunteers' skills. Some recent Peace Corps assignments have included educating locals in Malawi about HIV and AIDS, training people in computers and developing small businesses in Ukraine, and giving agricultural advice in Honduras. Of the 7,000 volunteers currently serving in the Peace Corps, more than 400 are over the age of 50, including some who are in their 80s. Volunteers with health concerns can be assigned to areas with adequate medical facilities and participants receive monthly living allowances, which do not interfere with Social Security benefits. And the Peace Corps work is expense-free for these long-term assignments, making it a wonderful way to travel and experience new cultures for those who also want to be doing something meaningful and beneficial at the same time.

The American office of Doctors Without Borders (www.doctorswithout borders.org), known internationally as *Médecins Sans Frontières*, sends about 120 volunteer doctors, nurses, and other medical professionals for six months to a year to more than 80 countries with poor healthcare facilities. Founded in 1971 by French physicians, Doctors Without Borders welcomes retirees, who may find themselves running an AIDS treatment clinic in Africa or operating in a Sri Lankan surgical unit. Participants receive housing, transportation, meals, and a monthly stipend.

Dr. Gildon Beall, 75, the former head of the AIDS clinic at Los Angeles County Harbor-UCLA Medical Center Hospital, spent a year in Thailand treating AIDS patients. He liked the feeling that he was doing useful work to stem the global AIDS crisis. "There was a big impact in terms of patients," Dr. Beall says. "Many wouldn't be alive if it weren't for our efforts." However, he said the size of the problem was so huge he sometimes felt as if he barely made a dent.

Short-term projects—a couple of weeks up to several months—tend to be better bets in some ways, because you can check out how you like volunteering before making a long commitment. Groups such as Cross-Cultural Solutions, Global Citizens Network, Elderhostel, Global Volunteers, Earthwatch, and Habitat for Humanity organize short-term trips with a dozen or so people. However, participants in these projects are usually responsible for airfare, and in some cases fees, which, including accommodation, meals, and donations to the community, can range from $700 to $3,000. Habitat runs two programs: the Global Village program, which attracts all age groups, and the RV-Caravaner program, which is made up mostly of retirees who travel by mobile homes and participate in builds in New Zealand and Newfoundland (and also the United States).

One notable exception is Volunteers For Peace (VFP), which charges about $200 to place volunteers in an international "workcamp." Volunteers pay for transportation, but meals and lodging are covered. The biggest difference is that the more expensive programs attract a large percentage of retirees, while

Volunteers For Peace participants are younger. The VFP program (www.vfp.org) does promote several "mixed age" camps and offers opportunities to teach English directly in a community, but you should ask about the makeup of a camp if bunking down with a group of college kids is not your thing.

And don't forget archaeological digs. The best way to learn more about these is to request the Archaeological Fieldwork Opportunities Bulletin from the Archaeological Institute of America (www.archeological.org), which provides contact information for excavations all over the world.

 ## HEALTHVIEWS

If you are going abroad, it is a good idea to get a medical checkup (and vaccines if necessary) six or eight weeks in advance of your departure. Prepare a clearly written list of important prescription medications you plan to carry. Also, find out what your insurance covers outside the United States and if you can purchase a supplemental travel policy. The Centers for Disease Control and Prevention (CDC) Web site shows vaccine requirements, information on specific illnesses, and more (www.cdc.gov/travel). The U.S. State Department Web site has requirements for passports, visas, and immunizations, and also some references to English-speaking doctors and country profiles (travel.state.gov/foreignentryreqs.html). A good general overview of travel tips is available from the American Academy of Family Physicians (www.familydoctor.org).

 ## YOUR MONEY MATTERS

Travel can be expensive, of course. If you're a trip-o-holic, here are some ways to do what you love without losing your shirt.

- **Destination:** You can save a bundle by choosing sites that are off the beaten path. If you love to ski, forget the Alps—try Bulgaria instead. Trade pricey hotel rooms in Cancún for a spot in quieter, cheaper, nearby Isla Mujeres.
- **Money:** Watching currency moves is another smart travel strategy. In 2003, costs in Argentina, Brazil, and Uruguay were a third of what they were in the late 1990s because of a severe economic downturn. A few years ago, the strong American dollar made Europe a steal for American tourists.

- **Deals:** Travel deals abound in the so-called off season and shoulder season, when tourists are few and sites uncrowded. Tuscany in January? Mexico in July? But you get what you pay for. European cities are cold in the winter and anywhere south of San Francisco can be deathly hot in the summer.
- **Special deals for seniors:** Some discounts start as young as age 50. Check out airline clubs, coupons, and other promotions especially for seniors. When booking hotels always ask for senior discounts and then compare them with other discounts for which you may be eligible; most hotel chains offer both, so shop the best deal.
- **Value for money:** Some tour operations run by internationals living in the United States deal only with their native regions—Sceptre Travel for Ireland, or Pacha Tours for Turkey, for example. Packages offered by these companies may be more in-depth, more varied, and less expensive than those destinations offered by the larger tour operators.

  Also, check publications such as *Consumer Reports*, which noted in a 2004 issue, for instance, that "blind" online travel services (where you say what you want at what price) don't save you money more than 50 percent of the time.
- **Air:** The Internet has exposed the wizard behind the curtain of travel agencies. Try www.orbitz.com, www.expedia.com, www.travelocity.com, and www.cheaptickets.com.
- **House Swaps:** A house swap is becoming an increasingly popular way to feel like a native in a foreign place. Two sites that pair up people and their houses are www.homeexchange.com and www.trading-homes.com.
- **Volunteer:** If you do have to shell out some cash for your trip, what's the best way to make it pay off? Why not try a volunteer vacation? As long as the majority of your trip is devoted to volunteering you can deduct the cost of airfare, hotel, and food from your taxes.

If you're reading this book for a spouse, friend, or parent . . . If you're going along on the trip, what fun! Travel that suits a person's pace and interests can't be beat—especially for active older parents. But if your retired spouse is desperate to see the world today, and you're still tied down or building that career, then there's a lot of discussion and compromise in your future.

Trips that Make You Think

Judie Fernandez is a 65-year-old retired lawyer, and her 72-year-old husband is a retired judge. They live in Menlo Park, California.

"We started taking European trips about fifteen years ago, traveling on our own at first, including driving in Europe. About six years ago, we wanted to go to Sicily but were unwilling to do it on our own, so we tried Elderhostel. Concerned we would be with 'old' people who aren't mobile and are cranky (what a bigot I was!), we were very happy to join the group of lively, stimulating people for the two-week program. It was great! I've been on nine Elderhostel trips since. In March we head to Portugal and Spain for three weeks.

"The first Elderhostel we took I was fifty-eight. I was scared—who will be on this trip? Will they be walking with walkers? Hard of hearing? But you meet really interesting people from all educational levels—engineers, journalists, doctors, lawyers, judges, teachers, librarians, homemakers, craftsmen, and small-business owners. And it's not a hostel-oriented group anymore. You stay in good hotels. In India they are five-star but in the U.S. or an expensive country they might be three-stars. The accommodations are pleasant and comfortable with on-site restaurants, hair dryers, and so forth in the rooms—but not swanky and elegant.

"They give you a broad view of everything—a little about folk art, music, literature, art, history, and architecture and contemporary politics. I've 'seen' London, Paris, and Rome. This is educationally oriented travel, more academic.

"In China we learned brush painting and about the development of pictograph language from ancient to modern. In India, a year after September 11, 2001, they brought us to the Gandhi Institute in New Delhi and the director spoke about what Gandhi would do in light of this new form of warfare, terrorism. In Russia we were out of the hotel by eight a.m. every day and came home at six or seven p.m. We had home visits, and lectures at Moscow University, two of them by economics professors. In Florence we had college-level lectures on art and architecture and how Brunelleschi's dome was built. I'd been to Florence five times and never gotten so much out of it. In Mongolia we stayed in tents called ger *(a yurt, in Russian).*

"These are not shopping trips; they make you think. Traveling on your own, you spend so much time trying to figure out how to get around—how to change money, where's the Internet café, where's the train to the Taj Mahal. At first, the thought of getting on the tour bus made me gag, but I got used to it. At the end of the day, when you're tired and have to figure out how to get back to the hotel, instead you just hop on the bus, take a nap, and you're there.

"You sit at big round tables for dinner with eight to ten people, so there's companionship at meals. The international Elderhostel trips are twenty-five to thirty percent single. Not entirely women, some are single men. I talked to one man who is eighty-seven and has taken sixty programs, mostly in the U.S. His wife died five years ago. So he basically goes home, checks the mail, pays the bills, and goes off on a trip every couple of months.

"I think of the trips as mini college courses that include travel. You feel like a college kid again but no exams, homework, or papers to do. I look at the Elderhostel catalogue and say, 'I want to do every one of them.'"

From Florida to Greece

Robbins Denham, who retired in 1992 at age 65, had worked as a contractor. His most recent job was home improvement in Tampa, Florida. In retirement, he became involved as a tutor at the local computer center and joined a program for peer education at the University of South Florida's Learning in Retirement Institute, where he began to write poetry, study conversational Spanish, and take courses as wide-ranging as the history of Islam and "What Everybody Should Know about the Weather." Among the thirty courses he took was one on ancient Greece, led by a retired surgeon who had developed an interest in Greece and the Holy Land and had been there about 15 times. That led to the trip of a lifetime: a ten-day land tour and island-hopping cruise in Greece.

"What did we learn? Man, we learned that the Greeks had it made, two thousand–plus years ago. It was just awesome to see the beauty of the culture;

the (ancient) places excavated and restored, and the museums that had been established on the actual sites. I appreciated this trip so much because I had been in a class on the history of Greece. We went to the temple of Poseidon, beautifully set on a hill overlooking the Aegean Sea, and you could imagine the ships coming in. In Piraeus we were eating in a restaurant on the seashore and the waiter threw breadcrumbs to the fish just ten feet away.

"It meant a great deal to have some knowledge of what I might see there. I remember going to Santorini. I thought, why build on the top of the hill? Of course then you realize that the hill is a steep cliff that goes straight up within two hundred yards of where we anchored and there's no place else to build. You can't build on the cliff. And it was wonderful seeing the windmills and the remains of Minoan civilization, three thousand or more years old, covered up by a volcano eruption and discovered in the last hundred years. They even had a groundwater and a toilet system. Amazing! You learn a lot and you learn in a way that you can fully appreciate what you've studied."

Resource Guide

PUBLICATIONS

Travel Unlimited: Uncommon Adventures for the Mature Traveler by Alison Gardner (Avalon Travel, 2000).

The World: Travels 1950-2000 by Jan Morris (W. W. Norton, 2003).

ORGANIZATIONS AND WEB SITES

Adventure

Leading online provider of information about active travel and the outdoor lifestyle: http://away.com

Elderhostel
11 Avenue de Lafayette
Boston, MA 02111-1746
877-426-8056
www.elderhostel.org

ElderTreks
597 Markham Street
Toronto ON M6G 2L7
800-741-7956
www.eldertreks.com

Discounted Fares

Cheapseats travel agent:
www.cheapseats.com

Expedia Travel:
www.expedia.com

Orbitz—The Travel Site:
www.orbitz.com

Travelocity:
www.travelocity.com

Educational Travel

(Note: Check museums, university alumni clubs, and professional associations. Elderhostel is listed under Adventure, page 205.)

Grand Circle Travel
800-959-0405
www.gct.com

Saga Holidays
1161 Boylston Street
Boston, MA 02215
800-343-0273
www.sagaholidays.com

Senior Summer School:
The Education Vacation
PO Box 4424
Deerfield Beach, FL 33442-4424
800-847-2466
www.seniorsummerschool.com

Health

American Academy of
Family Physicians:
www.familydoctor.org/311.xml

Centers for Disease Control:
www.cdc.gov/travel

U.S. State Department:
travel.state.gov/foreignentryreqs.html

Home Exchange

Home Exchange.com, Inc.
(with a special link for seniors):
www.homeexchange.com

Tracing Your Roots (Africa)

African American Journeys
1000 North Humphreys Street
Suite 222
PMB 181
Flagstaff, AZ 86001
800-231-9811
www.africanamericanjourneys.com

Henderson Travel & Tours
7961 Eastern Avenue
Silver Spring, MD 20910
800-327-2309
www.hend.com

Tracing Your Roots (Jewish)

ShtetlSchleppers
JewishGen, Inc.
2951 Marina Bay Drive
Suite 130-472
League City, TX 77573
281-535-2200
www.jewishgen.org/shtetlschleppers

Tracing Your Roots (Military)

Military Historical Tours, Inc.
4600 Duke Street, Suite 420
Alexandria, VA 22304
800-722-9501
www.miltours.com

Tracing Your Roots (United States and Northern Europe)

Federation of Genealogical Societies
PO Box 200940
Austin, TX 78720-0940
888-FGS-1500
www.fgs.org

National Genealogical Society
4527 17th Street North
Arlington, VA 22207-2399
800-473-0060
www.ngsgenealogy.org

Volunteering Long-Term

Doctors Without Borders
333 Seventh Avenue, 2nd Floor
New York, NY 10001-5004
212-679-6800
www.doctorswithoutborders.org

Peace Corps
The Paul D. Coverdell Peace Corps
    Headquarters
1111 20th Street NW
Washington, DC 20526
800-424-8580
www.peacecorps.gov

Volunteering Short-Term

Cross-Cultural Solutions
2 Clinton Place
New Rochelle, NY 10801
800-380-4777
www.crossculturalsolutions.org

Earthwatch Institute
3 Clock Tower Place, Suite 100
Box 75
Maynard, MA 01754
800-776-0188
www.earthwatch.org

Global Citizens Network
130 N. Howell Street
St. Paul, MN 55104
800-644-9292
www.globalcitizens.org

Global Volunteers
375 East Little Canada Road
St. Paul, MN 55117-1628
800-487-1074
www.globalvolunteers.org

Habitat For Humanity International
Global Village and RV-Caravaners
121 Habitat Street
Americus, GA 31709-3498
229-924-6935, Ext. 2551 or 2552
www.habitat.org

Volunteers For Peace
1034 Tiffany Road
Belmont, VT 05730
802-259-2759
www.vfp.org

CHAPTER 16

Spiritual Seeking

Writing about spirituality is like trying to describe smell or taste in words. Words are inadequate. The experience—of rightness, flow, discovery, connectedness, joy—is better suited to poetry or music than rational arguments or mundane language.

That said, the following is an attempt to scope out the spiritual landscape, because this is indeed a corner of THE RETIREMENT ZONE to which many people travel: In a survey conducted by the National Council on the Aging, two out of every three people over 65 rated spirituality as very important in having a meaningful, vital life.

SPIRITUALITY À LA CARTE

"I am in a Jubilee community, a Christian community," recounts Bill Bailey of North Carolina. "It has a different approach to worship than either the Protestant or Roman Catholic traditions. Jubilee offers a worship service that is a call to life and includes art, interpretive dancing, singing, and dramatic presentations."

There are an estimated 350,000 faith organizations in the United States—roughly one for every 800 Americans. And new ones—like Bill Bailey's—evolve all the time. "I have a deep passion that started with me in 1966 on the future church—of what it and spirituality would look like. I arrived at the conclusion that the shell we were living in for last 50 years was deteriorating rapidly. I came to Asheville to pursue avant-garde religious communities that are breaking new ground, new earth religions."

The needs of the soul may be eternal. Still, how people satisfy their individual soul cravings varies enormously across time and place. Princeton sociologist Robert Wuthnow, documenting the evolution of American spirituality, points out in his book, *After Heaven: Spirituality in America Since the 1950s* (University of California Press, 1998), how our spiritual search has changed. He notes a shift from a spirituality defined by geography—a specific house of worship in a specific neighborhood—to a "spirituality of seeking," which includes art and music, personal reflection, encounters with the sacred, and development of the inner self.

A 20th-century view would hold that retirement-age people will stick with their longstanding religious or spiritual practices, meaning that they will continue to go to that same church, in that same neighborhood. That may be true for those born in the 1930s, who came of age in the conservative 1950s. But as the baby boomers move along in years, their eclecticism will show up in choices of spiritual path, as well.

For now, you can enjoy spiritual options, a la carte. The minister's granddaughter now practices yoga and meditates; the rabbi's son has become a student of therapeutic massage. Approaching 80, and a practicing Quaker, Pennsylvanian Mary Wood says, "I am very interested in Buddhism, and I meditate daily. At the public library I pick out books—on Buddhism, psychology, religion and science, studies of Jesus, religious biography, and so on." The quest for the sacred and divine has moved beyond the confines of the religious traditions into which we were born.

There's a world of diversity. You can find information on African, Caribbean, Native American, and Far Eastern religions. There are history and practice guidelines for Islam, in both its American Black Muslim and Middle Eastern forms. New Agers can pick from a rainbow spectrum of beliefs, personal and group practice, and psychology loosely called "the human potential movement." Others may seek to experience and practice polytheistic earth religions; shamanism, witchcraft, voodoo, or delve into traditions such as Jewish and Sufi mysticism, and Hinduism. What comes from one context is sometimes unceremoniously slapped onto another. So for instance, as though a mischievous Puck were at work, spiritual freeform dancing becomes part of a standard Christian worship service in Boston.

This is a rich, rich smorgasbord of traditions. It entices with the aromas of different insights, exotic doors to revelation, greater personal meanings, and the allure of new community. And undergirding it all is that central bedrock American tenet: freedom of religion.

There are those for whom "spirituality" is so loosely defined that they'd seriously call a really fresh imported truffle mushroom—or a beautifully played rendition of "Rhapsody in Blue"—a "soulful experience." And who's to judge? If you're feeling spiritual hunger, don't assume it's the same old fare. The menu's been expanded.

WHAT IS "SPIRITUALITY?"

Thanks to communications technology there are religious messages everywhere: on television, on the Internet, in books, even in the music industry.

It's a noisy cacophony. Evangelical Christianity has made a huge impact on our society, from Jimmy Carter's public embrace of religion in his book *Living Faith* (Three Rivers Press, 1998) to a powerful conservative political block. Tens of millions of mainstream believers attend services, and buy books, tape recordings, and videos featuring religious themes. Others support a sizeable economy of alternative or New Age practices. We are deluged with divisive public debate about the role of religion in education, abortion law, and delivery of basic social services to the poor and needy.

But what is spirituality? It's hard to define. Medical researcher Dr. David Cella of Northwestern University, who has studied the effect of belief on cancer patients, says it's "that which allows a person to experience transcendent meaning in life, to put one's perspective of suffering into some broader context." Gallup's 2003 report on America's "Spiritual Index" points out that for some people, spiritual life is involved with "inner feelings," such as a connection to a higher power, while for others the focus is on "outer commitment," that is, service to the community, society, or individuals. In an informal survey for this book, people say they recognize the life of the soul, spirit, or universal psyche as

- a hunger for something beyond the day-to-day material world;
- a gut sense that something connects each of us to a greater whole, it spans generations, links humankind;
- an inner energy;
- an intuitive grasp that there's some larger pattern, beyond our individual smallness;
- a feeling of "rightness," "belonging," "flow," "discovery and joy."

Spirituality is no longer necessarily connected to religion or a deity, whether that's Allah, Jesus, Buddha, or another God figure. An elderly German Jewish immigrant regularly attends religious services and says, "I am very Jewish and very unreligious. I go, I sing the songs, I know the Hebrew prayers. But if you put a gun at my head and say, Is there a God? I would say I haven't the faintest idea."

As a minister, 72-year-old Bill Bailey says the measure of spirituality is inner change: "If you come to a church and leave the same way, you didn't gain anything. People often think worship starts in the church. Uh-uh. The church is a refueling station, it is a community where a person can remember, rehearse, share, and grow in their own spirituality and service to the world."

Making Time for It to Happen

Traditional wisdom holds that by setting aside definite times for your inner life, there's the opportunity for "something to happen." Which isn't to say that every time a person meditates, or does yoga, or prays, they feel enlightened. By making time, though, you are clearing the weeds so that something new can grow.

Paying Attention: Intentionality

Exploring your spiritual potential takes some investment of self, too. Whether you use chanting, drumming, meditation, ritual dance, prayer, or walking in the autumn leaves, the moment of spiritual connection doesn't often happen if you are looking elsewhere. Quaker Douglas Steere, in a 1967 pamphlet entitled "On Being Present Where You Are" (available free online from Pendle Hill publications, www.pendlehill.org/pendle_hill_pamphlets.htm), writes of being present "as a readiness to respect and to stand in wonder and openness before the mysterious life and influence of the other."

Coexistence of the Sacred and the Everyday

The intuitive, heart-oriented, intangible world of the soul can meld with fast paced 21st-century life. As a 58-year-old Jewish-Buddhist-atheist banker puts it, "Here I am, driving across the Golden Gate Bridge in my BMW convertible—graying hair, a business suit, cell phone, laptop in the back, on my way to a meeting with my investment portfolio manager. Before the meeting, I'm going to fit in a drumming session at the local ashram. As far as I'm concerned, it all fits."

How can these two dimensions, the spiritual and the mundane, coexist? One informs and enriches the other. "Nothing prevents you from being an insurance agent and going through different stages of the soul. The notion of 'return,' the last stage, is that you come back to ordinary life even after you've had profound experiences," says Harry R. Moody, co-author of *The Five Stages of the Soul: Charting the Spiritual Passages that Shape Our Lives* (Anchor Books, 1997).

Reaping the Rewards of an Inner Voyage: Understanding, Gratitude, Forgiveness

Talk to someone engaged in an active spiritual life, and they will tell you what the personal benefits are: a sense of peace, wonderful if sometimes fleeting; serenity; self-acceptance; insight; a broader perspective; and life with purpose. They may also add that the noisy demands of the ego, the inner voice—the one that criticizes, directs, demands, and chastises—quiets down somewhat.

A spiritual perspective can help deal with real challenges, such as forgiving old grudges and accepting life's injustices.

It provides a kind of guidance. As John Bell in Tennessee says, "I feel like God must have put me on this earth for some reason. I think we should utilize every day that we have, to do as much as we possibly can because, you know, there's a lot of need in this world. I think that sometimes we take for granted the blessing of good health or being able to financially do the things that you want to do."

And there are definite comforts to belonging to a spiritual community: friends and contacts, a place to celebrate traditions, comfort in time of need, and a place to go for perspective. This can be particularly wonderful for those of us who feel isolated after a life transition, whether that's leaving the full-time workforce or moving far from children or to a new community.

Pop singer Madonna's hit song "Material Girl" captured part of the American psyche. But as materialistic as we are, there's a parallel trend. National opinion polls conducted in 2002 and 2003 found that

- Six in ten Americans say that their faith is involved in every aspect of their lives, and almost that many report having talked about their faith at work in the past day.
- Nearly half consider themselves "religious," 40 percent consider themselves "spiritual," and about 10 percent consider themselves both. About half report attending services on a weekly basis.
- Seven in ten people say that their faith gives them meaning and purpose in daily life, that they belong to a religious group, and that they feel "the need to experience spiritual growth in their daily life."
- About six in ten people aged 30 to 49 and seven in ten of those 50 to 64 say they belong to a church, mosque, or synagogue.

Based on over a thousand interviews of people over 65 conducted in January 2000 for National Council on the Aging, Harris Interactive, Inc. shows that next to family and health, spirituality ranks third in importance as a key to a "meaningful, vital life."

 INSIDER'S GUIDE: 10 Pathways

1) SOLITUDE AND NATURE

A trip to the Grand Canyon certainly puts things in perspective. But you don't have to go that far to experience nature; even in the city, it's all around us. "If you can look at a tree and say, 'how beautiful,' you're lucky," says former dentist Ed Micone, an artist, poet, and gardening enthusiast from Summit, New Jersey, who calls his retirement "an age of sort of aesthetic excitement." Just take off your blinkers to get this pleasure from your everyday life. As Micone observes, "I play golf with corporate guys and I'll say, 'Well look at that beautiful tree,' and they'll say, 'Micone, what the hell's wrong with you? Hit the goddamn ball!' See, they don't take time to smell the roses."

2) MEDITATION 101

As one retiree explained, "Meditation is ideal for a person who is a seeker. You do it in the morning and you do it in the evening and you don't worry; you don't make a mood out of it. You just do it and go about your ordinary life. That appeals to me. It is so practical. It is just gaining rest to be ready for activity; forget the content of what you were doing and there you are."

John Ong, age 76, spent 24 years as a professor at the College of Engineering at the University of Wisconsin in Milwaukee, and also worked in industry. He became interested in the Transcendental Meditation technique shortly after his first wife suddenly died, leaving him with four adolescent girls to raise. As he describes it, "You sit quietly and just think the special sound, the mantra. Instead of your thoughts going continually from the source to the outside, the meditation takes it to the inside, then it gets interrupted by another thought; in that process of interrupting, deep diving in and coming out, stress in the nervous system is released."

He says that people often make the mistake of associating mental technique with exercise: "We're trying to relax, but if we force ourselves to relax, it is not going to protect us." He explains, "The alternation of rest and activity helps cement the experience of silence. Over the years more and more silence, serenity, quiet, peace, and healing, you name it, gets cemented into yourself." And, he adds, "Meditation helps develop spiritual qualities and caring. It retrains the mind to control thoughts and feelings. It's a tool for life."

There are many forms of meditation, some with mantras or other special rituals.

3) PERSONAL PRAYER

What could possibly be more daunting than addressing the divine? And half the battle is sustaining the effort despite your own uncertainty. Yet most Americans *do* pray, according to the pollsters. A 2003 Gallup survey projects that nearly 7 in 10 "find hope from faith" when faced with a crisis, and 3 in 4 believe "God is actively involved in their lives." In 2001, the same pollsters found that only about 40 percent of American adults attend religious services regularly—but twice as many pray frequently.

4) FAITH-BASED COMMUNITY SERVICE AND SOCIAL JUSTICE PROGRAMS

Over 100 million Americans provide service through their church, synagogue, mosque, or other religious group. Most religious congregations offer an avenue for service or activism.

At Manhattan's progressive B'nai Jeshurun synagogue, there's a great deal of focus on service, called *tikkun olam* (which is Hebrew for "repair of the world"). Their list of social action and justice projects reflects that of many religious organizations: assistance to the homeless, AIDS, holiday food deliveries and visits, food collection for the hungry, interfaith programs, tutoring, programs at nursing homes as well as environmental issues and peace activities.

Charitable efforts such as collecting goods for disaster relief, helping stock a food pantry, or working with abused women are important direct-service programs that aid individuals in crisis. But they won't change the system. That's why many faith communities also seek systemic change through what are commonly called social justice programs. For instance, the United Church of Christ Web site (www.ucc.org/justice/issues.htm) features an A-to-Z index of more than a hundred social issues, from "Appalachia" to "xenophobia." Staff and lay people from faith organizations lobby, write letters to newspaper editors, and speak at forums regarding such issues as environmental or civil rights policy. The National Council of the Churches of Christ in the USA, like many other groups, organizes national legislative campaigns in Washington (www.nccusa.org).

Many religious organizations organize programs abroad that combine community service or public education with community prayer.

5) CARING FOR THE GOOD EARTH

We all breathe the same air and are warmed by the same sun. Taking the initiative to care for the planet is yet another route toward spiritual connectedness.

In Texas, Sister Rosemary Cicchitti, now age 78, worked with Mexican immigrants in the Rio Grande Valley area for a dozen years, after retiring at age 65 from administration and teaching with the Missionary Sisters of the Immaculate Heart of Mary. In helping immigrants to develop a revolving loan fund to purchase their plot of land, she seized on an opportunity to help introduce technologies to conserve energy and water, such as a compost toilet, and a solar hot water heater and oven. She says, "I believed in the innate resources that people had, and that together we could make life and this little piece of earth a little bit better. My ministry was based on wanting to enhance the quality of life for people, to show that life is more than watching television or making money."

What can one person really do to make a difference? Nine things, says the Center for a New American Dream, and what's more, they prove it. "We don't have to shiver in the dark or droop in the heat in order to protect the environment," said Betsy Taylor, the Center's executive director. Cut out a 20-mile car trip once a week and save 1,000 pounds of carbon dioxide in a year, says the Maryland-based advocacy organization. Install water-saving devices and save almost 8,000 gallons of water a year. Install energy-efficient lightbulbs—and get your friends to do so, as well. "Americans care about the planet, and individually they are ready to change their behavior—they just need to know that their actions have a real impact," added Ms. Taylor. So you don't get discouraged, go to the Web site to see the environmental benefits of nine simple everyday actions using a real-time online calculator at www.newdream.org/faith.

It may not seem "spiritual" to change a lightbulb. But imagine, if every American cared enough to follow these recommendations for a decade, how much cleaner and greener would God's good earth be?

6) LETTING GO: FORGIVENESS, GRATITUDE, COMPASSION

For many, the challenges of relationships define the spiritual terrain. De-emphasizing of personal agendas: learning to forgive, to let go, and to accept can be life-changing transitions. Coming to terms with having transgressed or hurt someone, with having behaved immorally, or with another's immoral acts can be the first step toward acceptance, having richer, more honest relationships, and peace.

Learning from the wisdom of different great traditions—through stories, parables, and models—can pave the way. Traditionalists might be uplifted by *Candles in the Dark: A Treasury of the World's Most Inspiring Parables* by Todd Outcalt (John Wiley & Sons, 2002). *How Good Do We Have to Be? A New Understanding of Guilt and Forgiveness* by Harold S. Kushner (Back Bay Books, 1997) offers insights by a popular writer on spiritual themes. The topic of compassion alone has generated numerous writings, including an early book by the prolific Henri J. M. Nouwen, *Compassion: A Reflection on the Christian Life* (Image Books, 1983), whereas Lorne Ladner, PhD, presents a contemporary Eastern view in *The Lost Art of Compassion: Discovering the Practice of Happiness in the Meeting of Buddhism and Psychology* (Harper San Francisco, 2004).

How to start? This is an introspective process. Depending on your bent, you might want to peruse books such as these, or you might benefit from having a private conversation with a minister, rabbi, or mentor; attending a spiritual retreat (see the following section); or joining a spiritually oriented men's or women's discussion group.

7) RETREATS

A cornucopia of possibilities awaits the person seeking to try a formal retreat. There are luxurious retreats complete with massage, personal trainers, weight reduction programs, healthy eating, and gorgeous surroundings, along with the opportunity to take spiritual workshops. At Kalani Honua Conference and Retreat Center on Hawaii's Big Island (www.kalani.com) you can play on the beach, do t'ai chi, or take classes such as Painting Your Personal Mythology and Journey into Your Inner Power. Others adapt Native American practices, such as sweat lodges or Eastern religious practices. At some retreats you can participate in groups that talk about personal growth and spiritual issues; at others you observe silence. Or you might follow in the footsteps of painter Georgia O'Keeffe and live in an adobe casa, or camp out in the 20,000 acres mountain getaway of Ghost Ranch in New Mexico (www.ghostranch.org).

Christian monastic retreats: Historically the most rigorous of religious communities, monasteries have opened their doors to the serious novice. Expect monastic conditions, literally: simplicity of surroundings, physical labor, long periods of intensive prayer, contemplation, study, silence, and spiritual camaraderie. In New Mexico, Pecos Benedictine Monastery (www.pecosabbey.org), with roots in Siena, Italy, is open to visitors for hermitage, offering courses such as Are We Living in Apocalyptic Times/How Can We Prepare Ourselves? and Setting the Captives Free: An Experience of Healing. In Rochester, Minnesota, Assisi Community Center of the Franciscan Sisters (www.rochesterfranciscan.org) invites people of all religious faiths to a hermitage to participate in their holistic spiritual healing center, complete with massage, psychotherapists, and traditional meditation and prayer.

Eastern and Indian religious retreats: There's a sizeable network of retreats based on non-Western religions. Some Indian religious retreats base their practice on the tenets of Ayurvedic medicine, a centuries-old tradition of health care based in India. Ananda (www.ananda.org/ananda/village), for instance, offers on-site classes in multiple locations from Assisi, Italy, to Nevada City and Palo Alto. The Raj (www.mum.edu) in Fairfield, Iowa, provides individualized analyses of your mind-body balance and recommends a specific course of rejuvenating exercise, meals, and relaxation. A network of Zen Buddhism retreats dots the East and West coasts.

Other: There are many "niche" retreats. For instance, the Program for Creative Self-Development (www.zzapp.org/PCSDJoy/page2.htm) is a gay-positive, holistic learning community dedicated to the psychological, spiritual, and creative fulfillment of all gay or gay-friendly people.

8) FOLLOWING A COMMERCIALLY SUCCESSFUL "GURU"

Older baby boomers and other newcomers to THE RETIREMENT ZONE may recall the days of the 1960s when it was "far-out" to go to India or Nepal to study with a master. Since then, the phenomenon of people following a spiritual leader in the pathways of Eastern religions has become much less exotic. And you don't have to trek to another continent anymore, either. For instance, followers of best-selling author Deepak Chopra buy his books and tapes, watch him on TV, and may participate in any number of residential programs, held at different locations across the United States (www.chopra.com), promising life-altering self-discovery.

Other spiritual giants include Jack Kornfeld, who recently authored *After the Ecstasy, the Laundry: How the Heart Grows Wise on the Spiritual Path* (Bantam Books, 2000), Ram Dass (born as Richard Alpert), a popular Western spiritual teacher whose best-known book is *Be Here Now* (Three Rivers Press, 1981; www.ramdasstapes.org); and Tibetan Buddhist master Gelek Rinpoche.

9) LIVING IN A SPIRITUAL COMMUNITY

A handful of "intentional" communities dot the U.S. map. Most are not "communes" in the sense that they share finances, but many communities do share land and have daily meals together.

Some well-known destinations are Kripalu (www.kripalu.org) in Massachusetts, Ananda Village in California, Satchidananda Ashram (www.yogaville.org) in Virginia, Ananda Marga (www.anandamarga.org) in New York, and Maharishi University of Management (www.mum.edu) in Iowa.

Describing her Quaker continuing-care community of Kendal at Longwood (www.kendal.org/comm.htm) in Pennsylvania, 77-year-old Mary Wood says, "We have about eighty people who meet every Sunday for a Quaker meeting, for worship. We also have meetings to consider what we can do to move towards a more peaceful world and to improve and conserve the environment. There are local opportunities for people to practice whatever religious beliefs they wish. I happen to like a lot of silence; there's a lot of respect for that here. Book clubs, Bible study, and hymn singing are popular. I spend quite a bit of time reading and in silent meditation and just observing the natural world."

10) THE CREATIVE-SPIRITUAL NEXUS

Since the 1960s, people have become increasingly interested in the relationship between spirituality and individualistic creativity. One popular classic that's spun off groups of people working together is *The Artist's Way: A Spiritual Path to*

Higher Creativity by Julia Cameron (Jeremy P. Tarcher/Putnam, 2002). Among the practices encouraged are to have an intentional experience of nature, and the discipline to write on a regular basis. *Writing Down the Bones* by Natalie Goldberg (Shambhala Press, 1986) offers a lighthearted Zen approach to writing. A more analytical approach is provided by Robert Wuthnow in *Creative Spirituality: The Way of the Artist* (University of California Press, 2001).

 ## HEALTHVIEWS

Is belief good for your health? If there's really a "faith-health" connection, nobody yet understands precisely what it might be based on—the will to live, a mustering of inner energies, social support, and friendship that comes from belonging to a faith community, or a trusting and positive attitude that reduces stress.

Religion and spiritual pursuits are indeed a source of positive involvement with the world and can be powerful coping strategies at times of crisis. During times of good health, religious or spiritual involvement can engage you in many positive ways, imparting a sense of belonging to a community, the comforts of tradition, a system of ethics, and a way to think about transcending the mundane. And for those in pain or suffering, religious traditions and parables can provide exemplary models.

What is the precise relationship between religion and health? Some preliminary evidence suggests that attendance at religious services (rather than prayer or other individualistic elements of religious practice) has positive health effects, in certain conditions.

The National Cancer Institute and American Academy of Family Physicians, among others, have included recommendations for physicians on how to discuss a patient's religious and spiritual practice. Dozens of medical schools across the nation are offering courses on the connection between religion, spirituality, and health. And meanwhile, because the scientific mechanisms are murky and little understood, plenty of research into this topic is under way. According to a publication of the National Academy on an Aging Society (www.agingsociety.org), "Many dimensions of health and well-being have been studied in relation to religious involvement. Major ones include mortality, physical illness, disability, and mental health problems, especially depression."

But if you aren't religiously or spiritually inclined, should you become so to gain the health benefits? No. Columbia University Professor R. Sloan comments,

"People who already have a habit of attendance at religious services may be at reduced risk for illness, although this has not been conclusively demonstrated. But there is nothing to indicate that changing one's religious habits in order to promote one's health will yield any benefit."

Spirituality isn't aspirin. And religion is not medicine.

YOUR MONEY MATTERS:
The Cost of Spiritual Seeking

- **Dues:** Some portion of your church or synagogue donations is tax deductible. Ask the institution for a letter stating exactly how much you can write off. Specific, additional contributions such as those earmarked for a building fund or religious school are tax deductible.
- **Retreats:** Many spiritual retreat centers are run as not-for-profit enterprises. Ask if you can volunteer for a weekend or week of serving meals or checking in guests in exchange for attending classes and workshops. If you are looking for a spiritual adventure, opt for an ashram or retreat center in a part of the world where it's cheaper. The yoga is more authentic in Calcutta than it is in California, at a fraction of the cost.
- **Beware:** Sadly, charlatans and money grabbers still prey on people on a spiritual quest. Any organization or individual that ties your financial contributions to personal salvation should be avoided. Ask for the organization's audited statements for the last few years if you feel uncomfortable.

Chances are, if you are a serious seeker, the price tag has nothing to do with the quality of your experience. So if you are wondering about the meaning of life and want to take a little journey of self-discovery, don't assume that money is an obstacle.

> **If you're reading this book for a spouse, friend, or parent . . .** A spiritual perspective often helps people deal with life's challenges, and what Hamlet famously called "the slings and arrows of outrageous fortune." So, if he or she is spiritually or religiously inclined, encourage your loved one to participate.

Is this Me?

A SPIRITUALITY QUESTIONNAIRE

If you're not sure whether "spiritual seeker" describes you, perhaps this informal quiz will help you decide.

1) Do you belong to a formal institution, such as a church, synagogue, or mosque that you like and meets your needs?

2) Do you feel like there's something profoundly missing in your life, but you can't quite say what's missing? (Don't answer "yes" if what you know is missing is the fountain of youth, more sex, a better golf swing, or a winning lottery ticket.)

3) Would you describe yourself as someone seeking spirit? Seeking to break out of the straightjacket of your life?

4) Do you think about your inner life or how to navigate life's passages?

5) Are you interested in exploring religious traditions, either the one you were born into or other traditional religions or alternative practices?

6) Are there specific things you're thinking about—moral questions, major life decisions, issues of relationships—that bother you a great deal and about which you're feeling stuck, or could use some guidance?

7) Do you feel that your spiritual life is connected to how healthy you feel?

8) Did you stop practicing your religion, and feel the need for something else but don't know what that is?

9) Do you consider yourself a person who wants to have more of a spiritual life?

10) Do you have some curiosity or interest in "meaning of life" kinds of discussions but feel there's no place where you can comfortably talk about such things?

If you answered "yes" to the first or to the last question, and "no" to all the others, the chances are you're not a candidate for the pathways described in this chapter. Those who answered affirmatively to Question 1 are probably content with their current situation. If you answered "yes" to any of Questions 2 through 10, you might very well be a spiritual seeker.

When We Sort of Retired, We Didn't Retire: Instead, We Just Turned a Corner

David and Ellie Castle found a whole new life in retirement when they decided to move into a community. It just wasn't the "retirement community" they'd originally planned to move into! Born in the mid-1920s, David Castle had worked as a psychologist, pastor, college professor, and family therapist. His wife was a high-school teacher and social worker. They lived most of their married life in Iowa. While waiting to move into a Bucks County, Pennsylvania, retirement community, they visited an unusual community called Koinoinia. They decided to stay there instead.

Perhaps one of the earliest interracial egalitarian communities, Koinoinia, in Sumter County, Georgia, was the precursor to Habitat for Humanity (whose headquarters are located nearby, just down the road). It was founded in 1942, long before the civil rights movement, by a white Baptist minister, Clarence Jordan. The community built houses for impoverished local black families, bartering with supporters to supplement their materials, employed local African-American workers whom they paid wages equal to those of whites, and with whom they shared meals—behavior unheard of in the Deep South at that time. From the 1940s until the 1960s Koinoinia survived intimidations and attacks by white supremacists, investigations by the FBI, and boycotts by local businessmen. Located in a poor farming area of Georgia, it has been called "a demonstration plot for the Kingdom of God." Today, Koinoinia welcomes visitors and students, and is sustained financially by farming pecans.

"Our daily life is busy. We usually have between twenty-five and forty people; probably two thirds of them live here on campus. We meet every day for a short morning prayer and work assignments. Then off we go. There's office and maintenance work, keeping up thirty guest accommodations, taking care of visitors, and doing tours. At the noontime meal the community comes together. We stop for lunch, have a devotional period and wonderful music including classical and black gospel. That lunch period I think is the heart of our community. We share our joys. At one we go back to work till five. But we put

people ahead of product, so we take time to talk or help each other or go places to enhance our experience. We have a chapel service on Wednesday mornings.

"Koinoinia's founder, Clarence Jordan, was generous. And he believed in an abundant, loving, and forgiving God. So there's a really warm, open, welcoming spirit that visitors feel right away. Many people find something here that they don't feel in their churches at home. A lot of people come who are seeking. They find nothing like this in their rather closed institutional religious communities at home.

"We have a mile-and-a-half-long peace trail, like a meditation trail, so people can be by themselves. We try to avoid the misuse of resources. We have almost no air conditioning. We hang our clothes out instead of in the drier. Our furnishings are simple and clean. We think in terms of environmental stewardship of the earth. We do some organic gardening and follow the principles of simple living as much as we can. We have community decision making.

"Often when I am giving tours people ask what we do. I say we don't 'do' but we try to 'be.' Visitors want to do something for poor people, like build a house. We do that, but more—this place is a platform for learning, growing, and changing. Clarence Jordan was about turning your life around, not doing business as usual. We plant the seeds of God's love and grace and mercy, and people see how that can change their life. Hundreds, maybe thousands, come through here in the course of the year. We had a couple here on a tour for a few hours who said, 'We came with a burden and we left with the burden lifted, thank you very much.'

"At the end of the day we look at each other and say 'WOW, where else can you get this?'"

Resource Guide

PUBLICATIONS

After Ecstasy, the Laundry: How the Heart Grows Wise on the Spiritual Path by Jack Kornfield (Bantam Books, 2000).

Beyond Belief: The Secret Gospel of Thomas by Elaine Pagels (Random House, 2003).

The Five Stages of the Soul: Charting the Spiritual Passages that Shape Our Lives by Harry R. Moody, PhD, and David Carroll (Anchor Books, 1998).

The Four Agreements: A Practical Guide to Personal Freedom by Don Miguel Ruiz (Amber-Allen, 1997).

Illuminata, A Return to Prayer by Marianne Williamson (Riverhead Books, 1995).

Kitchen Table Wisdom: Stories that Heal by Rachel Naomi Remen, M.D. (Riverhead Books, 1996).

The Miracle of Mindfulness by Thich Nhat Hanh, translated by Mobi Ho (Beacon Press, 1999).

Pay Attention, for Goodness' Sake: Practicing the Perfections of the Heart, the Buddhist Path of Kindness by Sylvia Boorstein, PhD (Ballantine Books, 2003).

The Power of Now: A Guide to Spiritual Enlightenment by Eckhart Tolle (New World Library, 1999).

The Purpose-Driven Life: What on Earth Am I Here For? by Rick Warren (Zondervan, 2002).

Spiritual but Not Religious: Understanding Unchurched America by Robert C. Fuller (Oxford University Press, 2002).

Spiritual Marketplace: Baby Boomers and the Remaking of American Religion by Wade Clark Roof (Princeton University Press, 1999).

When Bad Things Happen to Good People by Harold S. Kushner (Schocken Books, 1981).

Who Wrote the Bible? by Richard E. Friedman (Prentice Hall, 1987).

Zen Mind, Beginner's Mind by Shunryu Suzuki-roshi; Trudy Dixon, ed. (Weatherhill, 1970).

ORGANIZATIONS AND WEB SITES

Note: There are hundreds of thousands of organizations devoted to spirituality and religions of all denominations across the United States, plus a rich supply of print and online information. Check local newspapers, telephone directories, and Internet listings for local contacts. The following is an eclectic list of faith-based social action organizations.

Church Women United
475 Riverside Drive, Suite 1626
New York, NY 10115
800-298-5551
www.churchwomen.org

Evangelical Lutheran Church
in America
8765 West Higgins Road
Chicago, IL 60631
800-638-3522
www.elca.org

Friends Committee on
National Legislation
245 Second Street NE
Washington, DC 20002-5795
800-630-1330
www.fcnl.org

Interfaith Alliance
1331 H Street NW
11th Floor
Washington, DC 20005
800-510-0969
www.interfaithalliance.org

National Council of Churches USA
475 Riverside Drive, Suite 880
New York, NY 10115
212-870-2227
www.ncccusa.org

Religious Action Center
of Reform Judaism
2027 Massachusetts Avenue NW
Washington, DC 20036
202-387-2800
www.rac.org/home-frame.html

Spiritual Eldering Institute
970 Aurora Avenue
Boulder, CO 80302
303-449-7243
www.spiritualeldering.org

Unitarian Universalist Association
25 Beacon Street
Boston, MA 02108
617-742-2100
www.uua.org

United Church of Christ
700 Prospect Avenue
Cleveland, OH 44115
866-822-8224
www.ucc.org

United Methodist Church
General Board of Church & Society
100 Maryland Avenue NE
Washington, DC 20002
202-488-5600
www.umc-gbcs.org

CHAPTER 17

Learning

NOT JUST FOR SCHOOL JUNKIES

Regardless of whether you were a college dropout or a perpetual student in your not-so-distant youth, you might consider going back to school, now that you have some time to yourself in THE RETIREMENT ZONE.

Love isn't the same the second time around, they say, and neither is school. At age 60, 74, or 82, there's no career pressure, no crushing student loans, and no competition over grades. Most mature students aren't taking exams, writing papers, or worrying about accumulating credits. There isn't anyone telling them to learn German or take calculus in order to get into graduate school.

"Unlike college kids, we aren't intimidated by professors. Because even if a lecturer is smarter, they're almost never older," jokes one octogenarian. He was on his way to a course called Mentors and Protégés: A Study in Intergenerational Relationships at American University in Washington, D.C.

Reentering the world of education isn't everybody's cup of tea. But Americans are voting with their feet for education—their own education, not the local school-bond issue—and are marching right back to school. Whether they are enrolling purely for pleasure, finishing a degree, or getting professional certification for a second career, they seem to enjoy a "second time around" as students.

CLASSROOM TALES

Sitting in a small classroom, a dozen students listen intently as two of their peers passionately debate human cloning. Nothing is unusual—except that these students, on average, are 70 years old. Since they last wore a cap and gown, most members of the class have had one (or more) careers, one (or more) marriages, raised families, and lived a life that started way back in the 20th century. The subject that so engages them at 10 A.M. on a dreary winter Monday is Bioethics and Genetic Engineering: Challenges of a Brave New World.

Sally, 65, recently retired from running a hotel catering business. Sitting at her computer at midnight after a late-night tennis game, Sally's not surfing the Internet. She's doing an online course offered by a university located 2,000 miles away from her Salt Lake City home. She's working toward a credential as a teacher of English as a second language. Her dream is to work part-time in Portugal, where she and her companion think they would like to retire. Teaching will give her a "bridge job," she says, between her career as a manager and full retirement.

He's on his way out the door to go to school—which for once isn't the same as going to work. Colin is an athletic 55-year-old basketball fanatic who took early retirement from his administrative job for a budget-squeezed education department in a major city. He's enrolled in the local continuing education program to sharpen his information technology skills. He has a new 30-year life plan: Using old contacts and new skills, he wants to build an educational consulting business. He hopes to sell the business at age 65, when his wife retires, so they can travel. When he hits 75, he expects to finish his career where he began, working with young children as a classroom volunteer. Meanwhile, when people ask what he's doing, he grins and says, "Information technology—I'm doing IT!"

Combining School and UN-Retiring

For men and women anticipating several decades of good health, education becomes a way to freshen up skills, pick up a new credential, and get ready for a different or a part-time career. The range is astonishing: the Bloomberg School of Public Health at Johns Hopkins University offers a Masters in Public Health using a combined in-person/online course schedule. The University of Nevada in Las Vegas offers a degree in senior theater. If you feel stuck in THE RETIREMENT ZONE and unsure of what's next, taking some courses is a safe, easy way to experiment. (See also Educational Travel and Ecotourism, page 191.)

RETIREMENT ZONE TRENDS:
Why School's Hot

Education is hot for the over-55 set.

What's the impetus behind the back-to-school trend? In 2000, more than a half million U.S. students over age 50, including 75,000 students over 65, were enrolled in universities, colleges, and two-year colleges. The number of older students continues to grow steadily. The over-50 student population increased by 50 percent since the early 1990s, and shows no sign of abating.

Some are retooling for a second, third, or fifth career. Others who return to school are pursuing new dreams and rekindling old passions. In Manhattan, a former publishing executive describes how he surprised even himself by enrolling for a class on architecture, an interest that he'd pushed aside in the midlife fray of working and raising a family. In Los Angeles, a 65-year-old retired music teacher "overcame a lifelong math anxiety" when she took a course that explored geometric patterns in nature—and fell in love with geometry. Some men and women, intrigued by what can be done in cyberspace (and wanting to keep up with the grandkids) are trying online courses.

You've watched TV and read the newspaper as the United States became desegregated, as the first men walked on the moon, as the Berlin Wall fell, and as the country ended and initiated armed conflict on different continents. You remember the first Barbie doll, Marlon Brando and Marilyn Monroe in their youth, and the passage of Roe *vs.* Wade. School offers an opportunity to review, read, and discuss these events of a lifetime.

And then there's the freedom of learning for its own sake. David B., nearly 80, draws a circle in the air with his hands and says, "What I learned in school up to now was always circumscribed. I was to study and learn things within that circle. Preparing for a career like mine, in law for example, you are required to learn things that are relevant to law, not art, literature, or philosophy. What I have now is complete freedom. Nobody is telling me I've got to learn this or that. I can spread my wings. The only purpose is what I find out."

Continuing education is *big* business. It's a subset of the education industry, complete with its own trade group (the National University Continuing Education Association www.ucea.edu) and career track (some university administrators specialize just in "adult" and "professional development" education). Some colleges are making significant financial investments in faculty, facilities, and programs to capture the adult student market. The result is often a professionally run adult educational institution with course offerings in almost every field, both for credit and on a non-credit basis.

Who takes adult education classes? *Everybody.* Housewives and lawyers, immigrants and Daughters of the American Revolution, great-grandparents and younger adults who, in addition to studying, are often juggling jobs and family responsibilities. So if your notion of "adult ed classes" is Aunt Millie taking basket weaving, look again.

12 Reasons to Give Education an "A" in THE RETIREMENT ZONE

REASON 1: There are tons of options. Study Chinese, take painting, get an MBA, delve into Dostoevsky, participate in an educational archaeological dig, or learn the skills to start a new business that will perk up your retirement income. There is a wealth of choices in terms of what you can study. Similarly, you have new options regarding *how* you get your education. You can sit at home in your kimono and learn online, join a community-based learning institution set up exclusively for older people, or mix it up with twenty-somethings at the local university. Got the travel bug? Take an educational travel program.

REASON 2: Education may improve the quality of your life. Personal development is hard to quantify. But students report that learning gives them a new perspective. One Vietnam vet and retired fireman describes taking an online art history course: "It's opened up incredible horizons."

REASON 3: It's fun. Maybe it's corny, but going back to school can be an adventure and a joy. Would you welcome an excuse to curl up and read all day long? Do you love the idea of engaging new ideas? Would you enjoy hanging around a university campus to see what those crazy students are wearing?

REASON 4: Education doesn't have to be expensive. Some online courses may cost you as much as taking the same course at a top-notch college. Alternatively, special programs for retirees called "Institutes for Learning in Retirement" charge as little as $10 a month. Some colleges enroll seniors in a course or two for free.

REASON 5: Everyone's doing it. An online-only version of the BW/Harris Poll of "relatively affluent Americans 45 and older" from *Business Week*, July 20, 1998, found that about half of the retirees surveyed are engaged in some kind of educational program, as shown in the following chart.

School Days Are Here Again

	NOT RETIRED	RETIRED
Older Adults Who Don't Plan to Go Back to School	39%	53%
Older Adults Who Do Plan to		
Other education	23%	30%
Take adult education courses	29%	18%
Audit college courses	12%	6%
Participate in Elderhostel program	14%	3%
Pursue graduate degree	6%	2%
Pursue undergraduate degree	3%	1%

REASON 6: You can retool for your next job. Faced with a roller-coaster economy, many people with decades of work experience are going back to school part-time to broaden their skills and polish up their resume, or get a certificate or degree.

REASON 7: It's flexible. You can structure your own schedule. If you're an early bird, sign up for a 9 A.M. class. If you're looking to fill your evenings, pencil in a weekly evening class. Online courses can be done anytime, anywhere.

REASON 8: It's not a job. You're not locked in. Some students dedicate 50 hours a week to their education, others spend only two. You can skip a summer, a semester, or a year—then pick it up again.

REASON 9: You're likely to meet interesting people. Educational settings are terrific for making new friends, even if they remain classroom-only relationships. People with higher levels of educational attainment tend to participate more in community and political affairs, volunteer organizations, sports, and hobby clubs, according to research.

REASON 10: You can go it alone or take a course with a spouse or a friend. It's easy to participate and make friends in a class without ever having to divulge your marital status. Some couples can, and do, study together. On the flip side, lots of married retirees are happy to have their "own thing" to do for a few hours a week.

REASON 11: It's cool to be a "student." Let's be honest, "being a student" suggests all kinds of appealing things: that you're inquiring, informal, active, and open. You may start reliving some of the things you loved best about your own college years—slouching around coffee shops and reading poetry, maybe. But don't be disappointed if you aren't carded when the class goes out for a beer.

REASON 12: And the doctor says it's good for you. Education is good for your brain, which is good for your body, too. It's no joke: learning can pay big health dividends. As 70-something Dr. Jay in Florida puts it, "If you have the chance, go to school, and exercise that muscle between your ears before it atrophies."

Your Local College and Other Resources

Suppose you are advising a friendly, education-starved Martian on what classes she might take in your area. Where are there computer classes? Is there a school of music? A poetry club or a fine arts center? Does the local school offer evening courses in foreign languages? Is there a study group at your church, synagogue, or mosque? How about a lecture series at the Y?

You may discover a rich vein of cultural enrichment options and foreign language courses, and also creative arts such as filmmaking and writing at a local college in any major city, or in most suburbs. The programs go by different names—"continuing education," "lifelong education," and "adult education."

Many colleges are sprouting satellite mini-centers. Urban colleges are opening satellites in the suburbs; uptown colleges are opening downtown mini-campuses; and community colleges are opening "off campus" centers. Taking a class can be as convenient as stopping at the supermarket.

If you live far from a campus, or if driving presents an obstacle, consider taking a course either online or by old-fashioned "snail mail." So-called "independent study enrollments" (they used to be called correspondence courses) attract a substantial number of students, and courses today are supplemented with audio and videotapes, and sometimes computer-assisted learning.

Also, check out courses offered by local museums, and chapters of your professional or trade associations, or union. You can find classes where people share interests: organizations for hobbyists, faith groups and churches, arts and crafts groups, and more. And, educational travel opportunities abound.

PRACTICAL TIP: There's no universal guide to the quality of continuing ed classes. Most are not taught by the professors who teach college undergraduates or graduates, but rather by people with professional experience in a given field. This can make for a stunningly interesting class—or a snoozer. Get word-of-mouth recommendations, or just talk to the teacher to see if it will be worthwhile.

FOR SENIORS ONLY:
Lifelong Learning Institutes

Members might be writing twenty-chapter memoirs, gazing at Jupiter through a telescope, studying Islam, and digging into the nuances of the First Amendment of the U.S. Constitution. Or they may be reading the texts of ancient Greece—and then pulling together a weeklong class cruise to the Aegean to visit the places they've studied. Some may be preparing to facilitate a seminar on a topic that they find interesting—even if they're rank amateurs.

If you ask a member of a Lifelong Learning Institute (LLI) or an "Institute for Learning in Retirement" (ILR) what it feels like to be a student again, he or she is likely to correct you by saying, "This is a collegial environment. It's wrong to say we are students. There are no 'students' and no 'professors.'"

What's This "LLI" Or "ILR" Thing?

An ILR or LLI (these are the same kinds of organizations, by different names) is an organization of retirement-age people who get together in an educational setting for the purposes of learning. Most are sponsored by a "host" college or university, but their members, not professional university administrators, run the programs. They attract people who like to read and discuss ideas. Usually, classes are small and styled after seminars. The organization is a local, grassroots nonprofit entity.

Don't feel left out if you've never heard of an "ILR" or an "LLI" before. Not many people have. That's because these programs generally don't advertise. People tend to find out about them through word-of-mouth. But if you like to explore new ideas, stretch your horizons, and spend time with mature peers (and don't want or need another credential) this might be your ticket.

Host institutions run the gamut from the nation's most prestigious universities to state university networks to community colleges. There are Lifelong Learning Institutes and ILRs in 40 states. Most are open to people over 50. The majority of members are in the 60 to 80 age range.

When you join, you become a "member." Dues average about $200 a year, but in some places they are as low as $10. Membership enables you to take courses, usually up to three (rules vary of course). Sometimes membership enables you to audit a regular university course for free. And members may join committees that make administrative decisions, such as what courses will be offered, who will "teach" them, and what will be part of outreach and social programming. Some Lifelong Learning Institutes or ILRs have a hired staff person, but many are run solely on volunteer power. So there are lots of volunteer opportunities that range from stuffing envelopes and answering phones to serving on long-range planning or curriculum committees. Due to space crunches at many colleges, classes often meet off-campus.

Typically, a Lifelong Learning Institute or an ILR offers ten to twenty study groups per term. Most members participate in one to three study groups per term. In most, at least half the study groups are developed and coordinated exclusively by members instead of professional faculty. At many institutes, for example at Harvard, the State University of New York programs, and Georgia College, virtually *all* study groups are member-coordinated. The coordinator's job, unpaid, is to do research, prepare a reading list, and be prepared to guide a weekly discussion of ten to twenty other members. Generally, the courses are college level, some at the level of graduate seminars.

Some well-known campus hosts include, in the Northeast, Harvard, Tufts, Dartmouth, and University of Maine; in the south, Duke and Emory; in the Midwest, Northwestern, Purdue, the University of Wisconsin, University of Cincinnati, and Washington University; in the Southwest, Baylor U. in Waco, Texas, and University of Arizona at Tucson; and in the West, UCLA and California State University, which has multiple ILR sites. You can find out if there's one near you by contacting the Elderhostel Institute Network (www.elder hostel.org/ein/intro.asp). Or if you live in the Western U.S., the Association for Learning in Retirement Organizations of the West (www.alirow.org). If you don't have an ILR close by, you can start your own! (See Resource Guide on page 245 for more contact information.)

Each program is a little different, reflecting what people in their individual communities want to do and learn. Here's a smattering of the courses that were peer-taught by members at UCLA's Plato Society, 2002: Great Anthropologists, The Controversial Fourteenth Amendment, Journey Into Physics, The Amazing World of the Ultra-Small Micromachines, Stories from Africa, Asia, and Latin America, Microprocessors & Nanotechnology, Presidents of the United States and their Legacies, Incredible Indonesia—Myth and Reality.

Who attends?

It's a brainy, inquisitive crowd: teachers, doctors, business executives, government officials, and lawyers. One administrator comments, "They are not going for a degree. They are not going back to work; it is not a career ladder that they are thinking of. They have the curiosity for learning and want to delve into subjects at a different level."

Kali Lightfoot, director of the University of Southern Maine's Senior College, Osher Lifelong Learning Institute (OLLI) says their 900-member program attracts ordinary lifelong Maine residents as well as highly accomplished individuals who've been drawn to retire in communities in the greater Portland area. Some are coming home from a way of life "away," and some are retiring to a place where they have spent many summers. She notes, "Among our students in the Maine Senior College Network, we've counted an ex-head of National Job Corps, a former Iran hostage, retired and current state legislators, published authors and working artists, ministers, rabbis, and a retired four-star general."

Anne Pearson, the 70-something volunteer coordinator of the program at California State University at Fullerton, talks about the importance of social life at the Institutes. "Even though I have four kids and eight grandkids, nobody likes being on the shelf and out of the mainstream," she says. "It's not just taking a class. That's missing the point. People come together in a learning organization with others who share their interests. There is a great deal of support, usually via email and online networks. That's one of the things you get—that group spirit."

Even the largest of the Lifelong Learning programs are intimate, with memberships from 60 to 300 people. Only about a dozen have enrollments over 1,000. Yvonne Wheeler, who codeveloped an Institute for Learning in Retirement in Denver in 1996, described her group: "The dynamics of a group of like-minded people are unbelievable. For instance, we offered a class on China. The group got together after the study group ended and traveled to China. They still have dinner once a month in people's homes and invite a speaker to talk about something to do with China. They've been doing it for seven years!"

"Nobody has their guard up, male or female," agrees an LLR administrator. "There's camaraderie in the classroom. We've had lots of e-mail friendships come out of it, and a few travel partnerships, too."

EXPLORING THE VIRTUAL CAMPUS

Thanks to the Internet, you can go to school without ever leaving home. What an opportunity for men and women in THE RETIREMENT ZONE! You can enroll in a university class while sitting in a fishing cabin in the Canadian Rockies or from your living room—maybe as respite from helping your spouse recover from a medical procedure. Some call it "e-education," others call it "online learning," "distance learning," or just the "virtual campus."

According to the U.S. Department of Education's National Center for Education Statistics, the majority of public colleges and universities offer distance-learning courses. In 2002, there were more than 3,000 programs at more than 1,100 accredited institutions of higher learning in the U.S. and Canada.

The programs are designed for different levels: working professionals, students pursuing academic credit, career-changers, and people seeking personal development. Like location, age is not a factor. Nobody asks. As of this writing, there are very few online courses offered exclusively for people in retirement, although AARP does offer access to a consortium program called FATHOM (www.fathom.com). You can find thousands of opportunities for study online.

What actually happens in an online course? An online is a course on virtually any topic that is delivered, wholly or partially, via the Internet to a student. Course materials and assignments are often sent via the Internet. Some courses simply give you the material and you learn on your own, at your own pace. Others are more interactive. Some courses are offered on a non-credit basis, so you aren't responsible for exams or submissions, and you don't receive a grade.

To communicate with your "class" via the Internet, you'll have to type messages, post responses, and otherwise communicate using your fingers. If you hate to type, or for some reason can't, e-learning may not be for you. If you're looking to meet people face to face, then check out your local resources: colleges, social clubs, or travel education programs. Keep in mind, though, that people can forge wonderful friendships over the Internet.

You can find non-credit online courses on all kinds of topics, from how to write mysteries to how to officiate a soccer game. There's even food for the soul. Taylor University (http://cll.taylor.edu), an evangelical Christian institution, offers distance-learning classes on theology. Many other organizations offer religion-based online courses as well. And some courses are highly technical in nature, like Carnegie Mellon's ten-course certification in software engineering (http://online.web.cmu.edu). You might log on for a seminar in architecture at the University of California, one on ethics at Brown University (www.brown.edu), and another in film studies at UCLA (www.uclaextension.edu). Some online courses are oriented toward master's degrees or professional certification. The course possibilities are extensive.

How to Get Started?

Your best bet is to use both hard-reference books and online information to find out what's available. Check out *Peterson's Guide to Distance Learning Programs.*

Almost all public education institutions offer online courses, and many private colleges and universities do, too. The University of Maryland and SUNY, the State University of New York system, offer an extensive number of online programs. Penn State is also a leader in the field, as are the University of Illinois and Stanford University. New York University's Virtual College, which has 4,000 students enrolled internationally, is among the largest of the private sector entrants in this field. Some small private colleges, like Skidmore, also offer interesting menus. You can easily access online catalogs for courses, degree programs, and/or professional education, organized by state and country, at the Web site of the University Continuing Education Association at www.ucea.edu/Distance02.htm.

Moreover, several consortiums of universities have joined forces online. FATHOM (www.fathom.com), spearheaded by Columbia University, offers courses from 14 prestigious partners, including the London School of Economics, Cambridge University Press, and the British Library.

The corporate world is joining the e-education bandwagon. UNext.com, a for-profit company, recently launched Cardean University (www.cardean.com), an online educator that it markets globally to large organizations and corporations. Also new to the scene are for-profit companies offering online business training for executives. Trade and professional associations, companies, and unions offer classes.

Try it! If you don't want to start with advanced electronic engineering, test the online waters by taking a course in a hobby. You can go to one of several university Web sites to do an online quiz to see if it's for you. For instance, see the Web site of the University of California at Berkeley (http://learn.berkeley.edu) or the Frequently Asked Questions section of the University of Illinois online learning program (http://www.online.uillinois.edu).

Quality Control

Surprisingly, you can't rely on name brands in this fast-changing field. A well-known institution may not necessarily offer more or better online courses than a small community college you've never heard of.

Ask questions. Ideally, online courses use the same learning materials (books notes, CD-ROMs, and other) as on-campus versions, are led by a faculty member, limit class size to 10 or 20, encourage interaction with other students, and can be completed without a visit to campus. Also check the listings on the Web site www.sloan-c.org, the "Sloan Consortium Catalog," a compilation of over 200 better online programs offered by universities, colleges, and community colleges.

 HEALTHVIEWS

In the nation's largest study of cognitive training, the Advanced Cognitive Training for Independent and Vital Elderly (ACTIVE) nationwide clinical trial, researchers at Johns Hopkins University found that training and practice improves the memory, concentration, and problem-solving abilities of people over age 65. The study, as reported in the November 2002 issue of *Journal of the American Medical Association* suggests that the advances may even be enough to make up for normal losses associated with later age.

And, your mature brain even has some advantages. Age brings a ripeness of understanding. Older students often savor subjects that make younger peers shudder: Shakespeare, art, and theoretical physics. Why? It's the "been there, done that" factor. Mature students can understand complex, even contradictory realities. Life experience gives you a better understanding of "poignant" or "bittersweet" than Webster's dictionary *ever* could.

"Older students have greater familiarity with names, places, and events, and some may have lived through what is being studied—the Great Depression, or

World War II, or the civil rights movement," says Anne Pearson, acting President of ALIROW (Association for Learning in Retirement Organizations in the West), an umbrella organization of senior colleges. "Even if they are not familiar with specific names and dates, older students understand the underlying fundamentals: power, ambition, ideology, failure. They just connect the dots better."

 YOUR MONEY MATTERS

- **Taxes:** Get familiar with what's known as Section 529 plans, especially if you have an inkling well in advance that you'll want to hit the books again later in life. Section 529 are college savings plans that offer an attractive way to build savings and provide tax benefits. "Withdrawals from a 529 plan can be used for tuition, fees, books, supplies, and equipment at most accredited institutions. Part-time attendees are included," according to Joseph Hurley, founder of the Internet site www.savingforcollege.com. The downside? Some 529 plans offer limited investment options. And there are penalties if the money is used for something other than tuition.

  For those retirees enrolling in college-degree programs, Lifetime Learning Credit is available to qualified students in full-time, half-time, and less-than-half-time programs. There are no restrictions on the number of years for which the credit can be claimed. The Lifetime credit may be used to acquire new skills or improve existing skills. The maximum credit for a tax year is $2,000 (20 percent of a maximum $10,000 of qualified tuition and expenses). As with all tax matters, these plans could change, so ask your accountant.

- **Special rates:** Veterans typically qualify for special tuition rates, and many colleges offer seniors cut-rate tuition (but ask about limitations based on available space, or the number of classes you can take). Some even offer scholarships.

  ILR (or LLI) programs offered to seniors charge a nominal membership fee and no charges for courses. Not only will you pay next to nothing for a course, but in many cases you gain priceless privileges to libraries and athletic facilities.

- **Online costs:** Fees for online programs vary substantially, from a few hundred dollars per course to many thousands, depending on the school and the study program. So shop around.

Think of this as an experiment. Look yourself straight in the eye in the bath-room mirror and say out loud what your inner self is starving to study (Chinese porcelain? primate mating habits? what made JFK tick? bicycle repair for the mechanically challenged? The saxophone?) and then go find a course on it. If you don't have a driving passion, then just select something convenient and reason-ably interesting, the same way you might select a movie on a rainy afternoon.

> **If you're reading this book for a spouse, friend, or parent . . .** Take a trip back to school with your loved one—it can be a wonderful way to connect again. So much can be done online, too. There's a course for everything from cooking to crafts to mind-bending academics. Why not do it together?

What to Study?

Use this worksheet to help find the educational choice that fits you.

EXERCISE 1: Second Chances

If you could be a teenager or college student again, what would you love to study—not for career advancement purposes, but because it really interests you? _____

_____

EXERCISE 2: Challenge Yourself

Some experts say that learning things you haven't yet mastered is one of the best ways to stimulate your brain. For instance, if you are adept at math and science, try music or a language; if you are a natural writer, take a course in math. It's the mental challenge that counts.

What are you *best* at doing? _____

In what areas do you feel *weakest*? _____

What are some things that you are interested in,

but think you can't master? _____

_____

EXERCISE 3: Making a Plan

What are you interested in learning and what educational resources are there in your community, or available to you online, where you might find instruction in your top ten list?

Things I'm interested in learning   Educational Resources available to me

Things I'm interested in learning	Educational Resources available to me
World War II	*community college*
Islam	*online courses (check out several)*

From Root Canal to Panama Canal

Roy Roistacher, a professor of dentistry who was born in 1922, is still going strong at 80. He says if he could, he would go back to work "in an instant." But he's thrilled with new avenues that have opened up to him at the New School University Institute for Retired Professionals (IRP), where he is preparing to coordinate a study group on the Panama Canal.

"I retired July 1, 2000, from a position I'd held for thirty-four years. Trained as a dentist, I moved into the academic world in 1964. I was asked to be chair of the Department of Dental Medicine at the Queens Hospital Center affiliate of the Mt. Sinai Medical School as a tenured clinical professor of the medical school. I left when I was seventy-seven years old. That world offered support on every level. When I left, I left all that behind: the secretaries who file, copying machines, the hundreds of people I knew, a pharmacy at my beck and call. All the support and ease. That's nothing to be sneezed at.

"How did I come to the New School? A physician friend who lives in my building said one of his retired friends, a psychiatrist, attended the IRP. He didn't know much about it. I filled out a rather detailed application, then I was called for a group interview. That was it.

"I've always been a reader, all my life. This activity, this learning, fills in much more than the two to four hours that you spend here, because you have to do the reading. You should do the reading. You want to do the reading. When I was a kid I'd roller-skate to the library. I never had enough time to read, through school and my career. At lunchtime today, I was saying to one of my colleagues here that I read all of Willa Cather before I was thirteen.

"This thing, the Institute for Retired Professionals, seemed from the beginning an opportunity to light up my brain again, in an unpressured environment. Nobody is telling you what to do. You can take whatever courses you want to take—Modern Plays, History of Medicine, Abraham Lincoln—it doesn't matter.

"I've had a long-standing interest in transportation. It fascinates me. Next year, I'm going to facilitate a study group on the Building of the Panama Canal. To have a reason to delve into it, to learn so much—it's an absolutely unique kind of thing.

"The New School program really was a savior for me. I get up at six A.M. I've been doing it for forty-five years. Whether I have to get up or not, I get up. I make my breakfast and then it is a quarter to seven. Then, what do I do? By eight I would have been in the car, going to work. Now, all of a sudden, I am still in my pajamas. That's a very disquieting feeling. Not only that I'm useless, but there's . . . nothing, no function for my day. What am I going to do? It's very difficult—until you find a place that sparks your interests.

"This intellectual environment is not for everyone. If you are not comfortable being verbal, it could be difficult. It's New York; everyone has something to say. I'm often the only male. At eighty, you find that a significant number of the people in the world you used to inhabit are dead. There are not many men. So all of a sudden another emptiness comes.

"I'm delighted to be here, to listen to the things people have done in their lives. This is an astounding opportunity. It fills in the niches of your appetite; you learn things you wouldn't otherwise, like reading Abe Lincoln! We do extraordinary things."

The Intimacy Of Anonymity

After the World Trade Center attacks and the sudden death of her father, Joyce W., 52, of New York felt the need to express herself.

"I was exploding with feelings and needed to write. I couldn't decide whether to take a class or try this online thing. I signed up for two fiction courses—one at a local university and an online course. I enrolled in the online writing course through an organization called the Writers' Studio. I could have taken the same course in person, just a few miles away, at the Writers' Studio Manhattan headquarters. But I was intrigued by the idea of doing it electronically. The online course was superb. We logged on for a 'meeting' every Monday at the same time in our own private chat room. The technology was fun—and my kids were impressed that I was 'Instant Message-ing' and doing all these cool Internet-based communications.

"There were two fascinating aspects to the course. Of my six fellow students, all professionals, and all other wannabe fiction writers, three lived far away. Jim from Scotland, who taught computer science, wrote a lot about being in the Royal Navy. A Cuban-American graphic designer from Miami wrote wonderful stories about growing up with dual nationalities. And there was an occasional Australian participant who logged in to our sessions from wherever she happened to be traveling in the world. The international flavor of the participants made the course tremendously exciting.

"It was so much easier to write freely knowing that I could 'listen' to classmates respond to my writing without seeing their faces. I'd always been terrified of writing fiction. The anonymity of the class, ironically, made it easier for me to bare my soul.

"The feedback that we got on our writing was intense. Everyone worked really diligently on commenting on one another's work. We'd e-mail our feedback. It was wonderful. I ran to my electronic inbox every morning to see what might be in it. I felt so unusually close to my classmates—which is strange, considering that I never actually met any of them. I will never forget that class.

"The university class was good. But next time, I think I'll take an online class."

Resource Guide

PUBLICATIONS

Guide to Distance Learning Programs, 7th Edition (Peterson's Guides, 2003).

ORGANIZATIONS AND WEB SITES

To find an Institute for Lifelong Learning in your area, contact two umbrella organizations:

ALIROW (an active association of independent Learning in Retirement LIR associations whose member directed activities are generally located on campuses of sponsoring universities and colleges of the Western United States). There is no office: Contact them through their Web site at www.alirow.org

Elderhostel Institute Network (EIN)
11 Avenue de Lafayette
Boston, MA 02111-1746
www.elderhostel.org/ein/intro.asp

Others include:

Fathom Knowledge Network:
www.fathom.com

529 Tax plans:
www.savingforcollege.com

National University Continuing Education Association
One Dupont Circle NW, Suite 615
Washington, DC 20036-1168
202-659-3130
www.ucea.edu

Peterson's Distance Learning:
www.petersons.com/distancelearning

Sloan Consortium Catalog:
www.sloan-c.org

CHAPTER 18

Loving Makes the World Go 'Round

If in the end it's people who count in life, then love is an important part of building a satisfying life in THE RETIREMENT ZONE. And under the broad umbrella of love, it's surely fair to count warm, intimate and close relationships of all kinds: family, friends, neighbors, colleagues, and fellow travelers of all sorts. Of the assorted relationships people pick up over a lifetime, family has a role like no other, and friends can provide oceans of love, emotional intimacy, and comfort. Still, romantic love is the ace of the pack. And this wonderful, impossible, extraordinary—what? *event*—in people's lives can, and certainly does, occur well past the age of blushing adolescence.

Here's what some famous people from earlier eras have had to say about love:

Love's like the measles—all the worse when it comes late in life.

—Douglas Jerrold, 1803-1857, English humorist

Never the time and the place/And the loved one all together!

—Robert Browning, 1812-1889, English poet

Love is the history of a woman's life; it is an episode in man's.

—Madame de Staël, 1766-1877, French writer

Love is a disease which fills you with a desire to be desired.

—Henri, Comte de Toulouse-Lautrec, 1864-1901, French painter

I love her and she loves me, and we hate each other with a wild hatred born of love.   —J. August Strindberg, 1849-1912, Swedish dramatist

What a recreation it is to be in love! It sets the heart aching so delicately, there's no taking a wink of sleep for the pleasure of the pain.

—George Colman, "the Younger," 1762-1836, English dramatist

WHEN ONLY HALF A COUPLE RETIRES

Imagine: One person in a marriage is retired and wants to try new things and travel, while the other person is still climbing that career ladder. Who does the laundry and household chores? Do jealousies arise when the non-working spouse makes a new daytime life, or becomes close to new friends? How many telephone calls should the retired husband make to the working wife during the course of the day? It has the makings of a sit-com.

There's no road map for how couples should retire, precisely because the generation now hitting their fifties and sixties is the first to have a majority of women, as well as men, in the workforce. As with so many other of society's arrangements that the baby boomers have reconfigured, couples entering THE RETIREMENT ZONE today are making it up as they go along.

Dr. Phyllis Moen, the McKnight Professor of Sociology at the University of Minnesota who studies retirement trends, says, "In second marriages, especially, many women are just starting back to work or they have gone back to school." Consequently, they don't feel "ready" to retire: "Some of it is about money. But equally important, psychologically stressful stuff happens when the wife feels the husband wants her to quit work, and she isn't ready to do so."

Experts say that both husband and wife rarely stop working simultaneously; often a two- to four-year lag separates his and her retirement.

Some marriages hit the skids over money. Tensions can run high when one spouse is working because the other was forced into early retirement, or when one is busy making money and the other is spending it in new ways, for instance, shopping or at a casino. Time management is another potential stress. What happens at the end of the day when she wants to collapse and he's ready to go out on the town? Most frequently, however, the pitfall is . . . housework. Who does the laundry and household chores? Even if he is doing the supermarket runs, is she still responsible for making the shopping list?

Most couples tend not to talk much about retirement except about the *date* of when they are going to retire, says Moen. "They don't talk about the ten to thirty years after that. Many will be married much longer in retirement than they were before retirement," she notes. Her advice? "*Talk* a lot," she says, adding, "You need to plan your lifestyle: How are you going to live? People talk about retirement like it's an *event*, not like it's going to be a *life*."

If talking about this is hard, an interesting approach to negotiating the parameters of daily married life can be gleaned from experts at the Harvard Negotiation Project in their book *Difficult Conversations: How to Discuss What Matters Most* by Douglas Stone, Bruce Patton, and co-authors (Penguin, 2000).

LOOKING FOR LOVE

The search for love continues throughout life; finding it is not so easy. And if you're a single, divorced, or widowed woman over 65, finding a male love partner is even more difficult. There are 146 unmarried women for every 100 unmarried men in the 45-to-64-year-old age range, and 315 unmarried women for every 100 unmarried men for people 65 and over in the U.S. If a picture speaks a thousand words, this graph tells the story:

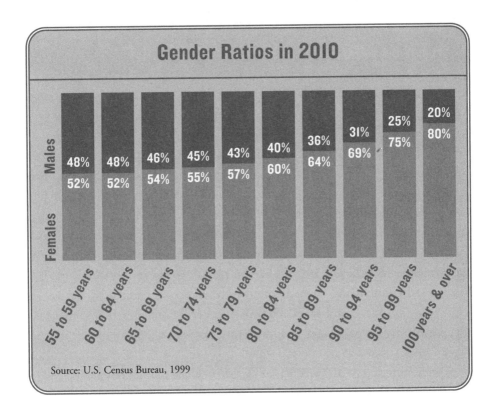

Gender Ratios in 2010

	55 to 59 years	60 to 64 years	65 to 69 years	70 to 74 years	75 to 79 years	80 to 84 years	85 to 89 years	90 to 94 years	95 to 99 years	100 years & over
Males	48%	48%	46%	45%	43%	40%	36%	31%	25%	20%
Females	52%	52%	54%	55%	57%	60%	64%	69%	75%	80%

Source: U.S. Census Bureau, 1999

This data brings to mind the title of the 1960s pop song "Where the Boys Are." Some enterprising single women have applied target marketing to this problem and come up with a solution: They've taken up fly fishing. Others have decided they're perfectly happy having mostly women as comrades, colleagues, neighbors, and friends. *The New York Times* reported in early 2004 that some women, anticipating the need for support and community as they age, are moving into retirement communities with other women on a sort of mutual support basis, working on the assumption that they won't find male companionship. And as noted above, friendship can involve love. Indeed, Lord Byron himself wrote, "Friendship is Love without his Wings!"

Still, if you're searching for romantic love, read on.

LOOKING FOR A MATE ONLINE

Some people try to meet others through blind dates, joining clubs, mall walking, and going to the gym, but you can also log on!

Since Sid Simon, 76, doesn't play tennis or golf in his community of Sanibel, Florida, he doesn't get a chance to meet many women. "I'm not a bar kind of person, and it doesn't feel like a big bountiful market," he says. Two friends who had met through match.com convinced him to join. Because he's very picky about whom he dates (she must be very fit and active), the retired professor appreciates being able to specify what he's looking for: a woman 55 to 65 (to keep up with him). "She must be sensual, alive intellectually, curious, still with wonder, and believing that she can make a difference in this world, too . . . Kissing and cuddling are very important to me. No cold fish need apply," he wrote in his profile. Through match.com, he's corresponded with and met several "interesting" women, and as of press time, he was scheduled to take one on a second date.

Despite a recent AARP survey that says that people in their 60s are most likely to be happier than other singles and be reluctant to get married, the seniors dating scene is more active than ever. In addition to the traditional mixers and trips, online dating is gaining popularity among the senior set. Of the approximately 6.8 million U.S. residents over 65 who are online, 1.1 million—about 17 percent—visited a personals site in an average month, according to industry sources in 2003. And the percentage of people using the Internet as an entrée to a new social life is only going to increase.

Seasoned users and relationship advisors say that success in the online world is a numbers game and that people should send many e-mails and not take it personally if others don't respond. After all, a profile is just that—a profile—and can't replace a face-to-face meeting.

While many seniors say they have been successful in meeting desirable people, online dating presents unique pitfalls. For example, people are tempted to lie about their age. Simon met one 65-year-old woman who wrote on her profile that she was 55. One 66-year-old woman from Alexandria, Virginia, said she hated the requirement of listing her age on dating sites. She says men have preconceived notions about her age.

Online dating introduces a whole new set of confusing social rules. Some men complain that women don't initiate contact, while some women report that men rarely respond when they do—instead preferring to be the pursuers. Then there's always the sting of rejection.

Dick Nipper, 73, a retired pipe fitter from south central Washington, hates the singles scene and tried online dating "out of curiosity." He was disappointed when three women he contacted didn't respond: "I wish she would say, 'I'm not interested' and leave it at that."

STAYING COOL

Romance-seeking seniors should also remember there are many ways to meet mates and not just rely on the Internet, urges Robin Gorman Newman, founder of love-coach.com. "Senior centers are happening places," she says. "There's a lot of socializing going on, due in part to the sense of community." She recommends checking out religious centers, adult-ed classes, dance lessons, or trips geared toward seniors. Other options, she says, are to volunteer or place a personal ad in a local newspaper.

Getting back into the dating scene can be daunting after being recently widowed or divorced. One 75-year-old widower from Melbourne, Florida, whose wife recently passed away after 53 years of marriage, said he felt like he was starting all over again, learning the rituals of dating.

Gorman Newman also suggests that seniors who are reentering the social market make it clear what they are looking for: "Some people want companionship more than romance. Not everyone is looking to get physical. It's good to be upfront, so there's no confusion."

Since adult children may be hesitant to encourage their parents to date again, Gorman Newman advises that senior daters take their time introducing their new love interests to their families.

Above all, take it easy and remember to have fun, she urges. "Love can happen at any age," she says. "Don't put more pressure on yourself than you have to. You don't have to look for Mr. or Ms. Right. Just look for a person whose company and conversation you enjoy."

YEE-HAH! THERE'S SEX AFTER 60

Yes, Martha. As people hit their 60s, 70s, and 80s, romance continues to blossom. So does sensuality. And—surprise!—sexual activity.

The comfortably asexual stereotype of that droopy older man or woman in a sloppy cardigan and sensible shoes may be not quite realistic. Your grown children may resent the "replacement" of their deceased or divorced parent with a newfound love. Your grandchildren might get squeamish and pronounce it "weird" or "yucky" to see you holding hands or smooching. They all might be horrified if you show up with a younger date or comment on someone's appearance. Well, they'll just have to get over it.

As one widower living in a Florida retirement community told his story, "There are a lot of wonderful people here, and the ratio of women to men is about two to one. I have met a couple of interesting women. I'm pushing 80 next month. I am amazed, I must confess, that I still have some of the urges I had many years ago. I didn't think this would be the case, but I guess it's natural."

Various surveys show that at least half of all Americans in the 60-plus age group are sexually active. That includes some late 70- and 80-year-olds, too. A 1999 report by the Palo Alto Medical Foundation of a study of more than 1,000 older men aged 58 to 94 found that "in the absence of social isolation and health issues, many older men show persistently active sexual lifestyles." Another small-

er survey of men and women whose average age was in the mid- to late 60s found "remarkably robust sex lives . . . even until advanced old age." A 1999 study by Brandeis University's National Center on Women and Aging found that nearly three quarters of women between the ages of 66 and 75 with annual household incomes of over $75,000 maintain sexual activity.

A surprising percentage of sexually active older adults report satisfaction. Among sexually active seniors, most (74 percent of the men and 70 percent of the women) said they were as satisfied or more satisfied with their sex lives, compared to when they were in their 40s, according to a 1998 study.

And sex sells, even the non-steamy, clinical sort. A book hailed by reviewers as the "best all-around sex manual for older adults," *The New Love and Sex after 60* by Dr. Robert Butler and Myrna I. Lewis has just been updated and rereleased—capping a 25-year run of popularity.

One study probed public attitudes toward whether a man or woman aged 75 can be considered sexy. Harris Interactive, Inc. conducted the interviews in January 2000, using a nationally representative sample of adults aged 18 and older. The survey includes an "over-sampling" of 1,155 persons aged 65 and older within the total adult sample (aged 18 and older) of 3,048. They found that over 80 percent of the whole sample, and slightly higher percentages of people over 65 years old, replied in the affirmative for both a 75-year-old man and woman.

CHALLENGES

Yet, there are challenges. There's cultural baggage. Women in particular may feel imperfect, "unsexy," or embarrassed over their decades-old, time-takes-a-toll bodies. Finding a partner can be hard. And there's the physiological challenge. The National Institute on Aging's (NIA) *Sexuality in Later Life* clinically spells out the common problems for men and women. To quote, "As men get older, impotence becomes more common. By age 65, about 15 to 25 percent of men have this problem at least one out of every four times they are having sex. This may happen in men with heart disease, high blood pressure, or diabetes—either because of the disease or the medicines used to treat it. . . ." As for women, it informs us, "The most common sexual difficulty of older women is dyspareunia, painful intercourse caused by poor vaginal lubrication. Your doctor or a pharmacist can suggest over-the-counter, water-based lubricants to use." (See www.niapublications.org/engagepages/sexuality.asp.)

GAY & GRAY

There are an estimated one to three million lesbian, gay, bisexual, and transgender (LGBT) Americans over the age of 65. By 2030, when 20 percent of Americans are over age 65, there will be about four million LGBT elders according to the National Gay and Lesbian Task Force Foundation.

In addition to the customary challenges of aging and retirement, this group also may confront discrimination in key areas: health services, benefits, retirement housing, and continuing-care communities. But sometimes out of lemons comes lemonade. A few dozen homes in a typical Florida retirement community, the Palms of Manasota, south of Tampa, have made history as the first all-gay retirement community. In Santa Fe, New Mexico, the nation's first full-service retirement community for lesbian, gay, bisexual, and transgender (LGBT) elders in the United States, called RainbowVision Properties, is slated for development in summer 2004. Plans are on the drawing board for several others, including the 75-unit Stonewall complex in Boston and a retirement resort called Our Town in California, both geared to LGBT seniors.

 ## HEALTHVIEWS

Safe Sex at Any Age

Experts warn that age does not protect you from sexually transmitted diseases. "Almost anyone who is sexually active is also at risk for being infected with HIV, the virus that causes AIDS. One out of every ten people diagnosed with AIDS in the United States is over age 50," according to the NIA. It further warns, "You are at risk if you have more than one sexual partner or are recently divorced or widowed and have started dating and having unprotected sex again. Always use a latex condom during sex, and talk to your doctor about ways to protect yourself from all sexually transmitted diseases. You are never too old to be at risk."

What To Do?

As at any age, communication with your partner is key to a good sexual relationship. There is a myriad of books and sex therapists who specialize in older adults. (One, Columbia University's Dr. Dagmar O'Connor, is a psychologist and the first woman sex therapist to be trained by Masters and Johnson in New York City.) Talk to your physician, but be aware that if you don't get the help you need, look elsewhere. That's because few internists are specially trained in the related fields of geriatrics or sexuality, let alone both.

To keep your sexual life simmering, the National Institute on Aging (NIA)'s *Sexuality in Later Life* advises, "Remember that sex does not have to include intercourse. Make your partner a high priority. Pay attention to his or her needs and wants. Take time to understand the changes you both are facing. Try different positions and new times, like having sex in the morning when you both may have more energy. Don't hurry—you or your partner may need to spend more time touching to become fully aroused." It further suggests, "Masturbation is a sexual activity that some older people, especially unmarried, widowed, or divorced people and those whose partners are ill or away, may find satisfying. If you do seem to have a problem that affects your sex life, talk to your doctor."

Want to feel sexy? Exercise!

Exercise is at the top of the list of what you can do to continue an active sex life, according to the NIA, which advises people to "exercise, eat good food, drink plenty of fluids like water or juices, don't smoke, and avoid alcohol. Try to reduce the stress in your life. See your doctor regularly. And keep a positive outlook on life."

 YOUR MONEY MATTERS

Some of the best things in life are, after all, free!

If you're reading this book for a friend or parent . . . here are two heads-ups: **1)** Don't fall into the stereotype trap. Remember, older folks have romantic urges, extramarital relationships, and sex lives, too. **2)** You may expect that without a full-time job, they'll spend more time with you or grandchildren. Don't be so sure! They may discover new relationships with peers.

Older Woman Meets Younger Man Online

After being widowed for a year and a half, Pat Weber, a spry, attractive 72-year-old who splits her residency between Milwaukee, Wisconsin, and Sun City, Arizona, received a solicitation from the Internet site Matchmaker.com while she was in Arizona.

They offered her a seven-day free trial. The curiosity of online dating led her to accept their offer. While in Arizona, she signed up for the Milwaukee area knowing she would be there shortly.

She read through the profiles of ALL the men, and one especially caught her eye . . . that of a 61-year-old man who wrote: "I am looking for a special lady that is bored with her life and wants a man that can make her feel like a very desired, happy, satisfied woman. I am an old fashioned romantic gentleman who likes to hug, hold hands, and be close. I'd like to call you just because I was thinking about you and wanted to hear your voice. I would love to pamper you. I think a woman of any age or size can be sexy and attractive. Sexy is not just appearance but an attitude, a presence, how you walk, the look in your eyes, your voice, your touch, and body language. I love to enjoy the essence of a woman, God's wonderful gift to man!"

"Wow . . . after reading that I was falling for him already," Weber admits. But she did nothing about contacting him because of the age difference. Her seven-day free trial ended and she thought no more about online dating, until Matchmaker offered her another seven-day trial a couple weeks later. So she went back into the site and was surprised to have received a message from the man whose profile had caught her eye. He said, "You sound like an interesting lady and I'd like to meet you." She wrote back and said she was flattered but felt he was too young for her. He replied, "I prefer older women because they are more mature, experienced, sensible, and don't come with all the baggage that younger ones do."

His attitude was a far cry from the usual one she heard around her competitive retirement community, where men of any age just wanted younger women. And they can get them! She says, "If a man can walk, he's got six women chasing him."

Well, since this fellow was in Milwaukee and she was in Sun City, the meeting had to wait for a few weeks. But meet they did, and thus began a whirlwind courtship of motorcycle rides, early-morning breakfasts, movies, great companionship, and a summer filled with activity and fun. "I never felt so important in my life," the former secretary said.

But all good things come to an end. Now she is back in Sun City, and he is still in Milwaukee; but his many phone calls and e-mails keep their romance blooming, and she is looking forward to next summer.

Weber credits the Internet with giving her the opportunity to meet people outside her local senior social scene. After she lost her husband, friends told her to get out and mingle. But she soon learned that wherever she went she was surrounded by couples or single women. If a man came along, you really didn't know a thing about him. With the Internet you learn his age, weight, height, religion, whether he smokes or drinks, where he grew up and the area he lives in now, his approximate annual income, his hobbies, and what he is looking for in a mate. His picture is also posted, so you get a fair idea of what he looks like. You feel like you know the person before you ever meet him.

You hear a lot of scary stories about meeting over the Internet, but Weber says you can tell a lot about a person by the way they write. She laughs about one 36-year-old who bombarded her with e-mails. "Now I know he didn't want my body so I will assume he wants my money. Got rid of him in a hurry!" But the men she met in her age category were all quality people—just looking for someone to share their free time with, just as she was.

Resource Guide

PUBLICATIONS

A Round-Heeled Woman: My Late-Life Adventures in Sex and Romance by Jane Juska (Villard, 2003).

Emotional Intelligence: Why It Can Matter More Than IQ by Daniel Goleman (Bantam Books, 1995).

Getting the Sex You Want: A Woman's Guide to Becoming Proud, Passionate, and Pleased in Bed by Sandra Leiblum, PhD, and Judith Sachs (Crown, 2002).

The New Love and Sex After 60 by Robert N. Butler, M.D., and Myrna I. Lewis, PhD (Ballantine Books, 2002).

Older Couples, New Romances: Finding & Keeping Love in Later Life by Edith Ankersmit Kemp, LCSW, and Jerrold E. Kemp, EdD (Celestial Arts, 2003).

Passionate Marriage: Love, Sex, and Intimacy in Emotionally Committed Relationships by David Schnarch (W. W. Norton, 1997).

Seasons of the Heart: Men and Women Talk About Love, Sex, and Romance After 60 by Zenith Henkin Gross (New World Library, 2000).

Still Doing It: Women and Men over Sixty Write About Their Sexuality by Joani Blank, ed. (Down There Press, 2000).

WEB SITES

In 2003, the "Most Popular Online Dating Sites for Seniors 65+" (according to comScore Media Metrix):

Tickle.com
Yahoo! Personals: personals.yahoo.com
Matchnet.com
Match.com
Singleme.com
Imatchup.com
Lavalife.com

Cupidjunction.com
Date.com
Cupidcams.com
Platinumromance.com
Datecam.com
Relationshipexchange.com
Romancepros.com

Others include:

50pluspersonals.com
gorgeousgrandma.com
lovecompass.com/special_dating/
    seniors
matchmaker.com
meetup.com
seniorfriendfinder.com
seniorscircle.com
seniorsinglefinder.com
seniorsmatch.com
seniorsweetheartz.com
singlesites.com/senior_dating.htm

PROBLEMS RELATED
TO SEXUALITY

AARP
601 E Street NW
Washington, DC 20049
888-687-2277
www.aarp.org

American Cancer Society
1599 Clifton Road NE
Atlanta, GA 30329
800-ACS-2345
www.cancer.org

American Foundation for Urologic
Disease, Inc.
1128 North Charles Street
Baltimore, MD 21201
800-242-2383
www.impotence.org

NIA Information Center
PO Box 8057
Gaithersburg, MD 20892-8057
800-222-2225
www.nia.nih.gov

GAY LESBIAN (LGBT) GROUPS

American Society on Aging Lesbian
and Gay Aging Issues Network
833 Market Street, Suite 511
San Francisco, CA 94103
800-537-9728
www.asaging.org/networks/lgain

Senior Action in a Gay Environment
SAGE
307 Seventh Avenue, 16th Floor
New York, NY 10001
212-741-2247
www.sageusa.org

CHAPTER 19

Grandparenting and Kids, Wonderful Kids

Polls tell us that when people talk about how they plan to spend their time in retirement, the item that tops the list is always "spend time with family." There's no reckoning how much of family time is, in fact, spent with children and teenagers. But ask most youngsters about their grandparents, or ask grandparents about their grandchildren, and instantly there's something—a spark, a longing, a pride.

In mobile 21st-century America, however, many people live at a distance (geographic or emotional) from the children they're biologically connected to. Others simply don't have young people in their family at all. That's the case, for instance, with many single people, gays and lesbians, and people from families that are small or not very close. Sometimes, like Wendy in *Peter Pan,* the children have simply grown up.

Aside from members of the immediate and extended family, there are lots of other ways to find a connection with youth. As with so many building blocks of life in THE RETIREMENT ZONE, you have some choices. Will you choose to live in an age-stratified community, where most people are more or less in the same stage of life? Many retirement communities have residential restrictions on children. If you choose to take a course at the local college, will you find one that caters to mature adults, or mix it up with the undergraduates? In your church or community, will you choose volunteer work that brings you closer to nature, that helps people in poverty, or that involves youth?

The following briefly addresses the grandparenting relationship and outlines a handful of intergenerational volunteer opportunities involving children.

GRANDCHILDREN: Kids Just Want to Have Fun

One thing is for sure: They grow up fast.

Whether you've got one, two, three grandchildren, or enough for an entire football team, the connection between older family members and kids can be powerful. The grandparent-grandchild bond stretches beyond, as the old joke goes, sharing a mutual enemy. Given the right moment, children are frequently fascinated to hear their great-grandparents' stories of that "Pleistocene" era, when "talking" movies (invented in 1923), air conditioning (1932), or helicopters (1939) were actually *news.* It's a strain for them, of course, to imagine a grandparent ever being their age. A 1950s prom dress stashed in the attic or some old pictures can help. Sharing an old photo album, love letters from a high-school crush, or a couple of Beatles albums dating to the Ed Sullivan era gives a sulky teenager something to chew on: personal history. *Your* stories become *their* stories. Even without resorting to the past, there are points of commonality. Kids and their grandparents can share a perceptive, piercing humor, and a curiosity about things that aren't "practical"—not to mention a mutual love of popcorn. The truism that grandparents reap the rewards, without the hassles, of parenthood obscures just how dynamic the intergenerational relationship can be.

It sounds obvious, but if you want to have a relationship with your grandchildren or great-grandchildren, it helps to take the time and make the effort to build a relationship. Keep in mind how tricky time is. A year represents, say, just 2 percent of your years if you're 50. That same calendar year represents a huge slice, fully 20 percent, of your five-year-old grandchild's life so far. It's like bending down to see what the world looks like from, say, three feet tall. Things—including you—look different from their perspective.

You may not be the only grandparent in their lives, either. American families are complicated by high divorce and remarriage rates, trends toward single parenting, and new reproductive technologies. Six-year-old Bella from Bend, Oregon, counts seven grandparents. She announces matter-of-factly, "I have five grannies: Oma, Granny Gladys, Lana, Audrey, and Momo. And two grandpas."

CAPTURING SPECIAL FAMILY LEGACIES

If you are a member of the "sandwich generation" (with responsibilities for both older and younger dependents) you may be aware of family legacies that deserve preservation. Video or audiotaping an older relative can be a meaningful family project. With a growing interest in oral histories, there are lots of resources you can find to help figure out how to proceed.

For instance, Gwynne Tomlan-Santiago, a retired actress and dance teacher, says, "Before I leave this earth I'd love to put together a documentary film with my mother about her experiences. While she's still on this planet, I want to do that for members of the family who will come after us." She explains, "In the Memphis and Jackson area, after Reconstruction, night riders went through black communities taking land. She's the eldest person alive on that side of the family; she was eight or ten years old when this happened. Her eyewitness recollection of the night riders coming to their house, burning the house down, and how the family were forced to become sharecroppers after their land was taken . . . All of her life that story was told over and over. So before, as they say, the energy wanes, my first retirement project is to begin videotaping."

It's easy to do this at home with a handheld video camera. Experts offer several tips: Use a tripod that's set up about six to eight feet away from the subject and video in good indoor light during the daytime. Do a trial run first with someone other than your subject, experiment with the zoom lens so you fill the frame, and check the sound. (If your built-in microphone isn't powerful enough, an external, wired microphone can be purchased for $35 to $70.) The most important thing, say the experts, is to keep it simple. Find a place where Grandma or Grandpa is comfortable, whether that's at the kitchen table or in a favorite chair. To get the conversation going, just ask him or her about a favorite story, relative, or beloved heirloom. Don't expect to film for hours. You may have to do several sessions of 20 or 30 minutes apiece to capture the whole story. If you have a digital video camera you can easily transfer the video to your computer, edit it, and create your own DVDs to send to family and friends.

PRACTICAL TIP: Playing with the Grandkids

Bond with your grandchildren: Get active and bake cookies; build model airplanes. Rediscover the simple wonders of tickles, pillow fights, new toys, the unexpected, unnecessary spoil-'em-rotten shopping trip, or trips to amusement parks. Waste time just "being." Teach them to play golf or poker; listen to music together; let them teach you an online game; play checkers.

Do the outrageous. "Old age is an excellent time for outrage. My goal is to say or do at least one outrageous thing every week," as Maggie Kuhn, founder of the Gray Panthers, once said. Without embarrassing yourself or your teen (good luck!), don't act your age. Get down on the floor and play with the baby. Send jokes or be pen pals with your pre-teen grandkids. Start a collection of stamps, rocks, comic books. Take trips to the zoo or theater. Have a sleepover party. Build (or be the overseer of construction) of a tree house. Play a practical joke on the parents, together. Join in the fun!

Or, pick a service project that you both care about, whether it's a local bike path, traffic safety, childhood hunger, or repainting the community room in your church.

Traveling with the Grandkids

A trip with the grandchildren can be a bonding adventure, and of course, can create memories of a lifetime. You can book with an upscale tour company, such as Grandtravel in Washington, D.C., which specializes in grandparent-grandchild trips, or plan your own. Common sense is your best guide here, but whether you take the kids for one day on a trip to a petting farm or for a month of museum-intensive, canal-boating, history-laden touring around the British Isles, be prepared. Oh, and never underestimate the power of shopping.

7 Practical Tips for Building an Itinerary with Grandkids

Whether you go to Paris or Podunk with your grandchildren (with or without their parents), you can have a marvelous time. But it does take a little planning.

1) Don't overschedule—for either of your sakes—and be flexible. Expect to make last-minute changes—kids are unpredictable.
2) Build the trip around one or two specific destinations, such as a national park, a museum, a play, or a visit to a farm.
3) Try to plan together, by looking at maps or sharing ideas.
4) Short is sweet—both in terms of the time away from home and how much you do in a day.
5) Make sure there's quiet-time equipment packed, such as books, videos, audio CDs, and art supplies.
6) Consider staying in a motel that has a swimming pool. A quick dip at the end of a long day can do wonders for a tired child or cranky teen.
7) Visit other relatives along the way–especially if they have children the same age.

BEYOND BLOOD TIES: Insider's Guide to Intergenerational Programs

Outside of your own family, there are a zillion ways you can reach out to children. Opportunities can be found locally for tutoring, mentoring, enrichment, and buddy programs. Depending on your talents, you may want to participate in

Children's museums They're weatherproof and usually offer clean bathrooms and a snack bar. Plus they are specifically built to accommodate children's needs to run, jump, touch, make noise, and play. Check ahead to make sure the museum has something for your grandchild's age group; most are geared to the six-to-twelve range. For instance, while in San Francisco, budding scientists should not miss the Exploratorium. In Madison, Wisconsin, kids can play farmer at the Madison Children's Museum. In Baltimore, there's lots of room for tumbling and climbing in a waterfront children's museum, Port Discovery.

organized, supervised extracurricular activities such as coaching, teaching art or music classes, or participating in a community choir. Churches and faith communities, along with local YMCA, usually run programs for children. Some social service agencies or hospitals may allow volunteers to work with abandoned or homeless at-risk children and teens (sick and indigent children, abused children, and children living in institutional care settings).

DOES IT MAKE A DIFFERENCE? Intergenerational programs can be wonderful for both groups involved. It's "validating for the older adults and exciting for the children," says Bronwyn Fees, an assistant professor at Kansas State University who studies intergenerational programs.

When successful, these programs can benefit the children, too. A national study by Public/Private Ventures of children who participated in the Big Brothers Big Sisters program found they were half as likely to skip a day of school or to start using drugs than peers who were not in the program. Other benefits were improved school performance and attendance, better grades, and greater self-confidence.

TUTORING is probably the single biggest point of interaction between volunteers and school-age children and teens. Many tutoring groups work in the school system.

New Jersey resident Clifton Arrington describes his experience: "I do a reading-buddy thing with elementary-grade children. I go in one or two days a week, usually for an hour or two. I'm assigned to a particular class as a teacher. The teacher will select students that may need some assistance in reading, or if they're working on a certain project they might need some assistance with that. I work with that particular young person. I find it exhilarating—the young people are phenomenal. It's the most fulfilling volunteer work I do. I feel that I'm making some kind of impact on a young person that just really influences his life, you know, somewhere down the road. I feel good about that. And I can see their delight in having someone just sit there, and encourage them, and be with them—and not be judgmental. Just accept them for who they are and try to help them."

Experience Corps (www.experiencecorps.org) members work as tutors and mentors to children in public schools in more than a dozen cities from Baltimore to San Francisco. The program describes its purpose, which is to "channel the talent and energy of growing numbers of older adults into public and community service." Members receive training in early childhood education and literacy, and work with teams, with the intent of making a positive contribution to the overall climate of a school.

> **PRACTICAL TIP:** When working as a volunteer in an intergenerational program, check to ensure that all the necessary legal forms, such as parental permission slips for minors, are in order. Some programs have recently demanded that volunteers even be fingerprinted! If you are not sure, then ask either the organization's lawyer or your own.

MENTORING may include academic tutoring, but it's a more all-around relationship in which an adult serves as a role model, friend, advisor, and informal advocate. The oldest and largest youth mentoring organization in the United States, Big Brothers Big Sisters (www.bbbsa.org), matches volunteers with children aged 5 to 18 in one-on-one relationships. It serves 200,000 children in 500 agencies across 5,000 communities. The children are enrolled usually on the recommendation of a teacher. Volunteers spend from one hour a week to several hours a month. The organization says that the "Bigs" and "Littles" are matched by trained professionals. As a volunteer, you might spend time on activities you and the child select, such as attending sporting events. For more information on mentoring, visit www.mentoring.org.

ASSISTING NEEDY GRANDPARENTS More than two million American children live in households headed by grandparents, according to the 2000 U.S. Census. And the stress levels among grandparents with the sole responsibility of raising youngsters is reflected in remarkably high rates of heart attacks. Various organizations assist needy grandparents and their grandchildren. For instance, Generations United, a membership organization focused on promoting intergenerational strategies, is a source of information about programs to help both children and their grandparents in this tough situation. Visit www.gu.org.

 ## HEALTHVIEWS

It's hard to quantify the number of people doing volunteer work with children in one capacity or another. However, what's clear is the need: There are an estimated 14 million children considered "at risk" in the U.S. due to poverty, homelessness, food insecurity, and other factors such as parents who are substance abusers or in prison. As for your own well-being, being connected, whether to your own family or to children through a volunteer program, is healthful.

 ## YOUR MONEY MATTERS

- **Count your change:** When working with children of any age, it's tempting to use little gifts as a way to move things along. That's fine, as long as it doesn't become the main currency of your relationship.
- **Taxes:** If you are volunteering to work with children, some of your expenses might be tax deductible. See Your Money Matters in Chapter 12, A Volunteering Primer, page 129.

> **If you're reading this book for a spouse, friend, or parent . . .** Whether the "child" in question is a relative, neighbor, or a pen pal, having a relationship with someone just starting out in life can be enriching for both the child and your loved one. Encourage your parent, sibling, or friend to find a way to relate to younger people—it can be a source of surprise and delight!

Grandfriends

Sandy Eggers is head of preschool at the Emmanuel United Methodist Kindergarten in Memphis, Tennessee. She says she became aware of the fact that, with living arrangements that keep different age groups separate from one another, children don't understand what it is like to age in our society. So she introduced into her kindergarten classes a program called "Grandfriends," recruiting about two dozen older adults living in a retirement community to come to class on a regular basis and interact with about 50 kindergartners.

"We paired them so there were two kids per adult, so bonds could be made," she recalls.

The rewards for the adults were many. First and foremost, she says, was "simple joyfulness and fun. It sounds trite, but the adults talked a lot about seeing the expressions on the six-year-olds' faces, and how much they enjoyed that." The experience made the older folks feel better about the next generation, too. Some said they now don't feel that children are as undisciplined as they expected. Some expressed a sense of purpose in helping. For instance, one person who loved to paint made a picture for her two children, noting that "they have lots of toys and material things, but they don't have their own personal painting."

For others, the benefits were in continuing to learn and be challenged. The adults, whose own grandchildren were older than the kids in the program, recalled how amazing it was to see "what those little minds have going on up there." One year, an autistic child was part of the program, and the adults were fascinated by the challenges she faced.

For some adult volunteers, the feeling of being wanted and needed was salient. One of the children was being raised by his own grandparents (whom he viewed as parents), so when he was assigned a Grandfriend, he was delighted, saying, "Now I have a grandmother." Some of these relationships have lasted for years. "Almost every apartment of a Grandfriend has art or letters from 'their children' on display," says Sandy.

Resource Guide

PUBLICATIONS

Amazing Grace: African American Grandmothers as Caregivers and Conveyors of Traditional Values by Dorothy Smith Ruiz (Praeger, 2004).

Grandloving: Making Memories with Your Grandchildren, 3rd Edition, by Sue Johnson and Julie Carlson (Heartstrings Press, 2003).

If I Knew It Was Going to Be This Much Fun, I Would Have Become a Grandparent First by Willard Scott and Friends (Hyperion, 2004).

Ordinary Resurrections: Children in the Years of Hope by Jonathan Kozol (Perennial, 2001).

ORGANIZATIONS AND WEB SITES

Community Arts Network
www.communityarts.net
(contact via Web site)

Experience Corps
2120 L Street NW, Suite 400
Washington, DC 20037
202-478-6190
www.experiencecorps.org

Foster Grandparents Program (FGP)
The Grandparent Caregiver
    Resource Center
New York City Department
    for the Aging
2 Lafayette Street
New York, NY 10007
212-442-3117 (program office)
www.nyc.gov/html/dfta/html/
    foster_grand.html

Generations United
1333 H Street NW, Suite 400 W
Washington, DC 20005
202-289-3979
www.gu.org

Grandparent Information Center
AARP
601 E Street NW
Washington, DC 20049
202-434-2296 (center office)
www.aarp.org/confacts/programs/gic.
html

Senior Corps/Corporation for
    National and Community
    Service Headquarters
1201 New York Avenue NW
Washington, DC 20525
800-424-8867
TTY: 800-833-3722
www.seniorcorps.org/joining/fgp

CHAPTER 20

Playing

HOBBIES AND PASSIONS

Gardening. Sky diving. Playing jazz. They're all play. But because we're grown-ups we call them "hobbies or passions."

The humble hobby is just something one does for relaxation and old-fashioned fun. A passion is a state of mind, and the subject of one's ardent devotion. People old enough to remember when passion was a code word for sex now routinely talk about their passion for, say, dark chocolate or hatha yoga. In our label-parsing, productivity-minded culture, it seems hipper, younger somehow to have a "passion" than a hobby. Still, both are forms of play. Both, too, are great post-work anchor activities. A person sometimes finds in their hobby/passion what was lost with the departure from a paid job: a rhythm and structure to the week; achievable goals; a door that opens up ways to participate in the world; meaningful work; tangible accomplishments, and sometimes friendship.

It may be tempting to trivialize a passion for golf, or scoff at knitting. But joy, energy, commitment, and imagination aren't yet wholly owned subsidiaries of corporate America. Nor are they owned by youth. And it's these powerful human qualities that one hears in the voices of people—older people—who are engaged in the business of their lives.

Doris Hallgren of Tampa, Florida, has a passion for genealogy. "My father's family was in the DAR," says the vivacious 77-year-old. "In 1997, I had two pieces of paper with little notes scribbled on them about family connections. Since we've put it on the computer, the family tree has just grown and grown. There are about a thousand people now on it."

Jean Andrews of Austin, Texas, talks about her recent travels abroad as if they were as easy as going to the mall: "Last year I spent about a month in Quizhou, China. My plans in April 2003 were canceled because of the Iraq war. I was going to Turkmenistan and Uzbekistan, and also to parts of Morocco where I haven't been before. So instead, in October I went up to northern Canada to see the polar bears, and then my daughter-in-law and I went to Eastern Europe, to Poland and the Czech Republic and Hungary." Jean Andrews is 80 years old.

TRENDS IN THE RETIREMENT ZONE: A Widening World of Hobbies and Passions

Throughout these chapters are discussions of a wide range of subjects, from social change to spirituality, about which some people are passionate. Here's a list of other interests; one of them might turn out to be a hobby for you, and a passion for someone else:

acting, archaeology, astronomy, bird-watching, boating, camping, cards, cars, ceramics, chorus, collecting, collecting at eBay, community newspapers, computers, cooking, dance competitions, doll-making, domestic arts, film-making, financial investing, finding and restoring antiques, fishing, flower arranging, flying, folk dancing, gambling, games, genealogy, golf, hiking, history, hunting, inventing, knitting, magic, model building, model trains, movies, needlework, painting/drawing, photography, playing and listening to music, playwriting, poetry, politics and advocacy, reading books alone and with book clubs, repairing musical instruments, restoration, sailing, senior beauty pageants, senior bodybuilding, sewing, singing, skiing, sports, storytelling, swimming, tap dancing, teaching, travel, square dancing, tennis, walking, water sports, wine tasting, writing.

Recent trends in the world of hobbies and passions:
- Women have taken up traditionally male-dominated hobbies, from running marathons to camping in national parks to fly fishing.
- More people over 60 participate in biking, running, triathlons, and other competitive sports than even a decade ago.
- The newest, hottest, biggest hobby is computers.
- There's information aplenty, both online and in specialized publications on the hobby of your choice, from antique cars to home decorating.
- Most hobbies and passions have a social element, if a person cares to seek it. An interested person can find, for instance, knitting circles, book clubs, speed-walking groups, wine-tasting classes, and organized group bird-watching trips.

ATHLETICS

Sports, of course, can be a passion. And amazing stories of aged athletic prowess emerge. Octogenarians who swim five miles a week. Ninety-year-old runners who start and finish marathons. Their acknowledgment by the Guinness World Records (www.guinnessworldrecords.com) in 2004 is a virtual salute to 77-year-old Canadian Jack MacKenzie, the oldest person to ski to the North Pole, and to 70-year-old Japanese Yuichiro Miura, who made history as the oldest person to scale Mount Everest.

Mature people are taking their places alongside twenty- and thirty-year-olds in competitive and noncompetitive sporting activities. For instance, the nation's largest race, the New York City Marathon, hosts 35,000 runners every year. The participation rate of older finishers has leaped in the past decade. In 2003, over a thousand runners over age 60 finished the 26.2-mile course, compared to just six over-60-year-old finishers in 1993. An astonishing 140 people in their seventies finished as well. (Among the 2003 finishers were 613 men and 123 women between ages 60 and 64; 44 men and 49 women between 65 and 70; 93 men and 16 women between 70 and 74; and 26 men and five women between ages 75 and 79.)

As with running, so it goes with many sports: swimming, walking, and cross-country skiing. For instance, take Harold Kessler, who may be one of the most accomplished older cyclists on the East Coast. "I was sixteen years old when I got hooked," says the Brooklyn-born octogenarian, who recalls watching bike races at Coney Island's indoor Velodrome track in the late 1930s and early 1940s. In his early years, Harold switched to motorcycles. But by age 60, after recuperation from an accident left him in need of exercise, he was back on a bicycle—and racing again. He says, "I was putting in forty miles every morning, usually six days a week. Up until I was seventy-five years old, I rode seven thousand miles a year. Every day. Except when it rained. Winter or summer. It was a matter of life or death; I just rode, no matter how cold it was. It keeps you young." He racked up dozens of bike racing medals over the years. Harold adds, "I won the last race I entered—a time trial at age seventy-five. There weren't many others my age. But I beat the seventy- and the sixty-five-year-olds."

Yes, it's possible.

THEATER

Carole Schweid was a member of the original Broadway cast of *A Chorus Line*. A graduate of Juilliard, she's been a singer, dancer, writer, and producer. At age 56 she joined the board of the Westport Arts Center. And recently she's worked as coproducer of an inventive midweek lunchtime theater series called *Play With Your Food*, which plays to sell-out crowds in her tony Connecticut town. "It's all about the theater for me. I don't care what I am doing in it," she says. "I am as happy ushering at the gala as being the ticket taker. I am as happy being the ticket taker as being the headliner. If it's theater, I just want to be there!" If Carole were a fish, the theater would be her pond.

The number of senior theater groups has doubled, compared to just a few years ago. The esprit de corps, the fun, and the opportunity to vent your emotions are all draws. Bonnie Vorenberg, director of ArtAge Publications in Portland, Oregon, explains senior theater's appeal: "It is such a thrill. Here you are at seventy or eighty and you put your words onstage or portray a character, and an audience stands up and applauds. There's no better thrill than having applause." It's seniors, too, who make up the audience.

The company names are telling: San Diego Late Bloomers Comedy Improv Troupe; Sarasota Senior Theatre; The InterActors of Milwaukee; the Better

Than Ever Independents of Sewickly, Pennsylvania; Footsteps of the Elders, from Columbus, Ohio; Encore Theatre of Eugene, Oregon. Some programs are university-based. At the University of Nevada in Las Vegas, a large campus with 23,000 students, a senior theater program founded in 1990 offers older students a variety of classes from acting and creative dramatics to directing and playwriting, as well as a first-in-the-nation Bachelor of Arts degree in senior adult theater.

ArtAge keeps a comprehensive database of senior theaters, and provides information, resources, and a directory. Not surprisingly, the senior theaters are generally small and are sponsored by some other organization (usually a community theater, sometimes a church). Their programming varies. Musicals, improvisation, oral histories, and drama are standards. Some also tackle relevant social issues such as elder abuse, bereavement, and ageism. "Raging Grannies," an activist group, uses street theater as a form of protest.

With 500 senior theaters in operation, and perhaps a hundred or several hundred people involved in each outfit, it would be a stretch to say that the senior theater movement is numerically significant. However, culture moves in mysterious ways. Perhaps Hollywood will take a cue and offer programming that's more reflective of the real-life issues and concerns of people over 40. Perhaps the findings of an NIH-funded study of theater and creativity in seniors—now under way—will catapult senior theater onto the front pages of health news. Will the quirky improv class of today become the hottest trend in "instant creativity" tomorrow? Will someone find that memorizing lines from Shakespeare is the most effective natural, drug-free memory-improvement regimen? Who knows? Anything could happen. After all, it's theater.

COMPUTERS

There's no underestimating the transformative power of a computer on a beginner. Not that most seniors are beginner computer users.

With every year that passes, more and more people over 65 are comfortable working online. Computers are a major hobby. One federal study found that over half of people 60 and under had access to the Internet, as did one third of people between 60 and 69, and slightly more than one in five people between ages 70 and 79.

From the users' experience, this hobby occurs in various phases: initiation, when the learning curve is steep; the first year or two of use, when users are in discovery mode; and then ongoing integration of the computer and its functions into a person's life.

For some, learning about the inner workings of the computer is fascinating. Others spend time learning about software or building Web sites. Or "putting their lives online" (not to be confused with putting their lives ON the line!), in terms of computerizing financial and health records, address books, photo albums, lists of possessions, and transferring hard copy to electronic records. Some people are taken with digital photo technology. Interactive opportunities as different as chat rooms and eBay have appeal, as does browsing, blogging, and shopping online.

Of course, there's the "stuff" itself: hardware, software, and streams and reams of information about user-friendliness, cost, and speed.

People who've crossed the Maginot Line from noncomputer to computerized will attest that at some indefinable point, it gets easier. Your keyboarding skills improve. You learn some shortcuts. You figure out how to find answers, do a refined search, and back up. Perhaps, after an initial investment of time, you will spend less, rather than more, time on the computer. You begin to feel like something's missing in your day if you haven't checked your e-mail account.

If you are thinking about returning to a salaried job, computer competence is essential in the workplace. SeniorNet is an organization specifically geared to helping seniors get online (www.seniornet.org). Courses are also offered at most public libraries, some senior centers, and at some colleges as well.

Note: Searching for information, especially about health and travel, can yield both excellent, useful information—and garbage. Before acting on information from the Internet, check to ensure that the source is reliable. This is particularly important in regard to health information. If the Web site you're looking at is from a U.S. or state government agency, an academic institution that you've heard of before, or a well-established nonprofit organization, chances are it's reliable. (If you're not sure about the latter, call your local library and inquire.)

CRAFTS

At 87, Natalie Grossman of Walpole, Massachusetts, is the kind of gal who, when asked in April to crochet an afghan, produces a lovely finished piece by July. A former accountant who retired at 68, she's been crocheting since she was 14. (To put this in perspective, Natalie was born in 1916, which was before Kleenex, Band-Aids, or hair dryers were invented. She learned to crochet as a teenager the year of the great stock market crash of 1929.) Her mother taught her, she says, and "I do it constantly." She adds, "It relaxes me, and it keeps my hands supple." She does needlepoint as well—and crossword puzzles.

Fred Faselt, 76, of Covington, Kentucky, retired in 1991 after working for 30 years as an industrial model maker. He said, "I wanted some wood products like bird feeders and some construction around the home. I couldn't afford to have it done, and I like to work with my hands anyway, so I just started buying equipment that I could use to work with, and if I didn't know how to do something, I'd go to the library and get a book or ask somebody. But in my work I used a lot of tools and I got familiar with woodworking. There are all kinds of feeders: suet, peanut, seed feeders, and thistle feeders. If I can pick up a buck or two, why, that's fine too. I don't have the money to travel like a lot of retired people do. I'm kind of a homebody anyway. I always enjoyed working and making things."

As though in the blood (or in the fingers), crafts have a peculiar way of linking generations. In her 50s, Erlene Carter retired from a career as a secretary and stenographer, moving with her husband from California to their home state of Arkansas, in part to help care for their aging parents. She found part-time secretarial work at a booking agency, which led to a job next door at the Arkansas Craft Guild: "There were all these people doing all these creative things: pottery, blacksmithing, leatherwork, woodwork—on and on. All of the pioneer survival crafts." She fell in love with one simple item: little dolls made from the dried husks of corn, their clothing made from colorful, hand-dyed shucks. "I just thought the corn-shuck dolls were beautiful. I really really wanted to make them," she recalls. Soon after, she learned to make corn-shuck dolls.

Erlene continues, "When I mentioned it to my mother, she said: 'Why didn't you say something, I made them all my life.' My mother's family had lived six or seven miles out in the country here in Stone County. It was rather isolated. My mother said, 'Corn-shuck dolls were just the kind that everybody had' when she was a child. If someone came to play when she was a child and didn't bring a doll, they went to the corncrib and made one."

Eighty-year-old Grace Voight of Bridgeport, Connecticut, retired after four decades working as a quality control inspector. She says she started ceramics 40 years ago. At home, she works on ceramics for three or four hours almost daily and goes to a local studio weekly. She says, "It keeps my mind active." Although her emphysema slows her down, she says, "I'd like to do ceramics for as long as I can. I have a lot of things in the works and I have to get them finished."

Dotti Plotkin, 69 years old, from Tucson, Arizona, is another ceramics hobbyist. Dotti is winding down her career as an insurance agent/financial planner. She spends about eight hours a week working out of her garage, where she has a kiln and wheel. She explains the allure: "It gives me quite a lot of satisfaction. I get involved with it. It's like you're away from your self. You get carried away." Both Dotti and Grace say they'd like to keep doing ceramics "forever."

Virtually every specific craft has an organization, Web site, and books dedicated to helping craftspeople find information and each other. Check the library, the Internet. or the Hobby Industry Association (www.hobby.org).

DANCE

Square dancing, jigs, samba, salsa, tango, and the jitterbug are wonderful. But if there's one kind of dance that attracts people in THE RETIREMENT ZONE, it's the line dance. Easy to do without a partner, fun, and sometimes challenging, the line dance is to people over 50 what the Twist used to be when they were teenagers. The simple reason why line dances are popular at parties, in aerobics classes, at senior centers, and high-end spa retreats is that they are fun.

At 77, Sylvia Polite still loves to dance. She always has, from the time she became old enough to get into the Savoy Ballroom in Harlem, where she grew up. Now that she's retired, she has more time to spend doing what she loves. "If you don't use it, you lose it," she's fond of saying. Before she retired, Sylvia worked for 26 years at a company in the Garment District, where she was shop steward and an accounts-payable assistant. Now that she's retired, with five grandchildren and three great-grandchildren, she's really enjoying life. Despite some health problems (she's also a breast cancer survivor), Sylvia's "life-is-a-ball-room-so-why-not-dance?" attitude keeps her on the move. She travels, goes places all the time, and every six months she proctors licensing exams for CPAs and attorneys. She's "open" to possibility. That's what got her onstage at the Golden Image Awards show for women over 60—just like Miss America, but without the bathing suits—where she modeled and danced.

Liz Lerman Dance Exchange is a national pioneer in engaging everyday people over the age of 65 in the creation and performance of contemporary dance. Based in suburban Washington, D.C., the troupe consists of performers whose ages span six decades, and their program often includes in-depth residencies in communities across the country (www.danceexchange.org.).

GARDENING

Digging in the dirt. Watching things grow. Making a beautiful little spot out of an ordinary corner of the yard. Gardening is spiritual, fun, artistic, and some-times good exercise, too. It gets you moving, gets you outdoors. No wonder it's a much-beloved pastime. If you're relocating to a new climatic zone—for instance, to warmer weather—expect to have fun learning about different plants and ecol-ogy. Gardening can be a year-round activity (during cold winters, one can always study, plan, and dream). It's a wonderful way to express yourself, share a passion with others, and to have a little private interaction with Mother Nature.

You can find wonderful photo books with detailed "how to" information in most bookstores (they are cheaper in secondhand shops) and an extraordinary amount of information in magazines and on the Internet. Check out www.gardenguides.com or www.taylorsgardeningguides.com, and Web sites for botan-ical gardens and cooperative extensions.

MUSIC

Music is a way of life. And it's a wonderful activity for people in THE RETIREMENT ZONE.

Oberlin, Ohio, may be one of the few places where it comes as no surprise when an octogenarian still plays in a jazz quartet. Oberlin College is home to one

of the nation's best-known university conservatories, and it's a place where there's music everywhere, about 400 concerts a year. Residents of the local retirement community participate in numerous chamber music groups and jazz ensembles, and attend performances at the college.

In New Jersey, Marvin Mausner, 79, a retired chemist, has been playing violin since he was a child. He also plays the viola. He met his wife, who plays cello, at about age 19 in the early 1940s, after the two joined the American Youth Orchestra conducted by Dean Dixon. Decades later, they both participate actively in community orchestras and spend as many as eight hours a week practicing.

The local music school or community college in your town or city is the best place to look for information on lessons. Or you can always start a rock band in your garage.

CREATIVE AND MEMOIR WRITING

Older people have always had stories to tell. What's new is that older writers now know that, if they choose, they can hold a finished product in their hand, whether that's a tiny volume of poetry or a 500-page history of the county jail. Rejection slips from publishers and magazines be damned; today there's more than one way to see your work in print. With the explosion of opportunities to "get published" (thanks to an industry of self-published books, independent and Internet marketing, and desktop publishing software), people of all ages and abilities are busily penning—or keyboarding—their memoirs, fantasies, mystery novels, and political tracts.

Jim Alter of Chicago worked in the family business, but he was always a writer. "I kept a journal for fifty years, a day-by-day journal," he said. "For our fiftieth anniversary last year, I reduced the eighteen thousand pages to four hundred fifty pages, had that printed in a hardcover book, and gave it to our kids as an anniversary gift. I called it *Joanne and Me*." He wrote a few mysteries, too, which he says, "are on the shelf." At age 81, Jim finished a memoir that he titled *We Were So Young*: "It was of my World War II experience in the Army Air Force. We flew thirty-one combat missions over Germany. It's about how frightened I was, and what we saw, and what we did. I have letters I'd written that my father had saved, and I have a pretty good data bank, and my memory is still pretty good." When no publishers nibbled, Jim decided to underwrite a small print run, and with help from family members, handle the marketing and distribution. He says with satisfaction, "When the first draft comes out of the printer, you set that down on your desk, and look at the several hundred pages. And you think, 'Did I really do that?'"

Local universities and colleges, and also online courses, offer tutorials in writing both fiction and nonfiction. Serious writers often attend writing conferences, which can last from a day to a week and feature workshops on everything from different writing genres to publicity; lectures by well-known writers, agents, and publishers; and networking opportunities. Some offer contest opportunities. You don't have to travel far to attend. You can find listings in writers' reference books such as the *Novel & Short Story Writer's Market* by Anne Bowling, Michael Schweer, and Vanessa Lyman, eds. (Writers Digest Books), which is updated annually and lists hundreds of conferences, organized by both location and month.

AND . . . IDEAS OF YOUR OWN

And people can develop a passion for anything. For instance: peppers.

"My life began at age forty-five," Jean Andrews, known locally in Austin as "The Pepper Lady," is fond of saying. By age 45, a 25-year marriage had ended. By age 50, in 1973, the petite artist-writer was enrolled in a doctoral program in art education at the University of North Texas. While trolling for a thesis topic, she stumbled on the fact that little was known about the pepper genus, *Capsicum*. She says, "I had discovered in growing peppers that I wanted to learn more about them, I was curious, but very little had been written about them. They were the most used spice and condiment in the world and had never been illustrated, so I decided I would illustrate that genus." First Jean practiced drawing technically accurate botanical renderings. Then she began drawing peppers. Painting from only live specimens, she then began to grow peppers, sometimes dozens of different varieties in a year. She drew the peppers she grew, despite suffering a retinal occlusion that affected her vision so badly she could only produce several drawings a year. "What really gives me my drive is an insatiable curiosity," she says, adding, "It took me seven years. First I had to determine which species to include in the illustrations. By the time I did all that, I had a book." The carefully illustrated, now-classic *Peppers: The Domesticated Capsicum* was, she says, "well-received; it's still the bible of peppers."

To understand how the pepper migrated from place to place, she started traveling for her research. Her investigations took her to virtually every continent, including China, the Middle East, Europe, and western Africa. "A lot of my traveling has been tracking Christopher Columbus. Columbus discovered the New World, opened it up, anyway," she explains, "and with that, all these New World plants started moving out. I have followed that migration throughout the world and written about it. I came up with a new theory on how they moved, and that theory has been accepted by the American Geographical Society." The resultant book was *The Pepper Trail: History and Recipes from Around the World*. "It won an international award as the most scholarly food book that year. I didn't touch much on the botanical aspect in that book, it was a history of how peppers moved around the world and affected different cuisines."

Over decades, Jean uncovered the private and public lives of the pepper plant: their insides and outsides, their form in bud and fruition, their many varieties, where they come from, how they got there, how they affected different international cuisines, and of course, what they look like, from the strict perspective of an accurate botanical drawing.

Having thoroughly plumbed the pepper plant, Jean's attentions now are on textiles. She's had a lifelong interest in embroidery, folk textiles, and folk art, and has amassed a large collection during her travels. A woman with a philanthropic streak, she's already endowed several visiting professorships at her alma mater, and has also donated her textile collection for study in the North Texas University's Jean Andrews Textile Study Room.

With a profile like that, one would expect Jean Andrews to say her passion is education or travel, if not peppers. But when asked, she says, "My main passion is the freedom to do my own thing and women's rights. I like to enable young women, and to encourage them to do things that my generation was completely denied. I don't think most people realize what we weren't able to do."

As for herself today, at age 80, she says, "I don't think I am doing anything surprising, I'm just doing what I am doing."

 ## HEALTHVIEWS

Hobbies and passions can be a wonderful way to keep mentally and physically active and socially engaged. Like eating a delicious, nutritious meal, you may not even bother to think about the fact that it's good for you. Researchers who work on a large federal study called the Health and Retirement Study tell us, "Many people believe that being active can help keep people physically healthy and keep their minds sharp. For example, doing things like exercising, doing crossword puzzles, and learning a new language might help keep your mind and body healthy. Over the years, researchers have found clues that suggest that this may be true." Remember: Like an L.L. Bean coat, some hobbies wear well: music, art, and theater, for example. Others may wear you (or your body parts) out, such as basketball.

 ## YOUR MONEY MATTERS

Hobbies can be expensive if they require equipment, classes, or trips. But in any given hobby area, you may find ways to cut costs. For instance, if you have a passion for museums, you can join the 100-year-old American Association of Museums (AAM) as non-paid museum staff. It is the nation's largest museum organization and for a $35 annual fee you can get a variety of discounts and a subscription to *Museum News*.

If you plan to pursue a hobby that's costly, give some thought—sooner rather than later—to ways to minimize the expenses long term. You might consider deducting contributions to nonprofit organizations or purchasing equipment secondhand. If you want to take music or acting lessons, and they're a bit expensive, perhaps you can barter some skill you have—painting furniture, accounting advice, a home cooked meal—for one lesson a month, thereby defraying the costs. Skilled hobbyists might be able to turn the hobby into a part-time business, for instance, by selling crafts you make, in which case some expenses may be tax-deductible.

> **If you're reading this book for a spouse, friend, or parent . . .** Staying engaged is one of the key elements to having a happy, successful life in THE RETIREMENT ZONE. So encourage your loved ones to get involved—or to expand long-standing interests—so that a solitary hobby becomes social, more fun, and a point of pride.

The Ladies in the Purple Jackets

Pat Lenny wasn't exactly a couch potato in her 50s. But she didn't see herself as a long-distance runner, either. Nobody's more surprised than she is at what she's been able to accomplish.

"I am shocked that I've finished eight marathons. I didn't know what a marathon was eight years ago. It's amazing—absolutely amazing to me. I am sixty-two. Every marathon is twenty-six point two miles; I finished the last one in six hours. Normally I am four fifty-five to four fifty-nine range, under five hours.

"I never ran seriously until we moved to New York from Cherry Hill, New Jersey. We lived close to Central Park and I saw the New York Marathon. Then I saw a five-K race in the park, and I said to my husband, "Wouldn't it be amazing to do that?" I set a goal for myself to get around the smallest loop—1.7 miles—in Central Park just once. I was fifty-five at that time. It wasn't easy. I was in okay shape, not great shape. I'd been taking aerobic classes. I wasn't thinking about a marathon.

"Eventually I tried to run three miles. When I could, I joined the New York Road Runners classes. My original goal was just to do a five-K race. I was amazed that I could do it. Then, I said, 'I could never do a ten-K.' One of the women in my running group said, 'You'll get caught up like everyone else, you start to love it so much.'

"She was right. When you run you do get that high. It is exhilarating. You can't really run unless you do love it. It can be hard, even gruesome sometimes, when you go out in all kinds of weather. I love the thrill of running around the park. I love being outside. You get to see everything.

"I'm now a member of a club called Mercury Masters. It's a team strictly for women over the age of fifty. It's an incredible group of thirty women, all in different professions—accomplished, interesting, fabulous women. We are the only team we know of in the country that is exclusively for women over fifty. I believe our oldest member who does marathons is sixty-four; she has done twenty-four marathons. The team has collectively completed over two hundred and twenty-seven marathons, in sixteen states, nine foreign countries, on five continents.

"We are all pre-Title IX. Most of us were not athletic in school. I went to an all-girls Catholic school; you almost weren't allowed to sweat. That's how it was, growing up in the 1950s and early 60s. And that's why it is exhilarating now. We don't take it for granted. Track didn't exist as a sport for us. The younger girls take it for granted. We don't. We didn't have this option.

"This is the most supportive group I have ever seen. We have classes. We communicate by e-mail. We meet in the park on Saturday mornings. Everybody runs at her own pace. Some are very fast; I am slow. We never know who will show up, but you hook up and do some mileage in all kinds of weather. We do at least five hours a week, average.

"My family's very supportive. My husband isn't a runner, but he takes photos of us all. I have three children. My oldest son is thirty-nine and my youngest is thirty-five. We celebrate Mother's Day in November, when the Marathon takes place, rather than in May. The kids come the night before. They work hard; my husband has it all mapped out, where to be at four different spots along the route, and they're there—cheering me and my friends on, holding big signs. We always have a big party afterwards.

"It's absolutely amazing every time you do it, no matter how hard it is out there. It's the feeling, 'I did it!' It's just unbelievable the first time. The joke is that for the next three weeks, in every single conversation you have for any reason, you manage to say you just did a marathon. The only question is how long it takes to work that in.

"I feel very young when I am out there. There's no question, when you come across that finish line you have the most incredible feeling. You feel like a kid.

"A lot of times when we are running, young girls will run up and say, 'You women are amazing,' or 'You're the only reason I can do this.' 'The Ladies in the Purple Jackets,' they call us. They say, 'You Ladies in the Purple Jackets!!!'"

Piano Lessons

Linda Moore, age 66, and a mother of three, describes herself as "basically a stay-at-home housewife for thirty-two years." After her marriage ended, she went to paralegal school and eventually became a full-time technical writer. She has been retired now for about five years.

"I take courses and I've been doing volunteer work in a public school, helping kids with reading and math. I am a library docent. I help people learn how to use library computers and databases in downtown Denver.

"And I am taking piano lessons.

"I started after I retired. It's new. Learning to sight-read and play is very hard compared with how quickly I used to learn things in my youth. That's painful. But I am very faithful to it. I practice about two hours a day. Is it possible for someone past 60 to take up the piano and do a decent job? I think so, but I see this as an experiment.

"I always wanted to play the piano, but we didn't have a piano at home. When we went to my grandma's, I would spend hours on the piano. I could read music pretty well in childhood, but not the entire range. I felt sort of deprived that I never had an instrument. So I bought a piano while I was still working, but I didn't get serious about it until I retired.

"Just now, after a long time, I feel I am making some real progress. I never think about looking at the clock. I love it so much. Every minute of practice is a pleasure."

Resource Guide

There are many specialized magazines, Web sites, and organizations dedicated to specific hobbies. Just a handful are listed here. For more information, check the library or Internet, or contact the trade association for that particular area.

ORGANIZATIONS AND WEB SITES

American Ceramic Society: www.ceramics.org

American Symphony Orchestra League: www.symphony.org

ArtAge Publications: www.seniortheatre.com

Collector Online worldwide marketplace for antiques, collectibles, and handmade items: www.collectoronline.com

Collectors News magazine: www.collectors-news.com

Family Tree magazine on genealogy: www.familytreemagazine.com

GardenGuides resource with bookshop, supplies, tips, articles, and discussions: www.gardenguides.com

Hobby Industry Association (HIA) 319 East 54th Street Elmwood Park, NJ 07407 201-794-1133 www.hobby.org

Popular Woodworking magazine: www.popularwoodworking.com

Quilt Town USA: www.quilttownusa.com

Woodshop News magazine: www.woodshopnews.com

PART IV

Managing Practical Matters

There's no escaping some of the practical realities of life. Three areas in particular claim the time and attention of many people in THE RETIREMENT ZONE. First and foremost is the question of money, both how much you have and how much you'll need. Another prominent concern is caregiving. You may be called upon to help care for a loved one. Or it may turn out that you yourself become the recipient of some kind of family care, whether for a short-term recuperation such as knee surgery, or a longer-term condition. Last, there's the question of home—of where you live and that common problem of too much clutter. The following chapters offer some practical information and advice, as well as some tips from an expert in each of these fields.

CHAPTER 21

Paying for Retirement

Finances are key in THE RETIREMENT ZONE. How much is enough? How much money will you need to be happy? Is it worth it to keep working for a while? And if so, how long?

Looking Forward offers a nonfinancial perspective on the wonderful and surprising range of things that people do in the years defined by THE RETIREMENT ZONE. But you can't ignore money. This chapter is geared sympathetically for those people who feel a rising panic or run for an aspirin when they see the words "financial planning." It spells out the basics. You'll find quizzes to assess your risk tolerance, your spending style, and your level of financial literacy.

Before your palms get sweaty worrying about money, take a mental break from the consumer culture. Think for a moment about who you are and what makes you happy. Mountains of possessions and a huge stash of cash don't necessary buy happiness. So whether you're a shop-a-holic Lucy or a frugal Fred, it's important to think honestly about what you need emotionally as opposed to what you might think you *want* materially. A five-day cruise might not be as satisfying as reestablishing a viable relationship with an estranged sibling.

That said, there's lot to learn about the financial aspects of retirement, and the majority of people over age 65 don't feel they know enough, according to studies by the National Council on the Aging. "Many workers struggle with making critical retirement savings decisions," notes Stephen Utkus, principal, Vanguard Center for Retirement Research. Sarah Sanford, executive director of the Society of Actuaries spells out the consequences of ducking realities. "Underplanning can have a severely detrimental effect on how people end up enjoying their retirement," she warns. "Without carefully considering future risks, retirees can face unexpected medical expenses, costs related to declining functional status, outliving their assets, decline in resources due to loss of a spouse, and the effects of inflation."

The initial part of this chapter is for people who are still receiving a salary.

The second part is for people who are no longer receiving a steady paycheck, and consider themselves retired, not unemployed.

And women, who traditionally are less financially experienced—and poorer on the whole than men—may see some of their own questions reflected in the Q/A with a leading women's financial consultant.

Please don't stop your financial education here, especially if you don't know the difference between a mutual fund and a mango tree. It's wise to also peruse the many available books and resources dedicated solely to questions of retirement financing. Take a course, or even consult an expert. This is one area you literally can't afford to ignore.

One good place to begin is by examining your own habits—starting with spending.

What's Your Spending Style?

When it comes to spending, do you have the urge to splurge? To suss out your spending style, no need to shop around—just take advantage of this quiz from Bankrate.com.

1) *Have you ever phoned friends later than you normally might, in order to save on long-distance calls?*
   a) Heck no.
   b) Yes, but I'm careful to phone only those who generally stay up late, anyway.
   c) Plenty of times.

2) *The shopping channels on TV are*
   a) Like the nature channel—I watch out of sociological interest.
   b) The best invention since sliced bread.
   c) A nice diversion—entertaining when I've got the time.

3) *During an amorous moment with your partner, you've fantasized about*
   a) Replacing your threadbare sheets as soon as there's a white sale.
   b) Being away at a nice vacation spot together.
   c) That TV show where contestants with a shopping cart get a two-minute spree.

4) *You receive an unsolicited credit card in the mail, so you*
   a) Stash it for emergencies.
   b) Make plastic confetti.
   c) Take it for a spin at the mall—just to make sure it works.

5) *When you go into the ritziest retail shop in your neighborhood*
   a) It's to see what's in style; more often than not, I'll get the look for less elsewhere.
   b) The manager does a jig of joy.
   c) Security tails me—sheesh, is there a limit as to how many times a person can just look?

6) *If you buy something on impulse, do you feel*
   a) Good (da-da, da-da, da-da, da, I knew that I would, now!)
   b) A little reckless and wanton, but I don't do this very often.
   c) Like breathing deeply into a brown paper bag.

7) *You're invited to a party. You hope*

   a) There'll be some real food—not those dopey little wieners in blankets.

   b) There'll be some really interesting guests.

   c) To find a new knockout outfit at the mall that'll keep everyone buzzing for weeks afterward.

8) *Speaking of clothing for special events, have you purchased anything for a one-time occasion, left the tags on, and returned it to the store later?*

   a) "What am I, Minnie Pearl?"

   b) No, but this is kind of tempting.

   c) Please, I'd be willing to risk setting off metal detectors if the clothing's plastic security devices were accidentally left on—discreetly wearing little paper tags is no big deal.

9) *OK, fantasy time again. Your favorite celebrity lust object speaks to you, and says, "Here are my . . ."*

   a) "Hotel-room keys."

   b) "Frequent-flyer miles."

   c) "Credit cards."

10) *You're at a celebratory dinner with friends at a fine restaurant, each of you responsible for your own share. You toast with a glass of*

   a) Champagne. A toast is not a toast without it.

   b) Sparkling wine, or some other festive fizzy.

   c) Water, tap, this year's vintage.

11) *Bringing your lunch to work makes you feel*

   a) Like a worker bee—boxed-in worker bee—which is why I don't do it.

   b) Like I'm doing a smart thing—but sometimes I go out with the gang.

   c) Good and virtuous.

12) *Have you ever cut open a used, flattened tube of toothpaste?*

   a) No. Why? Is there a prize inside?

   b) No. I prefer endeavors with a more favorable effort-to-savings ratio

   c) Sure. Waste not, want not.

©Bankrate.com. Used with permission.
To score, see key on page 316.

SHIFTING MIND-SETS:
From Spending to Saving

Whether you are already retired or contemplating your future, saving money is a good practice for those in THE RETIREMENT ZONE. You can start saving the very next time you set out to spend money. How? Price shop.

Most consumers underestimate the value of comparison shopping, according to research released by the Consumer Literacy Consortium, a group of consumer education leaders from government, consumer, and business organizations. "The fact is that shopping around for most products will yield savings far greater than ten percent," says Jack Gillis, director of Public Affairs of the Consumer Federation of America. Those who don't comparison shop say the time spent is not worth the money saved. "The fifty percent of consumers who don't shop around are losing out on thousands of dollars of potential savings," says Gillis.

Check this out: In the fall of 2002, students at Virginia Tech University participated in a comparison-shopping study to determine typical price savings gained by shopping around and the time it took to discover these savings. It took them just 73 minutes of phone shopping to rack up $390 of savings, albeit on fairly big-ticket items.

Search Time and Savings for Selected Products

Product	Median Savings	Search Time
RT, DC-Chicago Flight	$125	21 min.
RT, Houston-LA Flight	$139	15 min.
Car rental, two-day	$26	21 min.
Color TV	$100	16 min.

"Shopping—especially by phone or on the Internet—is easier than most consumers realize," said Robert Krughoff, president of Consumers' CHECKBOOK, a non-profit consumer information service. "For many products and services, consumers can save between one and nine dollars for every minute they devote to shopping. That's a much higher rate of return than most of us get on the job—and of course you don't have to pay taxes on money you save."

Shift your mind-set from spending to saving; what you save over the course of a year might be the equivalent of a big, fat raise.

FOR PRE-RETIREES:
If You're Still Working Full Time

After job-hopping through the 1980s and 1990s, you've amassed more than one 401(k) plan, a hodge-podge of investments, and possibly some real estate. If you haven't begun to think about the financial aspect of your long-term future, the time to do so is now. Retired attorney Judie Fernandez advises, "You need to plan four or five years in advance. Go, try out, read, and make a list of things you'd love to do, set goals, and make a wish list. You have to realize that someday is here, not five years from now, as you might not be healthy. Make a wish. Think about where you want to go and how much time to spend doing things. And crank that into your budget."

Lifestyle Scenarios

Do you need to work part time, full time, or can you quit soon? The answers are a matter of style, attitude, lifestyle, and comfort level about contingency planning.

How can you think that far ahead? Here's a method for organizing your thoughts on the subject, borrowing a concept from educational guidance counselors. High-school seniors competing to get into colleges are urged to think in terms of three categories of applications: "reach" schools that are their top picks, "target" schools that are in the realm of reasonable expectations, and "safety" schools, places where they are pretty sure of getting an acceptance. You can apply the same logic to other life transitions. Ask yourself: What's a reach—your dream retirement lifestyle—and how much will it cost? What's a target—a reasonable expectation of how you can live given your current resources and decent luck? And what's a safety scenario lifestyle—your most modest lifestyle—just in case things don't go quite your way? And for each, what's a thumbnail budget?

A HYPOTHETICAL CASE Take Mary, a hypothetical 60-year-old nurse supervisor who is divorced and living alone in the now mortgage-free family home. She's a new grandmother of twins. Let's say Mary's parents were German immigrants and she has an interest in German language and culture. She'd love to help out with the twins' college fund. Mary might array her options accordingly, and make a budget for each:

MARY'S DREAM SCENARIO

1) **Home/Car:** *Keep the family house, get new car*
2) **Work Status/Health Insurance:** *Stop working at 63; volunteer at church more instead! Pay health insurance premiums until Medicare eligible, look into long-term care insurance.*
3) **Luxury Item:** *Buy a small apartment in Berlin.*
4) **Family:** *Set up trust fund for grandkids' college education.*
5) **For me:** *Take summer language class in Germany; find relatives.*

MARY'S TARGET SCENARIO

1) **Home/Car:** *Downsize. Sell the family house, donate extra belongings, and move to a condo; keep car.*
2) **Work Status/Health Insurance:** *Try for promotion this year; shift into part-time work from age 63 to 68; stay on employer health plan as long as possible.*
3) **Luxury Item:** *Swap the condo for a little house in German country town during summer vacation.*
4) **Family:** *Contribute something annually to grandkids' college funds.*
5) **For me:** *Immersion course in German language. (Buy genealogy software and join a genealogy club.)*

MARY'S SAFETY SCENARIO

1) **Home/Car:** *Downsize. Sell the family home and belongings; move to a cheaper condo one town over while working; when retired, move to inexpensive place in Mexico.*
2) **Work Status/Health Insurance:** *Work overtime to pay off credit-card debt; shift into higher-paid private night nursing until age 69 (dinner and gas included). Rely on employer health plan, Medicare.*
3) **Luxury Item:** *Help organize small family reunion, invite German relatives to visit in U.S.*
4) **Family:** *Discuss with kids the idea of reverse mortgage on condo so have extra income to invest in college funds. Or, if move to Mexico, set up college fund sooner with proceeds from condo sale.*
5) **For me:** *Study German at community college.*

Now, just for fun, write down a few scenarios of your own:

Develop a Few Scenarios for your RETIREMENT ZONE

MY DREAM SCENARIO

1) Home/Car: _____
_____
_____

2) Work Status/Health Insurance: _____
_____
_____

3) Luxury Item: _____
_____
_____

4) Family: _____
_____
_____

5) For me: _____
_____
_____

MY TARGET SCENARIO

1) Home/Car: _____
_____
_____

2) Work Status/Health Insurance: _____
_____
_____

3) Luxury Item: _____
_____

4) Family: _____
_____
_____

5) For me: _____

_____

_____

MY SAFETY SCENARIO

1) Home/Car: _____

_____

2) Work Status/Health Insurance: _____

_____

3) Luxury Item: _____

_____

4) Family: _____

_____

5) For me: _____

_____

_____

Creating your own RETIREMENT ZONE scenarios may initially raise more questions than it answers. Which of these scenarios can you afford? How long will you need to keep working? Can you realize some of your wildest dreams in a way that costs less than you assume? But whichever scenario you aim for, the most basic question is:

HOW MUCH MONEY DO YOU NEED?

It's not a mystery. It's math. Call it the 80 percent rule of thumb. Many financial experts say that for every year in full retirement, you'll need about 80 percent of your pre-retirement annual income to support your lifestyle. In addition, some advisors recommend that you have from three months' to two years' worth of expenses readily available as an emergency fund—not cash under the mattress, but in such easily accessible investments as money market funds or Treasury bills.

The 80 percent rule means having saved and invested a considerable sum *before* you sever that umbilical cord to your paycheck. As of this writing, the most you can currently collect from Social Security is a bit more than $20,000 a year. Practically speaking, the question is: How much of your nest egg can you draw on every year after retirement and still have adequate money for your later years? And of course the big uncertainties include your own life span, future health and unforeseen expenses, and the performance of the economy, markets, and inflation.

Luckily, the calculations can be done fairly easily. A bevy of large investment firms offer free online investment calculators and a range of sophisticated service packages combining planning, investing, consumer education, and so on. To estimate what you'll need, you simply type in the following information: your current annual income requirements, the number of years until you retire, how long you think you will be retired, a guess on the rate of inflation, and what percent yield you think you can get on your investments. Their results may vary slightly (because they may use different underlying assumptions).

Retirement can bring you savings well beyond those ubiquitous senior-citizen discounts. For instance, assuming you are one of the four out of five householders over 65 who own the home they live in, free and clear, you could have the option of buying a smaller house, and even moving to a less-expensive area—and can garner a handy profit in the process. Smaller sources of savings add up, too. Typically, according to the U.S. Census Bureau, many people flip-flop their spending patterns in retirement. With no time pressure to buy prepared meals or lunch at work, you may eat in more often. And you may spend less money on clothing than when you were employed full time. And without needing to drive to work daily, you might trade in the SUV for a modest two-seater with greater fuel efficiency. On the other hand, there may be new expenses. In particular, it's wise to consider possible health care costs—and whether you might be paying some of your spouse's, parents,' or in-laws' medical expenses, too.

ESTIMATE YOUR FINANCIAL NEEDS . . . then try living on that fixed income.

If you aren't sure you are ready to live on what you've got saved for retirement, give it a trial run. That's the advice that ex-Boeing executive and retirement expert Henry K. Hebeler offers—along with free retirement planning tools—on his Web site, www.analyzenow.com: "During your last few working years, spend only the amount you can afford in retirement."

Practical Tips:
8 STEPS TO YOUR FINANCIAL FUTURE

1) **Make a plan and stick with it.** Think long and hard about your goals—and write them down. Planning is more than just the nuts and bolts of managing stocks, bonds, and funds. What is the range of things you might want to spend money on during your decades in THE RETIREMENT ZONE? Not just next year, but in five or ten? Consider the fact that your expenses will change over time.

2) **Know what you already have and where it is.** Collect and organize your papers. If you've job-hopped, you could have investments in numerous 401(k) plans, and consolidating them will doubtless involve headaches and paperwork. If you're not sure how to proceed, seek help. Find out when you will be eligible for government benefits such as Social Security and Medicare benefits, and file in a timely fashion; these don't just fall out of the sky on your 62nd or 65th birthday. Log on to the Social Security Online Web site for extensive, user-friendly information (www.socialsecurity.gov). To learn more about your Medicare coverage, you can log on to the official government Web site (www.medicare.gov) or contact the Medicare Rights Center (www.medicarerights.org).

3) **Clean up your personal money management act.** Like good personal hygiene, good personal financial management habits will serve you well. Do you take simple steps to save money and financial hassle—like balancing your checkbook, reconciling your bank statements, and paying your bills on time? Do you dispute charges, negotiate rates, and keep track of what others are doing with your money? A first step is to pay off all your double-digit credit card debt. For additional information, see the National Foundation for Credit Counseling Web site at www.debtadvice.org.

4) **Work out some numbers, and resist wishful thinking.** Do some projections using online calculators. Take advantage of retirement planning seminars at your place of employment, a local college, or faith-based organization. Or peruse the shelves at a bookstore or library for resources on this topic. When making financial assump-

tions—about inflation, or your rate of return—don't be a cockeyed optimist. Plan for emergencies and be realistic about factors that may diminish your nest egg—inflation, fees to financial advisors, taxes, and other investment costs.

5) **Know your own tolerance for risk.** Getting comfortable with your own risk-tolerance level is essential if you are going to formulate a well-crafted investment plan—and one that you'll stick to. If you are married or have a significant other with whom you are pooling funds, discuss this thoroughly. It helps to see the big picture. For instance, what financial generation are you? Depression-era men and women often feel permanently insecure financially. As Princeton, New Jersey, resident George Fox mused, "I was born in 1939, and the Depression was very real to my parents. I have a solid nest egg. What worries me is that I will be like Silas Marner and not want to spend, that I'll never think I have enough." On the other end of the spectrum, some baby boomers run up debt faster than a squirrel runs up a tree. Try to be realistic about your own assets and future needs. (See the Financial Risk Tolerance quiz on page 304.)

6) **If you're in THE RETIREMENT ZONE today, start thinking about _tomorrow_.** Rethink those expensive habits and make necessary lifestyle adjustments _now_.

7) **Is your interest or willpower already flagging? Give yourself an incentive.** Say you've always wanted to spend a year in a villa in rural France, à la Peter Mayle. One observer suggests this strategy: Tape up a photo of your dream scene in the place in your house or office where you make your financial decisions. Look at it periodically to remember why you're saving.

8) **Consider changing to a job with a pension plan that's better than what you've got.** As you are still working, you might consider whether the retirement benefits at your current job are as good as you can get. If not, consider a job switch. Or maybe now is the time to get started moonlighting and setting up that home-based business, something that perhaps you could grow into when you quit working full time.

Financial Literacy Quiz

Do you know the ABCs of personal finance management? Take this quiz and find out.

1) *How regularly do you keep an emergency fund of at least three months' living expenses?*
   a) all the time
   b) sometimes
   c) rarely
   d) never

2) *How regularly do you pay your bills on time?*
   a) all the time
   b) sometimes
   c) rarely
   d) never

3) *How regularly do you follow a monthly budget?*
   a) all the time
   b) sometimes
   c) rarely
   d) never

4) *Do you regularly contribute to a Retirement Account?*
   a) all the time
   b) sometimes
   c) rarely
   d) never

5) *How regularly do you read your bank account statements?*
   a) all the time
   b) sometimes
   c) rarely
   d) never

6) *Have you prepared a will?*
   a) yes
   b) no

7) *How regularly do you shop around for best insurance quotes/coverage?*

a) all the time

b) sometimes

c) rarely

d) never

8) *Do you check your credit report annually for accuracy?*

a) all the time

b) sometimes

c) rarely

d) never

9) *How regularly do you make more than minimum payments on your credit card bills?*

a) all the time

b) sometimes

c) rarely

d) never

10) *How regularly do you look for and switch to credit cards with lower rates or better terms?*

a) all the time

b) sometimes

c) rarely

d) never

11) *Did you comparison shop for the best deal on your mortgage?*

a) yes

b) no

12) *Do you adjust your W4 form annually to make sure you are not giving the government too much money?*

a) all the time

b) sometimes

c) rarely

d) never

©Bankrate.com. Used with permission.
To score, see key on page 317.

It's a good idea to put as much as you can into tax-deductible retirement plans while you are still employed. It adds up.

But, you may protest, it's impossible to save! Well, think carrot and stick. As a carrot, there are three good incentives to start saving for retirement now. First, you'll save a heap of money on taxes by squirreling away money now in retirement plans, especially if you invest up to the legal limits. Second, when you start drawing down on your money, you might find yourself in a lower tax bracket and hence pay lower taxes on distributions from accounts like IRAs. Third, upping your contributions, because they're in pretax dollars, may translate into lower taxes, since you'll only pay taxes on the income after the contribution.

As for the stick, without scaring yourself to death, just dwell for a moment on the uncertainties—such as the possibility that you may have to kick in more for health insurance, prescription drugs, and even eyeglasses in retirement than you do while you're covered by an employer health care plan.

If all else fails, consider tricking yourself into saving. You can set up an automatic transfer from your checking account into a mutual fund, for instance. If you don't see it, maybe you won't spend it.

3 Places to Save Money for Retirement
(NOT INCLUDING UNDER YOUR MATTRESS)

1) **401(k)s:** If you are an employee, the biggest piece of your retirement portfolio should be an employer-sponsored plan like the ubiquitous 401(k). Most 401(k) plans (if you work for a not-for-profit, your plan might be called a 403(b), but they're essentially the same) let you put away pretax dollars in an account that grows tax free until you start making withdrawals in retirement. Some plans offer matching contributions. You'd be foolish to pass up the match by not enrolling in the 401(k). It's free money! Think of it this way. Say your company offers a 50-cent match for every dollar you put in up to a limit, say $5,000. That's an immediate guaranteed 50 percent return on your investment. Ordinarily, you'd have to do something of dubious legality to get a 50 percent rate of return on your investment. Even if the investment choices offered are limited, the most important thing is to choose the best of the lot and to save.

2) **SEPS AND KEOGHS:** If you're self-employed, you've got to fund your retirement all by yourself. Simplified Employee Plan IRAs (SEP IRAs) and Keoghs are plans that let you squirrel away retirement assets in pretax dollars. Just like a 401(k), these investments grow tax free until withdrawal. They can be set up for self-employed people whether or not they have employees. The contribution limits are much higher for these types of retirement accounts, and are particularly useful for those who don't have access to a 401(k) plan.

3) **IRAS:** For years, the individual retirement account was the investment of choice of people saving for retirement. Though it's taken a backseat to the 401(k), the IRA is still a workhorse of retirement, and it is worth having. Unfortunately the annual limit on an IRA is a piddly $3000, though older savers can put away $3500 in a recently enacted "catch up" provision. A Roth IRA is best for most people because while you put in after-tax dollars, your investment grows tax free and withdrawals in retirement are also tax free. Over decades, you win back the amount that you paid in taxes many times over. (There are income limits for contributors to Roth IRAs. If your income is above these fairly high limits, then a regular IRA is your best option; it's best to have your individual situation reviewed by a professional financial planner or investment advisor.) Though an IRA is an important part of your investment plan, you should always contribute to a 401(k) plan first, since the contribution amounts are higher for most 401(k)s.

INVESTING FOR PRE-RETIREES

Experts stress that it's important to diversify. Think of it as protecting yourself from putting all your eggs in one basket. The usual ingredients that go into the mix are stocks, bonds, cash, and real estate, but you have to work out the precise allocation. One basic rule of thumb says that you should subtract your age from 110 and allocate that percentage of your investments to stocks. So, as Wall Street wisdom goes, a 70-year old would have 40 percent of his or her portfolio in stocks.

Of course, your personal risk tolerance will also be a factor. How would you feel if your investment declined by 10 percent a year? What about 20? If you're a moderate risk taker where your money is concerned, then you'll want a plan that has some risk, but not enough that it gives you a sick feeling each time you think about the stock market's huge swings. Conservative investors shouldn't be surprised that they won't make as much as the market when stocks start to zoom, but at least they don't stand the chance of losing their shirts when the closing bell marks a down day. And if you have an investment philosophy that is not dependent on how stocks are doing on any given day or any given year, you more easily stay the course for years on end.

What's Your Financial Risk Tolerance Level?

How much do you agree or disagree with the following questions?

1) Agree Strongly
2) Agree Somewhat
3) Maybe
4) Disagree Somewhat
5) Disagree Strongly

1) If I lost 20 percent or more on the value of my portfolio, I wouldn't sleep for a month. _____

2) I'm willing to give up some upside potential in my investments if that means my portfolio won't go the way of Enron. _____

3) Keeping the capital I have is more important to me than catching the next eBay or Microsoft. _____

4) I have enough liquidity in my portfolio (cash or other short-term, low-risk investments) to get me through six months' worth of expenses and maybe even a trip to Hawaii. _____

5) I will need my money some time in the next 5 to 10 years. _____

Where do you come out on the risk tolerance quiz?
To score, see key on page 317.

The Pre-retirement Investment Pie

STOCKS: Stocks should form the centerpiece of your investment portfolio, whether you're 10 years *from* retirement or 10 years *into* retirement. Remember that baby boomers today are expected to live, on average, well into their 70s and many will live to be 90 and 100 years old. Only stocks—not bonds or cash—can be expected to keep up with or outpace future rises in inflation.

Unless you're well versed in stock picking, consider investing in mutual funds. Just make sure you're well diversified across industries and investment styles so one blow-up won't take down your entire portfolio. Consider a portfolio of only index funds, which are investment vehicles that track different segments of the market like the Standard and Poor's 500 stock index or a benchmark of bonds.

Experts suggest that blue-chip stocks (like General Electric or Microsoft, for instance) should be at the core of your investment portfolio. Why? With some exceptions, the stocks of large, well-established companies tend to be more stable than those of start-ups. Certainly, small company stocks have an important place in a diversified portfolio, but they should play a supporting role, not take center-stage. A broadly invested mutual fund comprising many large company names that's also low-cost and keeps turnover to a minimum is the thing to look for. To round out your large stock holdings (i.e., stocks in large corporations), experts say, you'll also need to allocate about 20 percent of the stock portion of your portfolio to "small cap" stocks (i.e., stocks in small companies). In addition, take a helping of international stocks, also about 20 percent, and a slice of real-estate stocks, which generally don't move in the same direction as other equities.

BONDS: The other big piece of most investment portfolios is bonds. This asset class usually behaves differently from stocks, and therefore offers some protection from volatility. The same rules apply to bond investing as to stock buying. Pick a well-diversified fund that doesn't charge high operating expenses. Remember, bonds can take a hit if interest rates rise sharply. So it's safest to spread your risks among different bond types that don't all react the same way. And as you get older, increase the bond portion of your portfolio.

If You Hire a Pro, If You Manage Your Own Money...

Many people hire someone to help them decide how to manage their investments. You have a range of specialists from whom to choose, including investment advisors, CPAs, lawyers, and certified financial planners. Tempting though it is to hope that one advisor can perform all these different functions, there are risks in combining these roles. Make sure you find out what each one can and can't do, and how each one gets paid—fee, commissions, or whether they are based on performance, or some other basis. Try to personally meet the individual who will be managing your money. And always, always get references. You can start your search for a qualified professional on the Certified Financial Planner Standards Board Web site and other online sites. If you are seeking a consultant who will just help you get started with an investment strategy that meets your needs, you could expect to be charged between $1,000 and $2,000 for the equivalent of one day's consultation work.

If you choose to manage your own finances, there are ample sources of information to guide your investments. Here are three low-cost options:

- **Newsletters:** Find one you can—and will—follow. That means it's written so that you can understand it. But be certain you can make a commitment to following the advice, which means the philosophy should fit your own in regard to such strategies as trading versus buy-and-hold, market-timing, funds, stocks, bonds, gold, and exotic investments. Be aware of charlatans and hyperbolic claims of getting something for nothing, such as outstanding performance for low risk.

- **Investment Clubs:** Sharing information with others reduces the work and offers you new perspectives. For information on the pros and cons, as well as legal paperwork, tips on assembling a workable membership group, and so on, check both the National Association of Investors Corp. (www.better-investing.org).

- **Web sites:** The Internet offers a wealth of worksheets and calculators and can provide you with good historical information about investments. But be aware that the advice can come from any number of sources and may not be consistent. Experts suggest that you use the Web for calculators, but not actionable advice.

INVESTING FOR RETIREES: Now That You've Stopped Getting a Paycheck

You're retired, and have probably made some significant financial decisions already. However, ongoing post-retirement financial management is important, too. That's especially the case in the current era when the face of retirement is changing.

Retirees were always told that they should have their money mainly in bonds or certificates of deposit. Not anymore. The reason? Bonds rarely keep up with the pace of inflation because the income they generate is fixed. That holds doubly true for bank CDs, which typically produce even lower rates of income—substantially below the rate of inflation. And remember that some costs like health care and fuel rise at an even faster clip than inflation.

A portfolio that's comprised of 50 percent stocks is no longer considered risky and outrageous. Follow the general investment guidelines above for your stocks and place the bonds in a mixture of long-term bond funds on one end and short maturity bonds on the other in case you should need immediate access to your money.

REDUCING LIVING EXPENSES IN RETIREMENT

On the seesaw of income and expense, one way to influence the financial equation in your favor is to bring down your expenses. Throughout this book, you've seen "Your Money Matters" sections suggesting ways to save while in THE RETIREMENT ZONE, whether you're going back to school, traveling, or volunteering at a nonprofit organization. Also consider the following:

WHERE YOU LIVE: You might consider selling your home if you've lived there a long time and it's too big now or hard to keep up. It's probably appreciated quite a bit over the years. You'll be able to put the proceeds into a smaller house that requires less upkeep and less in taxes. Or you might think about moving to a less expensive area. It's no wonder that areas like St. George, Utah, and communities in Tennessee are drawing lots of transplants from the coasts. A 2004 survey by the development company Del Webb found that one in three baby boomers say they plan to relocate in retirement.

Hola, Mexico? Another option is to move abroad where Americans can raise their standard of living while paying less for it. La Paz and San Miguel de Allende are two such currently popular expatriate retiree havens in Mexico. You can continue to collect your Social Security check and pensions anywhere in the world. You won't be able to use Medicare to pay for health care, but costs for routine doctor visits are just a fraction of what they cost stateside. Just make sure you have emergency evacuation coverage in your health insurance to enable you to get home in a jiffy in case of a medical emergency.

Boomtowns abroad sometimes make for a good investment, too. If you bought a home early in the cycle, say, in Costa Rica, or Dublin, or Acapulco— before your neighbors back home made the same discovery—you would have benefited from rapid appreciation in value.

Online, you can find articles on moving and retiring overseas at two Web sites, www.escapeartist.com/retirement/havens.htm and www.liveabroad.com.

INSURANCE: Examine your insurance situation. Do you really need life insurance if you have no dependents and the house is paid for? You could take that money and put it into a long-term care policy that will pick up the cost of major medical bills should you get seriously ill. And if you're not driving as much, you can ask your insurance company for a rate reduction. Check your homeowners insurance, too, as your home is probably your biggest asset.

BARTER CLUBS: If you're an enterprising sort, you might consider bartering to get the goods and services you want in your area. Each member gets an account. You "sell" your goods or services for a certain amount of "money," which then gets deposited in your account. You can then spend those "dollars" for something you need. Why not trade gardening for dinner out at a Chinese restaurant or baby-sitting for a time share in Puerto Rico? Try finding barter situations on www.craigslist.org, a community message board. For those with businesses, products, or services to barter, check the International Reciprocal Trade Association, based in Rochester, New York (www.irta.com).

STAYING HEALTHY: An ounce of prevention saves a pound of cure, and thousands of dollars worth of doctors' bills as well. Living healthfully—quitting smoking, exercising regularly, watching your cholesterol and other basic health indicators—can result in real dollar savings. It's never too late to start.

OTHER SOURCES OF INCOME IN RETIREMENT

IRAs: As noted earlier in this chapter, you can start tapping into your retirement savings at age 59½ and you'll be required to take a minimum distribution at age 70½. But these don't have to be your sole sources of income.

HOME EQUITY LOANS: According to the U.S. Administration on Aging, about 80 percent of Americans over age 65 own their own homes. And in many cases, the homes have appreciated greatly in value. You can establish a line of home equity credit while you are still working (that will enhance your ability to obtain a good rate) and keep it for a rainy day. Check such details as "inactivity" fees, requirements for a draw-down within a certain period of time, and other fine print.

REVERSE MORTGAGE: This is certainly not for everyone, because in the end it's understood that the bank, not your heirs, will own your home. But it is a way to keep receiving checks. You can get a reverse mortgage if you've built up a significant amount of equity in your home, and the home is owner-occupied. The bank will pay you a monthly check, which may be tax free since it's principal plus interest, the same interest you would have written off on your taxes if you were paying a traditional mortgage. You do not have to leave your home once the reverse mortgage is paid off. When you die, the home is sold to pay the balance of what you owed the bank. The remainder, if any, goes to your estate. You must be 62 years or older to apply for a reverse mortgage. Remember to discuss this option with your heirs so that the first they hear that they won't be inheriting the family home isn't at the reading of the will. For more information, go to www.aarp.org/revmort.

EMPLOYMENT INCOME: Support your expensive lifestyle habits with a part-time job. An increasingly popular choice to perk up a paltry retirement account is extending the work years. Service jobs that were once filled by college and high-school kids have some appeal: a paycheck, possibly some benefits, and they lend structure to the week without the stresses of a full-time career.

Aside from keeping money coming in, you're also delaying the time that you need to start tapping into your capital. Delaying retirement by just two years can have a profound effect on your savings rate, enabling your 401(k) to grow a bit more and increasing your Social Security income later on.

SOCIAL SECURITY RETIREMENT BENEFITS: Currently, the "full retirement age" under Social Security is 65. Social Security retired-worker benefits are first available at age 62, but benefits that begin before the full retirement age are equal to 80 percent of the amount that the worker would have received at 65. Social Security full retirement age is being increased to 67 over time (effective for those born in 1962 and later).

Historically most people begin receiving Social Security retirement benefits before age 65. Approximately 75 percent of men and 80 percent of women who began receiving Social Security retired-worker benefits between 1990 and 1999 applied for benefits before age 65. Among women, this percentage has remained steady over the past 10 years, while among men, there was a slight increase in the proportion of applicants younger than 65 years.

When thinking about the potential value of your Social Security income, don't forget to factor in an average annual inflation rate of about 3 percent.

Women, in particular, should look into their Social Security benefits. Our Social Security system is based on anachronistic assumptions about family patterns that were characteristic of the mid-20th century, when few women worked. A fascinating if disturbing report called *Social Security: Out of Step with the Modern Family*, issued by the nonprofit Urban Institute in April 2000, documents how spousal and survivor benefits shortchange married working women across all income brackets, and also single working mothers. The report summarizes, "Social Security rules designed mainly for one-earner, married-couple families are out of place in today's world of two-earner families, single-parent households, short-lived marriages, and domestic relationships that don't involve marriage at all. This mismatch deters real benefit increases and may even increase poverty among the elderly—the exact opposite of what Social Security was designed to achieve" (see www.urban.org).

Special note for gay and lesbian seniors: Social Security pays survivor benefits to widows and widowers but not to surviving partners of same-sex life relationships. Similarly, Medicaid regulations protect the assets and homes of married spouses but offer no such protection to same-sex partners. Tax laws and other 401(k) and pension regulations do not recognize same-sex partners. As we go to press, these policies are being challenged by activists in California, New York, and elsewhere.

HEALTHVIEWS

Medical costs are the big black hole of just about every well-laid financial plan. The portions of hospitalization and surgery not covered by your health insurance or managed-care plan can gnaw away at carefully horded financial reserves. As we go to print, many employers have cut back on company-paid health benefits, requiring retirees to pay the full cost of their insurance.

If you or your loved one is facing recuperation from surgery or a debilitating chronic disease, professional care may be necessary. Medicare has very strict guidelines for covering home health care aides, based on a physician's diagnosis. Sometimes, families hire additional help through private agencies. These services average about $16 an hour, and are higher in urban areas.

There may be no viable alternative to a nursing home, if you or your loved one have multiple disabilities and need assistance with several activities of daily living, such as bathing, toileting, eating, and/or have a severe loss of mental cognition due to diseases such as Alzheimer's. The average age of a new admission to a nursing home is about 80; the average length of stay is under four years. Still, the costs can be astronomical. The average nursing home costs $55,000 annually, and can cost almost twice as much in a place like New York, AARP reports. Medicare will only cover a limited few months of nursing-home care. Then, without insurance, you're on your own. Medicaid will pick up the tab if you don't have any assets. To qualify, if you're married, your spouse can keep just $90,000 in assets (including your home) plus some $2,000 in monthly income. A visit to an elder-law attorney well in advance, while you are still healthy, can help you to plan a way around seeing your assets completely depleted by a nursing-home stay.

LONG-TERM CARE INSURANCE: PROS AND CONS Long-term care insurance is a product offered by commercial companies to help cover future expenses related to home care, nursing care, and nursing home care. It's appealing because these costs can mount to as much as a quarter of a million dollars for an elderly person's extended bout of sickness or disability in the last years of life. According to a report in the financial weekly *Barrons*, in early 2004, long-term care insurance sales are up, driven by buyers in their late 50s. The average age of buyers in 1990 was 72, dropping to age 58 in 2003.

Long-term care insurance sounds like a good idea, and it may be in some cases. However, the November 2003 issue of *Consumer Reports* magazine gives a yellow light to long-term care insurance policies. Their view is that for most people, "long-term-care insurance is too risky and too expensive," and that it is so complicated "it can stymie the most conscientious consumer." They also question the financial stability of some long-term care insurers. Highlights of their 2003 investigation of 47 policies, all in California, are sobering:

Future costs: Projected average rate for a private room in a nursing home will be about $175,200 annually by the year 2021.

Age Matters: Long-term care insurance should not be considered before age 60 except by those with chronic diseases, according to *Consumer Reports*.

Hidden Costs: Long-term care insurance generally pays a daily benefit for nursing-home care. But drugs supplies, and special services aren't necessarily covered; they can add 20 percent or more to the bill. Further, notes *Consumer Reports*, policies have deductibles in the form of "elimination periods" during which you must pay for nursing-home care out of your own pocket—and that the daily benefit you buy today will pay for a smaller percentage of the cost years from now, when care is needed, because of inflation and rising costs.

A booklet entitled *Do You Need Long-Term-Care Insurance?* is available free at www.ConsumerReports.org.

PHILANTHROPY AND TAX-DEDUCTIBLE CHARITABLE CONTRIBUTIONS

Retirement is a good time to review your charitable contributions. Often, over time, individuals and couples end up contributing fairly substantial sums in bits and pieces, often to programs that are more important to their friends or colleagues than to themselves. If you're giving away what seems like a sizeable amount of money but in a dispersed fashion, that's fine—as long as it's a conscious decision and fits in with your new life in THE RETIREMENT ZONE.

It's nice to know what you are funding: What is the organization's mission? What percentage of individual contributions goes to overhead versus programming? You don't have to be content with glossy brochures and fancy Web sites; pick up the phone to inquire. Before you contribute money to a smaller outfit, make sure the recipient is a nonprofit organization registered as such with the Internal Revenue Service, if you want to take the contribution as a tax deduction.

If you find that you're giving away sizeable amounts and it is time-consuming, or if you are searching for a different way to contribute financially, consider these two options:

Family foundations and Community Trusts: The National Center for Family Philanthropy estimates that there are more than 30,000 family foundations operating in the United States; two thirds of larger family foundations were formed in the 1980s and 1990s. This growth is part of an anticipated intergenerational transfer of wealth which has been estimated to reach mammoth proportions—up to $41 trillion—by the middle of the 21st century, according to projections made by professors at Boston College. To learn more about different approaches to individual or family philanthropy and community trusts, contact the Foundation Center (www.fdncenter.org) or the National Center for Family Philanthropy (www.ncfp.org).

Grassroots "Giving Circles": Giving Circles, which started in Maryland with assistance from the Association of Baltimore Area Grantmakers, bring friends or like-minded people together around a specific common interest, such as health or women's issues. Each participant contributes to the kitty, and together they review requests and make allocations. One big advantage: You don't have to make a huge contribution to make a difference.

If you're reading this book for a spouse or parent . . . and you haven't had "the" conversation about finances, it may be time. (Actually, it is not one but a series of conversations.) For adult children, family discussions about money are often tricky. One easy way to start is to discuss the legal matters first: estate planning and wills, as well as health care advance directives. For spouses and partners, you do need to have a shared understanding of your assets and lifestyle expectations for the future together, as well as your partner's ability to continue to earn income in current or future part-time or full-time jobs.

Q & A: Retirement and Money—Especially for Women

An interview with Jennifer Openshaw, CEO, Family Financial Network and founder, Women's Financial Network (www.familyfn.com)

Q: *Do women have different retirement planning needs from those of men?*
A: You bet! Women live longer, earn less, save less, and, unfortunately, even pay more for needs ranging from health care to nylons for our jobs! So, we have to make our money go a heck of a lot further. Women out-live men by seven years on average. Because women are in and out of the workforce caring for kids and aging parents, their pensions and savings are generally much lower than men's. And if anyone is counting on Social Security, think again: A woman's average benefit check is about 25 percent less than that for a man, and the average income for a woman over 65 is about $15,000 compared to $28,000 for a man. These greater needs suggest that women need to be more aggressive when it comes to investing and managing their money. Sadly, it is often a lack of knowledge or even our fear of losing money that prevents women from investing smart. I like to remind women that we take risks with our hearts in relationships and with our lives when we step into cars. If we can learn how to manage and use risk in our investments, we'll be much more likely to meet our retirement needs while reducing the chances of losing our money. Yes, this is possible.

Q: *Why do women invest more conservatively?*
A: We're definitely less confident when it comes to handling money. Men, having traditionally been the primary breadwinner earning a paycheck over many years, see money as a stream to be replenished. Women see it as a faucet that can be turned off. After all, we haven't always had our money and, when we do, something else—a parent or child's needs—can call us back home. Studies show that women have a greater portion of their savings sitting in conservative places like bonds or a bank account at a whopping 1 percent.

Q: *What prevents women from saving as much as men do if they're more conservative in how they approach money?*

A: Women don't save either, because someone else always did the saving for them, or because they simply didn't realize how important it is. Women are also still earning less than men—about 72 cents for every dollar earned by a man on average. The unfortunate truth, though, is that as people start earning more, they simply spend more. Studies show that women are much more likely than men to buy things when they don't need them or when they're on sale. You know, that "make me feel good" kind of shopping of which many are guilty after a bad day.

But because men are more confident in their stock-picking abilities, they tend to trade their stocks 45 percent more than women, according to a study by University of California Davis. That higher trading actually results in the average woman's portfolio performing 1 percent better than the average man's. That may not sound like much, but that 1 percent can easily translate into thousands of dollars over time.

Q: *What are women's specific financial concerns in retirement?*

A: Planning and investing for her longer life span is concern number one. She also needs to make sure that she and her spouse have appropriate insurance to guard against an illness depleting their finances. The bottom line is that when it comes to retirement planning, I like to play it conservative. Don't assume that Uncle Sam will be there, or your husband, or an inheritance. Assume the worst, then hope for the best—and you can rest easier at night.

Q: *How can women do a better job of saving?*

A: Women should, at a minimum, put at least a good 10 percent of their income straight into savings. No second thoughts. Little steps can go a long way. Take bottled water. If we put that $1.50 spent each day on bottled water into our savings, we'd find our account replenished to the tune of nearly $70,000 in 30 years, assuming an 8 percent average annual rate of return. All from this one little change. Dining out is another great example. Cut just $40 each week and tuck it away, and in 30 years you'd have over $200,000.

ANSWER KEY

To score quiz on page 290, "What's Your Spending Style?"

1. a=3, b=2, c=1
2. a=1, b=3, c=2
3. a=1, b=2, c=3
4. a=2, b=1, c=3
5. a=2, b=3, c=1
6. a=3, b=2, c=1
7. a=1, b=2, c=3
8. a=3, b=2, c=1
9. a=2, b=1, c=3
10. a=3, b=2, c=1
11. a=3, b=2, c=1
12. a=3, b=2, c=1

0 to 16 points: Wild 'n' wanton spending is not your style. Saving and sacrificing are more your mode. Consider the roots of your reluctance to loosen those purse strings. It may be that you come from a home where parsimony was prized, perhaps out of necessity, practicality, or choice. Is this really your choice now? Or are you simply playing out patterns that don't apply anymore? Some reflection may reorder the use of your resources?

17 to 28 points: You are a sane and sensible spender. When it comes to your currency, you know when to hold 'em, and know when to fold 'em.

29 to 36 points: You may get a kick from champagne, but what makes you even more buoyant is spending beaucoup bucks. A surfeit of spending and securing of "stuff" may be a way to self-medicate. Explore other feel-good options that require little or no cash—and have fewer dire consequences.

ANSWER KEYS

To score quiz on page 300, "Financial Literacy Quiz"
Score responses as follows and add up points:
"All the Time"/"Yes" = 3
"Sometimes" = 2
"Rarely" = 1
"Never"/"No" = 0

Divide by the number of questions you answered to get an average points per question. Your average will range from 0 to 3. Multiple this figure by 33.333 to convert it into a 100-point scale. Now you have your numeric score. Grade yourself on the standard 100-point scale, with 90-100 = A, 80-89 = B, and so on. (Note: Some questions may not apply to you. For example, if you have already paid off your mortgage and don't intend to move, just add up your total points from those questions that ARE applicable to you.)

To score quiz on page 304, "What's Your Financial Risk Tolerance Level?"
Tally up your score. Where do you come out on the risk tolerance quiz?

20-25: You're an aggressive investor with a long-time horizon. You're comfortable putting money into aggressive investments that may lose money as long as the potential pay-off is big.

15-19: You know that stocks are the way to go, but you're not comfortable throwing all of your money into a risky investment, even if the windfall could be huge. You'd prefer a little mix of bonds and cash in addition to your core stock positions.

10-14: You think that both stocks and bonds have their proper place in a well-diversified portfolio, so you're careful to make sure all of your bases are covered. Stocks are great, but bonds let you sleep at night when the market tanks.

5-9: You recognize that the stock market is a scary place, so you'd rather focus your efforts on a sure thing. You've got just a touch of equities for some zip, but for the most part, you leave it to the daredevils.

1-4: Admit it, you're a scaredy cat. But as the saying goes: No pain, no gain. You must take some risk if you want a return that's higher than what's offered by your mattress.

Resource Guide

PUBLICATIONS

Baby Boomer Retirement: 65 Simple Ways to Protect Your Future by Don Silver (Adams-Hall, 1998).

The 8 Biggest Mistakes People Make with Their Finances Before and After Retirement by Terrence L. Reed, CFP (Dearborn Trade, 2001).

Ernst & Young's Retirement Planning Guide by Ernst & Young LLP, et al. (Wiley, 2002).

Everyone's Money Book on Retirement Planning by Jordan E. Goodman (Dearborn Trade, 2002).

Feathering Your Nest: The Retirement Planner by Lisa Berger (Workman, 1993).

How to Plan for a Secure Retirement, Revised and Updated Edition by Elias M. Zuckerman, Trudy Lieberman, and Barry Dickman (Consumer Reports, 1998).

Kiplinger's Retire Worry Free by the staff of *Kiplinger's Personal Finance* magazine (Kiplinger Books, 1998).

Unbelievably Good Deals and Great Adventures That You Absolutely Can't Get Unless You're Over 50 by Joan Rattner Heilman (Contemporary Books, published yearly).

FREE GUIDE

66 Ways to Save Money by the Consumer Literacy Consortium (Consumers Union, 1999). Free illustrated booklet available online at www.waytosave-money.org or write to the Consumer Federation of America, PO Box 12099, Washington, DC 20005.

ORGANIZATIONS AND WEB SITES

Consumers' CHECKBOOK
733 15th Street NW, Suite 820
Washington, DC 20005
800-213-SAVE (7283)
www.checkbook.org

Medicare Rights Center
1460 Broadway, 17th Floor
New York, NY 10036
212-869-3850, Ext. 19
www.medicarerights.org

Elder Law

SeniorLaw Home Page:
www.seniorlaw.com

Financial Planning

Bankrate Inc., consumer finance
marketplace; features loans and
calculators: www.bankrate.com

CNN Money, from *Money* magazine,
personal finance: www.money.com

General strategies from T. Rowe
Price: www.troweprice.com;
www.vanguard.com

Morningstar analyst reports
on stocks and mutual funds:
www.morningstar.com

Long-term Care Insurance

Caregiver.com magazine:
www.caregiver.com/articles/tips_buy_
Itci.htm

Philanthropy

National Center for Family
Philanthropy: www.ncfp.org

Reverse Mortgages

AARP: www.aarp.org/revmort

Federal Trade Commission:
www.ftc.gov/bcp/conline/pubs/
homes/rms.htm

Taxes and Donations

Kiplinger.com:
www.kiplinger.com/basics/archives/
2003/03/taxrecords.html

CHAPTER 22

Caregiving

A GENERATION OF JUGGLERS, A NATION OF CAREGIVERS

If a fairy godmother bestowed upon you three golden wishes that would come true during retirement, giving—or receiving care— probably wouldn't be on your wish list. After all, everybody hopes for good health. But there's some chance that caregiving will be part of your future as you move into your 50s and 60s and beyond.

That's particularly the case if you are married to a person in their middle to late 70s, or have a parent or close relative that age or older. This chapter seeks to shed some light on the experience of caregiving (just in case your fairy godmother doesn't show up).

Like travel, volunteering, and the dozen or more "anchor activities" described in Part III of this book, caregiving can be an anchor in the sense that it's something in your post-work life to which you devote substantial time, focus, and even financial commitment. Indeed, sometimes people go into retirement in order to better respond to a family member in need of care. Still, it's important to realize that you do have choices in this realm, too. That's especially the case for long-distance situations—for instance, when your parent has had a hip replacement but lives 1,000 miles away.

Like rearing children, the day-to-day responsibility of being a caregiver is hard to imagine unless you've done it. Sure, an outsider might have a general idea. "If you haven't walked in caregiving shoes, you can't truly comprehend what it is all about," Suzanne Mintz, president and cofounder, National Family Caregivers Association, is fond of saying. So, first a word on who's *getting* and who's *giving* the care, and what that care actually entails.

Today, about one in four caregivers in the United States are 50 to 64. Twelve percent are over 65. Put another way, about 50 million people—or one in four American households—provide unpaid care of some sort to an elderly, ailing friend or relative. The help might involve shopping and transportation, or personal care such as eating, bathing, and dressing. Family caregivers provide more than 80 percent of all home-care services.

As for the people receiving care, the average age of those in need of some kind of assistance—driving, shopping, or personal care—is 77. In general, the conditions that lead to an older person needing care in the practical matters of life are, in decreasing order of frequency, those generally related to aging, lack of mobility, dementia, heart conditions, cancer, and stroke. Others include arthritis, diabetes, lung disease, vision loss, mental illness, broken or brittle bones, or neurological problems. Thankfully, some of the most widespread chronic conditions, such as arthritis, don't often greatly limit a person's independence.

It's not just the condition per se, it's what happens to one's mobility that can be devastating. Take, for instance, not being able to drive a car. Transportation—or lack thereof—becomes a looming problem for getting the most basic things, like food. And the extent to which the basics of living become difficult for the physically impaired only increases for people who suffer cognitive impairments.

"Caregiving" is one of those catch-all words, like "parenting," that covers a wide range of tasks, determined by the needs of another. Some fairly simple tasks include: picking up a few groceries or running errands, a ride to the doctor, a brief friendly visit, or help paying the bills. Sometimes it involves a great deal more: administering medications, helping a person eat, bathe, or dress; relocating to a different kind of living situation; and running the business of someone's life, including medical decision making. More than two in five family caregivers provide some level of nursing support and over half provide help with daily living activities such as dressing and toileting, according to surveys.

The challenge can be emotional, logistical, and financial, too. With caregiving comes stress and—if you are the person actually doing the hands-on care—the risk of burnout.

AN OPTIMIST'S VIEW OF THE "CAREGIVER'S BURDEN"

The rewards of providing love and much-needed care to a close relative—not to mention "doing the right thing"—are immeasurable. People who help, serve, console, and comfort in times of illness and despair can emerge from their experience with a profound satisfaction. In some traditional cultures, it's understood that ailing relatives, especially older relatives, will be cared for by the extended family; to do so is considered an obligation and a point of honor. Caregiving isn't "fun" in a superficial way. But many adults caring for a parent or spouse report feeling loved, appreciated, and proud, surveys find. Four in five family caregivers report that one thing they all provide is emotional support: company, encouragement, sharing a joke or reminiscence, and hope. The majority of family caregivers say they haven't suffered mental or physical problems as a result of their caregiving.

The role of caregiver doesn't last forever. That's a bittersweet reality. The average duration of caregiving is about four years, and most people end up as caregivers for only one individual, according to the report *Caregiving in the US* by the National Alliance for Caregiving and AARP.

Yes, it is hard work. It can be emotionally draining. And depending on the situation, terribly sad. But caring is part of life, and—for all its challenges—it comes with laughter, tears, memories, and moments of truth. Taking care of one another is part of what human beings and families do and have done for generations. And in that sense, as tough as the task may be, the silver lining is that there's a joy in living—and in the opportunity to give.

Technology holds real promise. Take the story of 68-year-old Peter S., a three-pack-a-day smoker for years. Peter's lung disease was so bad that the slightest chill in the air or touch of humidity would affect his lungs severely. In a single year, he'd been admitted to the emergency room 48 times and had 9 hospital stays. Peter's hobby had been raising award-winning roses. But his recurring bronchitis took a lot out of him. He couldn't get out into the yard; his beautiful rose garden was in total disarray. His wife, aged 65 or so, had left him alone once, and while she was out, he'd had an attack. After that she rarely left the house again, not even to go shopping. She depended on others for that.

Peter's health care providers enrolled him in a home-care monitoring program through the local VA hospital. The home system had a stethoscope to listen to heart and lungs, a blood pressure and pulse gauge, a monitor for the level of oxygen in his blood, and a weight scale. Through the monitor's audio-video system they could communicate directly, so the medical staff was able to identify and treat symptoms, saving trips to the emergency room. Peter began to build up his physical and emotional health, and started venturing into his garden (initially for only twenty minutes and eventually for longer periods of time). He also got an electric scooter for long-distance travel. He showed up unannounced at the hospital one day with an armful of roses from his garden that he had planted and nurtured and picked. His wife? Well, she was out shopping. He's still got a condition, but he has scaled back from in-hospital care to in-home, monitored care. That's a remarkable improvement.

 ## INSIDER'S GUIDE:
12 Ways to Avoid Feeling Like Silly Putty

You get bounced from doctor's waiting room to doctor's waiting room, and twisted around the menacing fingers of an invisible, unkind giant of an insurance company. You get stretched from here to there mercilessly until you snap—and then you get it together again for the next round. And at the end of the day, you roll up in a little ball and tuck yourself away for a few hours before the next day's assault. In a crisis, family caregivers can feel like putty. Following are some tips on getting oriented, getting help, and taking care of yourself.

1) BE READY FOR ON-THE-JOB TRAINING. Unless you're a trained health professional, the caregiving experience involves a great deal of on-the-job learning. So, the experts say, while it is important to be educated and aware of resource people and materials, don't feel frustrated if you do not have all the answers in advance.

2) GET ORGANIZED. Yes, you'll be juggling. But you know how to do this, even if it's stressful. Both baby boomers and the Eisenhower generation have multi-tasked their way through jobs, relationships, children, family, technology, and finances for decades.

Things that might help: Make lists of contact information for physicians, insurance plans, neighbors, and other local facilities that might help. Don't make an extra trip. Whenever you do your own shopping, shop for your parent or neighbor then. Don't waste your precious personal days: schedule your own doctor visit on the same day you take your father. Bargain, barter, and delegate: make your teen's Saturday-night car privileges contingent upon running the Saturday-morning errands so you can do your own and your aunt's paperwork without racing to the bank or dry cleaners. (Useful note: Seniors can request that copies of their medical/insurance bills be automatically sent to a designated caregiver.)

3) SCOPE OUT THE ISSUES. Learn about the condition or disease that's become an unwelcome member of your family. Start with nonprofit organizations, such as the American Cancer Society, that provide information for family caregivers. Don't believe everything you read on the Internet; rely only on well-known organizations to ensure that the information is accurate.

And, find out about resources. Know that there's a vast amount of literature documenting the "caregiver burden" and a network of respite programs and local caregiver support organizations. You'll want to determine precisely what kinds of care are and are not covered by Medicare and/or any private insurance plan your loved one might have.

Also, it pays to learn the lingo. Professionals distinguish between two different levels of care. One has to do with such activities as preparing meals, shopping, paying bills, managing money, and doing light or heavy housework, known by the acronym IADL ("instrumental activities of daily living"). The other has to do with eating, toileting, bathing, dressing, and other personal-care activities, called ADL ("activities of daily living"). The number of ADLs and IADLs with which a person needs assistance is used as a measure of their need for caregiving support. Medicare, Medicaid, and insurance plans analyze benefit eligibility according to diagnosis and ADL and IADL status.

4) COMMUNICATE! It's important for relatives to discuss who should be providing care, and what coverage is available to pay for it. It's timely to clarify a patient's end-of-life wishes, and whether interventions such as respirators, resuscitation, and other "heroic measures" are desirable. It is best to communicate before an urgent or drastic situation arises. Ask your doctor or lawyer about two kinds of advance directives, a living will and health-care proxy. A living will is a legal document stating a patient's wishes, in advance, in regard to medical treatment preferences if and when the individual becomes unconscious or incompetent and is no longer able to make decisions for him- or herself. A living will is only applicable to terminal or irreversible illnesses and is subject to the judgment of the patient's physician. Using a living will, family members can follow the patient's wishes and avoid agonizing life or death decisions regarding whether to refuse life-sustaining treatments. A durable power of attorney for health care, or health-care proxy, appoints someone else to make medical decisions on behalf of a patient.

5) WHEN YOU HIRE HELP, LOOK BEFORE YOU LEAP. Many adult children find themselves in a pinch when their parents become ill and in need of care. One obvious solution is to hire professional help. Try to interview candidates in person. Agree on the details of the job, for instance if they must drive, cook certain foods (or not), do light laundry, and shop. Ask for references, of course. Also, arrange to get a full report when you call. And if you like the aide, be generous with praise and even tips; caregiving is a difficult, underpaid job. If it doesn't work out with one person, try another.

6) CONSIDER THE OPTIONS: There's a broad spectrum of living arrangements available at many different levels of expense.

A "continuing care community" generally offers two or three levels of facilities to meet the needs of people as their capacity for independent life declines. "Independent living" accommodations are usually small apartments with a kitchen and bath, with congregate dining options for dinner and breakfast. Some look more like a resort hotel than a "facility." Others feel institutional. Most offer on-site nurses, on-call physicians, transportation to shopping areas, and such activities as movies, exercise classes, and physical therapy. The living units are fitted with such safety features as bars in the showers and emergency pull-cords. "Assisted living" offers more intensive one-on-one care for residents who need help eating, dressing, bathing, or with other activities of daily life. Some facilities offer a third, more intensive level of care for patients with dementia.

Take into consideration your loved one's special circumstances. For instance, the Veteran's Administration runs some assisted living facilities. Some continuing-care communities offer kosher food.

7) UTILIZE SUPPORT SERVICES. You don't have to go it alone. You might find excellent support from a social worker, private care manager, or respite service. If the person needing care has been recently discharged from the hospital, contact the hospital's discharge planning nurse or the health insurance plan for suggestions of community-based services. The National Association of Professional Geriatric Care Managers network (www. caremanager.org) consists of social workers with experience working with an elderly population. They know the system and can help you understand your options regarding home-care agencies and living arrangements.

Consider using faith-based support services. (Two out of five family caregivers who report needing help from outside sources prefer to rely on a local community or religious organization.)

Finally, if a friend or family member cannot spot you while you take a mental health break from caregiving, respite care can be arranged in the home and through adult-care facilities.

8) CONSIDER JOINING A CAREGIVER SUPPORT GROUP. You can find in-person support groups through the local hospital. Online support groups are relatively new, and offer the convenience of being accessible from home. Mitch Golant, PhD, vice president, Research and Development, the Wellness Community, describes research showing that family caregivers of Parkinson's patients had a significant decrease in symptoms of hopelessness, anxiety, and depression after participating for five months in a professionally moderated online support group. "Instead of repressing their emotions, they began to talk about the needs of their patients, (and) what caregiving was doing to their own lives. They began to open up," he says.

9) IF YOU ARE PROVIDING CARE, CONSIDER THIS. Watch your own mental-health barometer. If you see signs that you're getting a serious case of the blues—get some help!

Fighting a chronic disease and facing declines in cognitive and physical ability can erode marriages, cause rifts among siblings, and create intense isolation and deep exhaustion on the part of the caregiver. *Caregiving in the U.S.*, a report by the National Alliance for Caregiving and AARP, paints a realistic picture: One in three caregivers say they have experienced physical or mental health problems as a result of caregiving. The greatest stress occurs when one person alone is providing care 40 or more hours a week and the care involves intensive personal needs as well as housework, shopping, cooking, and so on. Certain diagnoses—notably Alzheimer's and other forms of dementia—can create tremendous strain because the patient may become combative, or wander outside the home into harm's way, among other things. One in five family caregivers says they take care of someone with Alzheimer's, confusion, or dementia as a primary or secondary illness.

If you find yourself in this situation, don't underestimate the challenge. It's worthwhile to seek support, explore community resources, and organize a support system for yourself, including respite care.

A special note regarding employment: Many family caregivers have considered changing a job as a result of their family responsibilities. If you are still working, take time to learn about your company's policies regarding family leave and flextime (preferably *before* you speak with your boss about it). Read your employee handbook (if your company has one) or speak to a human resources representative. If you're thinking about going back to work or starting a new job, consider asking for flextime.

10) APPRECIATE YOUR OWN EFFORTS. If you are providing care to someone in need, it's a good deed. And it can be a privilege to care for someone. Look for the silver lining, the moments of connection, humor, and love. It's okay to give yourself a pat on the back.

11) HUMOR HELPS. There's nothing funny at all about someone who's debilitated or very ill. But humor is a great healer, and it can help all concerned to get through tough times. So find your funny bone. Log on to your favorite cartoon. Share a joke. Have a good laugh, at least once a day; it's healthy!

12) A TIME FOR ACTIVISM? Caregiving information and services are fragmented. Some of the most basic services are inadequate, experts agree: the *National Study of Adult Day Services* finds that there are 60 percent fewer adult day centers than needed to meet the demands of the growing elderly population. Dr. Dennis Shea, professor of health policy at the University of Georgia, warns, "Baby boomers who are assisting their parents or preparing for their own retirement need to be aware of the consequences of current national health care policy. We direct very few of our public resources towards providing help with these needs out in the community."

Make your voice heard on this issue. Write a letter to your Congressional representative; if you're not sure who that is, log onto www.congress.com.

POLICY CHALLENGE IN THE RETIREMENT ZONE:
Technology to the Rescue?

"If the U.S. keeps institutionalizing people at the current rate, our entire GDP will soon be dedicated to health care for the elderly," according to Jonathan Perlin, of the U.S. Department of Veterans Affairs. Our health care system can't afford to continue to provide institutionalized care at the present rate. People age 85 and older are the single fastest-growing age category in the United States. It is also the group most likely to need intensive medical care, hospitalization, and—if current patterns persist—nursing home facilities.

Some people see alternatives in smaller, friendlier institutions, or more government support to enable the frail elderly to maintain their independence. Reformers such as the Eden Alternative (www.edenalt.com) are experimenting with smaller, homier, and "greener" environments. Disability rights advocates argue that federal and state governments should allocate more funds to supporting community-based care—for instance, reimbursing relatives who work as "personal assistants"—rather than institutional solutions.

Just when it seems there won't be enough resources for caregiving in the future, a new generation of health-related electronic wizardry that promises to increase independence among the elderly is coming online. New in-home technologies include computer-driven gizmos to measure your blood pressure, pulse, and, for diabetics, glucose levels—and relay the information to health providers miles away. "Instead of running to the emergency room or doctor's office with symptoms, the patient can communicate from home—not just how he or she feels, but all the vital information that a nurse would obtain through doing blood pressure, pulse, and so on," explains Rita Kobb, lead gerontological nurse practitioner at the North Florida/South Georgia Veterans Health System in Lake City, Florida. "This is a tremendous way to flag problems before they become serious. You can get medication adjustments before you have to go to the emergency room. The technology increases access to care, promotes self care, and reduces health care consumption." Judith Tabolt Matthews of the University of Pittsburgh, one of the universities developing a pilot nurse robot, says, "The support that can be offered through robotics may greatly improve the quality of life for frail elderly people who want to continue to live independently. Robots are just coming of age. As the baby boomers approach the golden years, they and their robots may mature gracefully together."

In the future, your live-in robot may smile and bring you your pills while the TV tells you it's time to stretch and exercise. Your bathroom scale may tattle on you electronically at the nurses' station in the hospital, logging in your daily weight, body-fat index, blood pressure, and pulse. And if you should slip in the middle of the night, sensors in the floor of your electronically wired "smart home" may "hear" the thump, and alert health professionals and family care providers.

It's possible that, by the time you hit the ripe old age of 90, you won't think twice about wearing "healthy" underwear and shirts with tiny, tiny sensors that can monitor your vital signs. Meanwhile, personal attention, love, and hands-on care remain the bottom line in caring for someone.

 ## HEALTHVIEWS

Let's face it, caregiving is a double whammy of worry.

The first worrying question is, "Who will I be responsible for? My spouse, my parents, my in-laws? Will I have what it takes, financially, emotionally, and time-wise, to provide the care if and when they need it?" Half of adults taking care of a parent say they worry. More than one in four expresses frustration or feels overwhelmed.

The second is, "Who will be responsible for me? " One in every four adults says that the single worst thing about having a long-term health need would be losing independence and being a burden. Yet seven in ten believe that the physical decline that occurs with aging is due to things over which an individual has control.

You can't control your luck or your genetic inheritance, but your lifestyle choices and attitude surely can influence your long-term health. Here's a review of some ways to take a pro-active stance.

PLANNING FOR YOURSELF
1) Stay healthy, engaged, and proactive in caring for yourself.
2) If you are married, watch out for each other's health: the majority of older caregivers are caring for their ailing husband or wife.
3) Lose or maintain weight, if appropriate.
4) Tend to the paperwork: do wills, designate a health care surrogate, powers of attorney, etc.

5) Talk to your family about what you do and don't want, so they know your wishes should something befall you or your spouse. And be prepared to assert your elders' wishes, too.

6) Analyze whether long-term care insurance is for you (see page 311).

PLANNING FOR YOUR SPOUSE OR RELATIVE

1) Do all of the above!

2) Secure the legal right to carry out an elder's wishes if he or she is incapacitated, and get a health-care power of attorney.

3) Look into the resources available for family caregivers.

 YOUR MONEY MATTERS

The financial burdens of caregiving can be far-ranging. Almost half of all caregivers contributed an average of $273 per month in unreimbursed expenses, or nearly $3,300 pcr year, as caregivers, according to *Sons at Work: Balancing Employment and Eldercare*, a June 2003 study conducted by Metlife. An earlier study found that 10 percent of caregivers didn't know how much they spent out of pocket on caregiving. The money is going to prescriptions, home-care attendants, home safety modifications (such as bathtub rails and water temperature guards), and long-distance travel to visit an ailing relative. Other costs might include days lost from work and canceling activities, outings, and vacations.

> **If you're reading this book for a spouse, friend, or parent . . .** It's wise to attend to all legal paperwork early on: wills, estate planning, designation of power of attorney, and a half dozen health care directives, including health care surrogate, living wills, and organ donation. Caregiving, along with money, is one of the big issues of aging that often causes conflict, grief, and stress in a family unit.

Q & A: Caregiving's a Reality

An interview with Suzanne Mintz, president and cofounder, National Family Caregivers Association (www.nfcacares.org)

Q: *As baby boomers move along in years, what are the two or three most important things they should know about caregiving?*
A: First: caregiving will be part of your life. Second: don't try and do it all by yourself.

Q: *What do you recommend to adult children who live far away from their aging parents, in terms of trying to manage a long-distance caregiving situation?*
A: I'd advise finding a geriatric care manager to assess the situation and to be your eyes and ears. They know the terrain and can save you a great deal of time and grief. Contact the local department of Elder Affairs or Area Agency on Aging where your folks live, or the National Association of Geriatric Care Managers in Tucson, Arizona.

Q: *How do you know if a paid caregiver you meet briefly, or who comes through an agency, will take good care of your loved one?*
A: Our "Home Health Care Primer" suggests you ask such questions as, Is it certified for Medicare (and Medicaid) programs? How long has it been serving the community? Is it accredited by the Joint Commission on Accreditation of Healthcare Agencies or another recognized body? Does it provide an initial assessment to determine if the patient would be appropriate for home care and what those services might be? How does it choose its employees? There's a lot to ask.

Q: *Statistics show that the pool of family caregivers is dwindling. Who will pick up the slack? What do you foresee in, say, 2020?*
A: There are fewer members of the X generation than there are boomers. That's a fact. We are also experiencing a direct-care workforce shortage in this country, so this is a significant concern. So many people quip about not knowing their neighbors. As we age and as caregiving enters our lives, we all need to develop support systems.

Resource Guide

PUBLICATIONS

And Thou Shalt Honor: The Caregiver's Companion by Beth Witrogen McLeod, ed. (Rodale, 2002).

The Complete Eldercare Planner, Second Edition: Where to Start, Which Questions to Ask, and How to Find Help by Joy Loverde (Three Rivers Press, 2000).

Consumer Reports Complete Guide to Health Services for Seniors: What Your Family Needs to Know about Finding and Financing Medicare, Assisted Living, Nursing Homes, Home Care, Adult Day Care by Trudy Lieberman and the editors of Consumer Reports (Three Rivers Press, 2000).

Coping with Your Difficult Older Parent: A Guide for Stressed-Out Children by Grace Lebow and Barbara Kane with Irwin Lebow (Avon Books, 1999).

Keeping Them Healthy, Keeping Them Home: How to Care for Your Loved Ones at Home by Ellen M. Caruso, R.N. (Health Information Press, 1998).

ORGANIZATIONS AND WEB SITES

Aging Network Services, LLC
Topaz House
4400 East-West Highway, Suite 907
Bethesda, MD 20814
301-657-4329
www.agingnets.com

Medicare:
www.medicare.gov

National Academy of Elder Law Attorneys, Inc.
1604 North Country Club Road
Tucson, AZ 85716-3102
520-881-4005
www.naela.com

National Association of Area Agencies on Aging
1730 Rhode Island Avenue NW, Suite 1200
Washington, DC 20036
202-872-0888
www.n4a.org

National Association of Professional Geriatric Care Managers (GCM)
1604 North Country Club Road
Tucson, AZ 85716-3102
520-881-8008
www.caremanager.org

National Family Caregivers
  Association
10400 Connecticut Avenue, #500
Kensington, MD 20895-3944
800-896-3650
www.nfca.org

Alternative long-term care

Eden Alternative:
www.edenalternative.com

Greenhouse Project:
www.thegreenhouseproject.com

Thou Shalt Honor:
www.thoushalthonor.org

CHAPTER 23

De-Cluttering and Moving

Florida and Arizona are bursting at the seams with older folks, so it seems. And more are arriving every day. Or so the stereotype goes. In truth, fewer than one in five Americans move out of state full time after retirement. You absolutely, positively don't have to pick up roots and start all over again to enjoy your life in THE RETIREMENT ZONE. Still, for many people, moving is a desirable option or a financial necessity. But first, a word on one headache that can delay or even keep you from moving to your dream house, that small condo with easier upkeep, or relocating to Hawaii. That impediment is:

CLUTTER

Life's ironic. Some of what you strive to GET when you're in midlife you find yourself aching to get RID of later in life. The clothes. The kitchenware. The knickknacks. The old sports equipment. The almost-antiques. And the old furniture. And yes, the papers. To help in your downsizing decision making, here are a few questions to ask yourself about your belongings. (Please take care, however. The experts suggest mounting a de-cluttering campaign—for it's nothing less than that—on a gradual, room-by-room basis, to preserve your sanity.)

 ## Practical Tips:
7 QUESTIONS TO ASK YOURSELF ABOUT YOUR STUFF

1) Is it useful?
2) Is it valuable (such as silver or china)?
3) Does it give you pleasure?
4) Does it represent your true self in some way?
5) Does it remind you of some part of your life you'd like to remember?
6) Do you think you might use it in the future?
7) Do you think that if you get rid of something, you're being irresponsible to your parents, grandparents, or other relatives past or future?

WHAT TO DO WITH ALL THAT EXTRA STUFF

There are three basic options. You can give it to a family member or friend. (It's wise to make sure the recipient actually wants the item. Goods in reasonable shape can be donated to a Salvation Army, Goodwill, homeless shelter, or music and arts organizations, libraries, museums, schools, or the local historical society. You can try to sell it, although often people don't get as high a price as they think their goods deserve. Garage sales are popular; however, finding, cleaning, displaying, pricing, selling, and then disposing of unsold items isn't a small task.

If some of your possessions might be valuable, consult a professional appraiser, via Web sites such as www.appraisers.org or www.appraisers-association.org.

A word about selling on eBay, the online marketplace: The volume and range of goods that is bought and sold through eBay boggles the mind. Entire books have been written on it. If you're not computer literate (or don't want to spend hours on eBay), the company enables "trading assistants" to sell goods for others. The arrangements between clients and trading assistants are made independently of eBay, which simply serves as the marketplace. It's like hiring someone to sell your goods at a flea market, with similar details to be worked out: what their fee is based on, how long you want the goods to be "up for sale," what happens to the unsold items, and so on. There's information on this system on the eBay Web site (http://pages.ebay.com).

TO MOVE OR NOT TO MOVE?

Whether you're relocating across town or to another country, moving entails change. And while relocating can clean out the cobwebs in your brain (not to mention your garage), it also rates high on the stress scale. So, before embarking, it's helpful to be clear about *why* you're moving. As obvious as that sounds, some people decide to relocate as a way of avoiding other, more troublesome issues, such as strains in a marriage. Others resist moving because of what seem to be insurmountable obstacles, like telling your 90-year-old mother in Chicago that you're fed up with cold winters and she's moving with you to Florida.

Use the most basic decision-making tool this side of indecision, the pros-and-cons list. By getting it down on paper, you and your significant other can clarify your goals.

Think about different parts of your life—finances, family, and friends—and of course, factor in cost-of-living issues, keeping in mind that profits from the sale of your residence might subsidize future retirement years. But also take into consideration your interests, community affiliations, and habits. Take out a notebook and pen and write it all down. And discuss, discuss, discuss!

WHERE TO GO?

According to an Associated Press report in 2004, Census Bureau statistics show rapid growth of the retiree population well beyond Florida and Arizona, the sunny retirement meccas of the last century. Colorado, Idaho, Utah, and New

Mexico are new frontiers of THE RETIREMENT ZONE. Nevada is a big draw—its retirement population increased by 15 percent in just a few years. And people are moving to Alaska, too, where there's inexpensive land, few people, and an abundance of natural beauty.

The main factors to consider after location, location, location are: affordability; community life; access to outdoor recreation; proximity to family; access to medical facilities; access to transportation, both local and long distance; recreational and cultural offerings; a promising environment for getting a job or launching a second business, if relevant; and cost of living.

You can learn a great deal about what different places have to offer by thumbing your reference books. If it's price that's driving your decision, check out books such as *Where to Retire: America's Best and Most Affordable Places* by John Howells (Globe Pequot Press, 2003). If you have specific interests, search around for a guide that addresses them, such as *Choose a College Town for Retirement: Retirement Discoveries for Every Budget* by Joseph M. Lubow (Globe Pequot Press, 1999). The May/June 2004 issue of *AARP, The Magazine* cited fifteen most desirable retirement communities, namely: Loveland/Fort Collins, Colorado; Bellingham, Washington; Raleigh/Durham/Chapel Hill, North Carolina; Sarasota, Florida; Fayetteville, Arkansas; Charleston, South Carolina; Asheville, North Carolina; San Diego, California; San Antonio, Texas; Santa Fe, New Mexico; Gainesville, Florida; Iowa City, Iowa; Portsmouth, New Hampshire; Spokane, Washington; and Ashland, Oregon. Of course, once a community is so named, you can bet that the average housing price leaps up.

As baby boomers age in droves, there'll be increased demand for retirement housing and therefore prices in desirable locations will also rise. As of this writing, for instance, in the Hawaii area near Diamond Head, $400,000 will buy a 1400 square foot, two-bedroom condo in a beachfront building without an ocean view. Add $750 monthly association dues plus $1100 per month payment on a ground lease, totaling $1850 per month. A smaller, ocean-view condo exclusive of association dues lists at $750,000. It's not cheap, and prices are going up.

Once you know why you're moving, and you've narrowed your options down to a few towns or neighborhoods, try to spend as much time as possible there. Meanwhile, be an information sponge. Subscribe to the local newspaper, or read it online. Get information about community activities by contacting local civic organizations, churches or other faith organizations, political groups, dog or home owners associations, or whatever thing interests you. Pepper your real-estate agent with questions. And if you are not certain, then rent before you buy.

Practical Tips:
A WORD TO THE WISE ABOUT MOVING COMPANIES

To avoid a financial, emotional, or logistical nightmare, when dealing with moving companies, plan ahead.

1) Price Shop. Moving company prices vary widely, so ask for an estimate and whether the estimate is binding. If not, ask how costs might increase after the move and whether fees are based on hours, weight, distance, waiting or travel time, and so on.) If you can, negotiate a cap on how much the moves can charge above their estimate. *Get everything in writing.*

2) Go with a professional mover. Price is important, but so is quality, unless you don't care whether there's a big black footprint on your new white sofa. Check references. Get the name of the company that will move you in writing; the company name on your initial agreement should match the name on the bill of lading you sign on the day of the move. This is important because sometimes one mover will make arrangements for a move and then subcontract the actual move to an entirely different moving company.

3) Get insurance. There's a risk of damage to goods that have been shipped, so ask what kind of insurance the mover offers (probably minimal), check your homeowners insurance and, if necessary, buy more. The Federal Highway Administration Web site provides useful information under *Your Rights and Responsibilities When You Move* (www.fmcsa. dot.gov/factsfigs/moving.htm).

4) Make a photo and written inventory. Before you pack even one sock, take photos of expensive objects and any items of personal importance. Photos are valuable proof in the event that you need to make a claim due to damage caused in the move. If you do the packing, write a detailed inventory of what is in every box to review with the movers as they are loading up. If the movers pack you, they should prepare an inventory that you agree with. State the condition of your goods, as in, "six-foot dining table, no scratches on top or legs." When you receive the shipment, make sure you have the inventory on hand so you can ensure that everything you sent has arrived, and is in good shape.

5) Pay attention to the bill of lading. The bill of lading is the most important document needed to obtain reimbursement of claims. It's like a contract with the moving company. Make sure you and the mover agree on the inventory list of what's being shipped before you sign.

6) Act promptly. Hopefully, everything will go fine. But just in case, have a camera ready when the goods arrive in their new home, so you can document any damage. Experts suggest saving the packing material surrounding the damaged goods for further proof. Call the moving company immediately to file claims; if you have problems, consult the American Moving and Shipping Association at www.moving.org.

 ## HEALTHVIEWS

Moving is an invitation to the unknown; that's what's exciting about it! Make sure you potentially have social networks, meaningful activities, good health-care facilities, and a fun way to exercise in your new location.

Also take the time to ensure that where you're moving is accident-proof and accessible to visitors with disabilities, who may be navigating using wheelchairs, walkers, or canes. An ounce of prevention may protect your older spouse, mature friends, and elderly relatives from falls, burns, and inconvenience. The National Association of Home Builders recommends:

- Having at least one bedroom and bathroom on the first floor, allowing you to adapt the lower floor for possible one-level living.
- Having at least one entry without steps for easier access for everyone, regardless of their ability.
- Installing easy-to-use features such as lever door handles, electrical switches positioned slightly lower, and thermostats with large, easy-to-read numbers.
- And of course, getting rid of clutter that might cause someone to trip, or that could be a fire hazard.

For more information, see www.seniorsafehome.com, www.ageinplace.org, and www.nahb.org.

Q & A: Once You've Seen One Mess, You've Seen them All

An interview with professional organizer Ann Sullivan, author of *The Learning Annex Presents Uncluttering Your Space.*

Q: *Why should I bother de-cluttering my life as I'm thinking about retirement?*
A: One, peace of mind. Managing a lot of stuff takes energy. Two, it saves time. Statistics indicate that disorganization may cost us up to one hour a day. Three, it saves money. Disorganization could account for as much as 15 percent of your budget: buying duplicates, last-minute shopping at premium prices, and late fees on bills. Four, it improves your health, because clutter causes stress.

Q: *When's the best time to start?*
A: Now. Start now. De-cluttering is a continuous process. Americans accumulate stuff without even trying. You have to keep up with it. We get more paper in a year than our grandparents did in a lifetime.

Q: *How do I get started?*
A: First, choose the room that causes you the most stress, and then within that room, what area, and start there. Second, edit your belongings. You'll need boxes marked "toss," "give to family or friends," "donate," "repair," and "place elsewhere." Sort items into like categories, inventory what you have, and get rid of what you no longer use. Third, place items you're going to keep where the activity that they relate to takes place.

Organizing important papers is the most important task. Consult your attorney and accountant about what papers you should keep and where. Have a detailed instruction sheet that advises your representative of how to proceed in the case of an emergency or death. Make sure someone knows where all your important documents are being stored, such as medical records, wills, medical power of attorney, property deeds, and insurance papers. For insurance purposes, video the house and your belongings and put the tape in your safe deposit box in case of fire or burglary. The more documented you are, the better.

Q: *But I love to shop!*

A: How do you want to spend your money? If you know you are going to downsize in five years, think twice about getting new possessions. Ask yourself before you buy something, "Is this really beautiful or useful? Do I need to own it? What will it cost to maintain it, clean it, or find space for it?"

Q: *How do I make some money from what I get rid of?*

A: First, evaluate the time, effort, and money it will cost you to sell various items. Here are the options: 1) Consignment shops. 2) Yard sales, garage sales, flea markets, auctions, and online, eBay. 3) Estate sales: Hire a pro to come in and hold a sale in your house. 4) Tax write-offs. You can make tax-deductible donations to thrift shops or donate to charitable organizations. (For information on how this works, log on to www itsdeductible.com.)

Pick an organization you have a connection to and ask if they'd like a contribution. For instance, if you have a strong feeling about wanting to help battered women, or cancer survivors, or the local YMCA or YWCA, call to see if they take contributions. A lot of them will pick up. But whatever you contribute should be in good shape: be respectful.

Q: *I'm afraid I will give things—and then regret it.*

A: If you cannot decide about a particular item, put it in a box marked "undecided" with the date on it. When the box is full of such items, seal it. In six months' time, if you have not missed any of the items, without further evaluation get rid of the contents.

No matter how old you are, there are obstacles, psychological and otherwise, to getting organized and editing your possessions. But I have not seen a situation where someone has gotten rid of something and regretted it. I've only seen people feeling really liberated—and motivated to get rid of even more.

Q: *What do the "before" I get organized and "after" I get organized pictures look like?*

A: Before: Chaos. Oppression. Crisis.

After: Relief. Calm. Liberation. Freedom.

If you're reading this book for a spouse, friend, or parent . . . you might consider helping them weed through their belongings *well in advance* of relocation or crisis. Make it a family affair: one weekend every few months when you all get together, cook up a big batch of chili or a quick pasta dinner, and sort, box, toss, give away, or get ready for the sale of unwanted items.

Spouses might start to "weed out" a smallish, neutral space (not *his* workshop or her clothing closet). Pick a do-able job, finish it, and celebrate when you are done!

Adult children can use this opportunity to identify which items they'd love to inherit (or not). Ask them! Just beginning a dialogue about "stuff" helps people focus on the fact that it's the relationships, not the material stuff in their lives, that are most meaningful.

Resource Guide

PUBLICATIONS

De-cluttering

The Learning Annex Presents Uncluttering Your Space by Ann T. Sullivan (John Wiley & Sons, 2003).

Organizing from the Inside Out, 2nd Edition: The Foolproof System for Organizing Your Home, Your Office, and Your Life by Julie Morgenstern (Owl Books, 2004).

Moving

America's 100 Best Places to Retire, 3rd Edition by Elizabeth Armstrong, ed. (Vacation, 2002).

Choose a College Town for Retirement: Retirement Discoveries for Every Budget by Joseph M. Lubow (Globe Pequot Press, 1999).

The Insiders' Guide to Relocation by Beverly D. Roman and John Howells (Globe Pequot Press, 2004).

Moving On: A Practical Guide to Downsizing the Family Home by Linda Hetzer and Janet Hulstrand (Stewart, Tabori & Chang, 2004).

Where to Retire: America's Best and Most Affordable Places, 5th Edition, by John Howells (Globe Pequot Press, 2003).

ORGANIZATIONS AND WEB SITES

American Moving and
  Storage Association
1611 Duke Street
Alexandria, VA 22314
703-683-7410
www.moving.org

Seeds of Simplicity
PO Box 9955
Glendale, CA 91226
1-877-UNSTUFF
www.simpleliving.net/seedsofsimplicity

The Simple Society Alliance
  for Human Empowerment
303 Amherst Street, No. 7
Nashua, NH 03063
603-889-0111
www.simsoc.org

Large Flea Markets across the United States
(www.fleamarketguide.com)

Arizona: Tanque Verde Swap Market

Florida: FleaMasters Flea Market, Fort Myers

Kentucky: Kentucky Flea Market in Louisville

Minnesota: Gold Rush—Olmstead County

New York: Ceasar's Bazaar

Texas: First Monday Flea Market in Canton

Virginia: Happy's Flea Market, Roanoke

Washington State: Midway Swap and Shop, Kent

Conclusion

What happens in life isn't all up to you, of course. But remember that you *can* make choices to try to shape your future. And one way or another, your lifestyle may influence your physical health and sense of well-being, and perhaps even how long you live. You have the chance to engage in activities that are meaningful to you, that offer opportunities for socializing and fun, and that might help others.

For baby boomers and our older sibs, there's opportunity aplenty in THE RETIREMENT ZONE. With a little dreaming, a dose of courage, and some thoughtful planning, you can begin to plot a fulfilling course for your future. You're experienced in the journey of life, having traveled quite a distance already. And, thinking like an optimist, there are not just good years, but good *decades*, still ahead.

Looking forward, how will you use your gift of time?

GENERAL RETIREMENT RESOURCES

RECOMMENDED READING

Age Power: How the 21st Century Will Be Ruled by the New Old by Ken Dychtwald, PhD (Jeremy P. Tarcher/Putnam, 1999).

Merck Manual of Health and Aging by Mark H. Beers (Pocket Books, 2004).

My Time: Making the Most of the Rest of Your Life by Abigail Trafford (Basic Books, 2003).

The Savvy Senior: The Ultimate Guide to Health, Family, and Finances for Senior Citizens by Jim Miller (Hyperion, 2004).

The Third Age: Six Principles for Personal Growth and Renewal after Forty by William A. Sadler, PhD (Perseus Books, 2000).

Too Young to Retire: 101 Ways to Start the Rest of Your Life by Marika and Howard Stone (Plume, 2004).

ORGANIZATIONS AND WEB SITES

AARP
601 E Street NW
Washington, DC 20049
888-867-2277
www.aarp.org

Experience Corps
2120 L Street NW, Suite 400
Washington, DC 20037
202-478-6190
www.experiencecorps.org

Gray Panthers
733 15th Street NW, Suite 437
Washington, DC 20005
800-280-5362
www.graypanthers.org

National Institute on Aging
Information Center
PO Box 8057
Gaithersburg, MD 20892-8057
800-222-2225
www.nia.nih.gov

Others include:

Age Wave team home page:
www.agewave.com

Elderhostel educational travel:
www.elderhostel.org

Government seniors pages:
www.seniors.gov

MaturityWorks, web-recruitment
initiative based in London:
www.maturityworks.com

Not Yet Retired, information,
products, and services for people
50 and up: www.notyetretired.com

www.positiveaging.com

SCORE, "Counselors to America's
Small Business": www.score.org

Senior Link, nonprofit that connects
older adults with services:
www.seniorlink.org

Senior Net, nonprofit organization
bringing computer technologies
to older adults: www.seniornet.org

Senior Women Web:
www.seniorwomen.com

Third Age Inc., online media and
direct marketing: www.thirdage.com

Too Young to Retire, newsletter:
www.2young2retire.com

SELECTED SOURCES

Many sources were used in writing this book. The following four elements provided both the foundation and basic information for most chapters.

1) **INTERVIEWS:** Approximately 200 interviews were conducted between spring 2002 and February 2003. These included 140 one-on-one telephone interviews, averaging about 40 minutes in length, with a diverse group of retirees across the United States; three focus groups conducted in New York City; and dozens of telephone and in-person interviews with experts in demographics, health, psychology, and other fields.

2) **DEMOGRAPHIC, ATTITUDINAL, AND HEALTH RESEARCH:** Material distilled from a broad span of academic and professional literature including journals in gerontology, public health, and related fields such as *Gerontologist, Journal of Active Aging,* and the *New England Journal of Medicine,* as well as research produced by a wide range of nonprofit organizations and government agencies, including (but not limited to) AARP, American Society on Aging, American Public Health Association, Centers for Disease Control (CDC), Gerontological Society of America, National Council on Aging (NCOA), National Institute on Aging, U.S. Administration on Aging, U.S. Census Bureau, and U.S. Bureau of Labor Statistics. Some material comes from the Web sites of these and other organizations, in addition to unpublished research presented at academic conferences concerned with health and aging. A useful link to dozens of professional resources was facilitated through the online Resource Directory for Older People, a joint effort by the federal Administration on Aging and National Institute on the Aging (www.nia.nih.gov/rd/toc.html).

One study, American Perceptions of Aging in the 21st Century by the National Council on the Aging, is cited frequently and is the source for charts in various chapters. Harris Interactive, Inc. conducted the interviews in January 2000, using a nationally representative sample of adults aged 18 and older. The survey includes an "over-sampling" of 1,155 persons aged 65+ within the total adult (aged 18 and older) sample of 3,048.

3) **GENERAL MEDIA:** Major American newspapers, wire services, and magazines, retrieved through a Nexis search dating 1998-2003.

4) **STANDARD REFERENCE:** Includes *The World Almanac 2004*, and trade reference directories such as *Peterson's Guides* to educational opportunities. Generational benchmarks were readily available through Internet searches and books celebrating the 2000 millennium, including *The Century* by Peter Jennings and Todd Brewster (Doubleday, 1998). Internet search engines proved very helpful.

Additional sources for individual chapters appear below:

WELCOME TO THE RETIREMENT ZONE

Publications

The Creative Age: Awakening Human Potential in the Second Half of Life by Gene D. Cohen, M.D., PhD (Avon Books, 2000).

Prime Time: How Baby Boomers Will Revolutionize Retirement and Transform America by Marc Freedman (PublicAffairs, 1999).

The Third Act: Reinventing Yourself After Retirement by Edgar M. Bronfman with Catherine Whitney (G. P. Putnam, 2003).

ONE LITTLE CHAPTER ON FOUR BIG ISSUES

Publications

The Longevity Strategy: How to Live to 100 Using the Brain-Body Connection by David Mahoney and Richard M. Restak, M.D. (John Wiley & Sons, 1998).

U.S. Senate Select Committee on Aging, September 3, 2003, session, "How to Retain and Keep an Aging Workforce Productive."

Organizations

Gerontological Society of America (Washington, DC)

International Longevity Center-USA (New York)

SPRY Foundation (Washington, DC)

U.S. Census Bureau (Washington, DC)

U.S. Department of Labor (Washington, DC)

ATTITUDE: ACCENTUATE THE POSITIVE

Publications

Aging Well: Surprising Guideposts to a Happier Life from the Landmark Harvard Study of Adult Development by George E. Vaillant, M.D. (Little Brown & Company, 2002).

Successful Aging by John Wallis Rowe, M.D., and Robert L. Kahn, PhD (Dell, 1998).

HEART: ANCHORING YOUR SOCIAL LIFE

Publications

"The Social Portfolio, the Role of Activity in Mental Wellness as People Age" in *Mental Wellness in Aging* by J. Ronch, PhD, and J. Goldfield, MSW, eds. (Health Profession Press, 2003).

HEAD: TAKE YOUR BRAIN TO THE GYM

Publications

Aging with Grace: What the Nun Study Teaches Us About Leading Longer, Healthier, and More Meaningful Lives by David Snowdon, PhD (Bantam, 2001).

Journal of the American Geriatrics Society (various issues).

Journal of Geriatric Psychology (various issues).

Keep Your Brain Young: The Complete Guide to Physical and Emotional Health and Longevity by Guy McKhann, M.D., and Marilyn Albert, PhD (John Wiley & Sons, 2002).

Organizations

American Heart Association (Dallas, TX)

Dana Alliance for Brain Initiatives (New York, NY)

Society for Neuroscience (Washington, DC)

BODY: EXERCISE IS FOR EVERYBODY

Publications

Exercise: A Guide from the National Institute on Aging by a panel put together from the U.S. Department of Health.

Increasing Physical Activity Among Adults Age 50 and Older: National Blueprint, CDC, AARP, NIA, et al. (Robert Wood Johnson Foundation, 2001).

Special Recommendations for Older Adults, National Center for Chronic Disease Prevention and Health Promotion (Bethesda, MD).

ZEN AND THE ART OF MEANING

The Creative Age: Awakening Human Potential in the Second Half of Life by Gene D. Cohen, M.D., PhD (Avon Books, 2000).

The Third Act: Reinventing Yourself After Retirement by Edgar M. Bronfman with Catherine Whitney (Putnam, 2002).

Zen and the Art of Motorcycle Maintenance: An Inquiry into Values by Robert M. Pirsig (William Morrow, 1974).

A TALE OF TWO (OR TWO HUNDRED) TRANSITIONS

Organizations

Gerontological Society of America

BEFORE YOU MOVE TO FLORIDA: KNOW THYSELF, A WORKBOOK

Organizations

U.S. Department of Labor (Washington, DC)

MORE WAYS TO KNOW THYSELF:
TESTS, COACHES, AND PROFESSIONAL GUIDANCE

Organizations

Coach University (Steamboat Springs, CO)

International Coaching Federation (Washington, DC)

University of North Carolina Center for Creative Retirement (Asheville, NC)

U.S. Department of Labor (Washington, DC)

WORKING FOR PAY (AND FUN)

Publications

American Work Ethic in Retirement, nationwide survey conducted for Strong Financial Services (August 2003).

Cornell Study of Employer Phased Retirement Policies: A Report on Key Findings (Cornell University, 2003).

Staying Ahead of the Curve 2003: The AARP Working in Retirement Study (AARP, 2003).

A VOLUNTEERING PRIMER
VOLUNTEERING GUIDE: 10 WAYS TO PITCH IN, FROM ANIMALS TO POLITICS
SOCIAL ENTREPRENEURSHIP

Publications

The Journals of Gerontology B Series: Psychological and Social Sciences (Gerontological Society of America, May 2003), and numerous other health journals

Statistical Abstract of the United States by the U.S. Census Bureau (last revised April 6, 2004).

Volunteering in the United States, news release by the U.S. Bureau of Labor Statistics (December 17, 2003).

Organizations

AARP (Washington, DC)

Foundation Center (New York, NY)

Independent Sector (Washington, DC)

TRAVELING

Organizations

Travel Industry of America (Washington, DC)

U.S. Office of Travel and Tourism Industries (Washington, DC)

SPIRITUAL SEEKING

Publications

After Heaven: Spirituality in America Since the 1950s by Robert Wuthnow (University of California Press, 1998).

"The Links Between Religion and Health: Are They Real?" by Linda George, in *Public Policy and Aging Report* (National Academy on an Aging Society, Sept. 20, 2002).

"Should Physicians Prescribe Religious Activities?" by R. P. Sloan, in *New England Journal of Medicine* (June 22, 2000).

Spiritual, but not Religious: Understanding Unchurched America by Robert C. Fuller (Oxford University Press, 2002).

Spiritual Marketplace: Baby Boomers and the Remaking of American Religion by Wade Clark Roof (Princeton University Press, 1999).

Spiritual State of the Union 2003, a poll conducted by the Center for Research on Religion and Civil Society, Gallup Organization, and Urban Civil Society.

Organizations

Center for Study of Religion (Princeton, NJ)

LEARNING: NOT JUST FOR SCHOOL JUNKIES

Publications

Guide to Distance Learning Programs 2004 (Peterson's Guides, 2003).

Lifelong Learning Trends: A Profile of Continuing Higher Education by Peter Gwynn, ed. (National University Continuing Education Association, biennial).

Organizations

ALIROW (the Association of Independent Learning in Retirement of the Western U.S., online)

Elderhostel Institute Network (EIN) (Boston, MA)

National Center for Education Statistics, National University Continuing Education Association (Washington, DC)

LOVING MAKES THE WORLD GO 'ROUND

Publications

Outing Age: Public Policy Issues Affecting Gay, Lesbian, Bisexual and Transgender Elders by Sean Cahill, PhD, Rev. Ken South, and Jane Spade (Policy Institute of the National Gay and Lesbian Task Force Foundation, 2000).

"Sex and the Elderly Woman," ABC News report (March 16, 2000).

Sexuality in Later Life, an NIA "Age Page" (August 2002).

GRANDPARENTING AND KIDS, WONDERFUL KIDS

Organizations

Big Brothers Big Sisters (Philadelphia, PA)

Center for Intergenerational Learning at Temple University (Philadelphia, PA)

Experience Corps (Washington, DC)

Generations United (Washington, DC)

PLAYING: HOBBIES AND PASSIONS

Organizations

AARP (Washington, DC)

Hobby Industry of America (Elmwood Park, NJ)

PAYING FOR RETIREMENT

Publications

2001 Retirement Risk Survey by Matthew Greenwald and Associates, Inc., and the Employee Benefit Research Institute (Society of Actuaries, 2002).

Organizations

Bankrate.com (North Palm Beach, FL)

Certified Financial Planner Standards Board (Washington, DC)

Consumers' CHECKBOOK (Washington, DC)

Consumers Union, Inc. (Yonkers, NY)

Family Financial Network (Los Angeles, CA)

Strong Financial Advisors (Menomonee Falls, WI)

T. Rowe Price (Baltimore, MD)

Vanguard Group (Valley Forge, PA)

CAREGIVING: A GENERATION OF JUGGLERS, A NATION OF CAREGIVERS

Publications

American Medical Association Guide to Home Caregiving by the AMA (Wiley, 2001).

Chronic Care in America: A 21st-Century Challenge by the Institute for Health and Aging (Robert Wood Johnson Foundation, 1996).

Computer-based Technology and Caregiving for Older Adults Conference (SPRY Foundation, 2003).

Internet Health Resources by Susannah Fox and Deborah Fellows (Pew Internet & American Life Project, July 2003).

The Metlife Study of Sons at Work: Balancing Employment and Eldercare from the National Alliance for Caregiving and the Center for Productive Aging (Mature Market Institute, 2003).

Organizations

AARP (Washington, DC)

MIT Age Lab (Cambridge, MA)

National Family Caregivers Association (Kensington, MD)

Rehabilitation Engineering Research Center University of Florida (Gainesville, FL)

DE-CLUTTERING AND MOVING

Publications

The Learning Annex Presents Uncluttering Your Space by Ann T. Sullivan (John Wiley & Sons, 2003).

Where to Retire: America's Best and Most Affordable Places, 5th edition, by John Howells (Globe Pequot Press, 2003).

Index